WHEN THE GIANTS WERE GIANTS

Also by Peter Williams

The Joe Williams Baseball Reader

WHEN THE
GIANTS
WERE
GIANTS

Bill Terry and the

Golden Age of

New York Baseball

by Peter Williams

with an introduction

by W. P. Kinsella

1994

Algonquin Books of Chapel Hill

Published by
ALGONQUIN BOOKS OF CHAPEL HILL
Post Office Box 2225
Chapel Hill, North Carolina 27515-2225

a division of
WORKMAN PUBLISHING COMPANY, INC.
708 Broadway
New York, New York 10003

Library of Congress Cataloging-in-Publication Data

Williams, Peter, 1937 Jan. 30-
When the Giants Were Giants: Bill Terry and the Golden Age of New York
Baseball / by Peter Williams; with an introduction by W. P. Kinsella.
p. cm.
Includes bibliographical references and index.
ISBN 0-945575-02-5
1. Terry, Bill, 1898-1989. 2. Baseball players—United States—Biography.
3. New York Giants (Baseball team)—History.
4. Baseball—New York (N.Y.)—History—20th century.
I. Kinsella, W. P. II. Title.
GV865.T42W55 1994
796.357'092—dc20
[B]
94-1019
CIP

10 9 8 7 6 5 4 3 2 1
First Edition

for

Joe Williams and Bill Terry

a couple of
tough-minded Memphians
who should have been
better friends

CONTENTS

PART IV

Nice Guys Finish Last

ILLUSTRATIONS

Following page 129

ACKNOWLEDGMENTS

I'd like to thank the following people and organizations for their generous help: in Atlanta, the Georgia Department of Archives and History, Joe Gerson of the Georgia Hall of Fame, Franklin M. Garrett and Frank Wheeler of the Atlanta Historical Society, and that city's fine senior sports writer, Furman Bisher; in Memphis, the management of the Peabody Hotel, Jerry Armour of the National Cotton Council, the volunteers at St. Luke's Episcopal Church, the Rev. Lewis McKee and, in the area of formal research, Ed Frank of the Mississippi Valley Collection at Memphis State University, Patricia La Point of the Memphis Collection at the Memphis-Shelby County Library, and Mike Freeman for access to his thesis on Clarence Saunders; elsewhere in the country, Bruce Rubenstein of the University of Michigan at Flint, the Hollywood actress Ruth Terry and some more first-rate sports journalists, Red Barber of Tallahassee, Bob Broeg of St. Louis, Fred Russell of Nashville, and Larry Ritter and Bill Bloome of New York. I also want to acknowledge the crucial help of two of the most dedicated editors around, Louis D. Rubin, Jr., who was as much parent as obstetrician to this book, and Robert A. Rubin, who nursed it through infancy.

As grateful as I am to all of the above, however, my deepest thanks have to go to the following men: Hal Schumacher, who complained about the stench of Cy Young's cigars, then immediately said, "Boy, did you see that home run Bo Jackson hit yesterday?"; Ted Williams, who interrupted our outdoor conversation to fire at a bird with an imaginary rifle (I could hear the bird, but I couldn't see it); Harry Danning, who made me turn off my tape recorder whenever he told a shady joke (they were pretty funny, too); Joe Moore, who was a little irritated at his doctor for telling him maybe he shouldn't rope and tie his own cattle anymore; Buddy Hassett, who went way out of his way to do me a personal favor (I still owe him a beer); Bob Thomson, who never complained when my over-affectionate hound shed hair all over his dark suit, and whose wife passed on her recipe for foolproof meringue; Al Lopez, who acted out the game in which he caught the hog-calling Pea Ridge Day, and who seemed actually to be back in Ebbets Field during the demonstration; John Mize, who filled me in on both the stinginess of Branch Rickey and the hilarious baseball life of Johnny King; Clydell Castleman, who says Whitey Ford stole his nickname ("Slick"); the cheerful San Francisco announcer and ex-Terryman, Joe Orengo; Edward "Doc" Marshall, who, like so many of Terry's Giants, became a very successful businessman; Billy Herman, who pointed out that even the players who didn't like Terry always respected him; Terry Moore; Mel Harder, Bob Feller, and Denny Galehouse, whose memories of barnstorming with the Giants are both vivid and affectionate; Babe Phelps, who along with many other people, misses the Brooklyn of Ebbets Field; Dick Bartell, who loved Terry; Rube Fischer, who didn't; Alex Kampouris and Lonnie Frey, who admit they still can't stand Bartell; Don Gutteridge; Bill Lohrman, who used to go to the movies with Ott and Hubbell (Bill would always wind up sitting with Carl, because Mel insisted on marching all the way up front); Bill Jurges, who not only survived encounters with George Magerkurth and an enraged and pistol-packing woman, but even a couple with Bartell; Bob Seeds, a man of few words; Harry Gumbert, who noted that, when Dizzy Dean got in trouble, he threw faster, but when Hubbell got in trouble, he slowed up; Frank Crosetti, who figures his hit against Fitzsimmons in the 1936 Series was good and clean; Bill Dickey, who says his hit against Hubbell in the 1934 All-Star game was also clean, but modestly insists he was lucky; Burgess Whitehead, who thinks he, Terry, and the Giants did not do badly at all in that 1936 Series; Harry Craft, who graciously thanked *me* for contacting *him*; Leo Durocher, who was among the many people who couldn't believe Terry was as fast a runner as he was; and Bill Terry, because he didn't hesitate to pick up the lunch check.

INTRODUCTION

by W. P. Kinsella

Could the magnificent New York Giants teams of the Twenties, with Bill Terry as a player, and the perhaps-even-greater Giants of the Thirties, with Terry as manager, step onto the grass at Candlestick Park today and compete with the best of them? Without a doubt. Bill Terry would hit the ball in the gap, while Carl Hubbell would have present-day baseball players lunging hopelessly at his screwball.

There is no other team sport where this premise is applicable. In football, basketball, and hockey, teams from as late as the 1960s and 1970s would be humiliated by their present-day counterparts. These games have become more sophisticated, the players larger and faster. But Hubbell or Christy Mathewson would be twenty-game winners today, and Bill Terry would still hit over .300. Current players might have a slight advantage in the field, but the Giants of the Golden Age would give today's Braves a run to the wire.

That continuity with today's game is one reason why Peter Williams' *When the Giants Were Giants* will appeal to baseball fans, baseball history buffs, and lovers of excellent storytelling. The book chronicles the life of New York Giants superstar Bill Terry, the last National Leaguer to hit .400. But it is far more than a biography. It is the story of two eras—the Roaring Twenties and the Dirty Thirties.

The career of Bill Terry is a vehicle for the reader to travel through the boisterous, high-living Twenties, a time when a star like Terry could hold out and win against the likes of John McGraw and Giants owner Charles Stoneham. Then came the dark days of the Depression. Strangely, the popularity of baseball did not decline. People may not have been able to afford to go to the park as often, but they followed the game closely in the newspapers and by means of that new phenomenon, radio.

"Memphis Bill" Terry is also interesting as one of the first major-league players who created a life for himself outside baseball. By finding stable employment with Standard Oil, he became invulnerable to scheming and penny-pinching owners, who even in good times cried poverty and perennially underpaid their players. Terry seems to have been born understanding supply and demand. More than once he told owner Stoneham and manager McGraw he would quit baseball if he wasn't properly compensated, and because he had other work to fall back on, he meant it. Those of us who have tried to live off of what we can earn from our art can sympathize—though he loved baseball with a passion, he considered it, first and foremost, a way to make a living, and he demanded that he be properly compensated. Art for art's sake, or baseball without a dignified salary, was not for Bill Terry.

Terry understood the American work ethic. As a player he worked harder than anyone else, which was difficult in the expansive Twenties when the sports heroes were gargantuans like Ruth, and in golf, Walter Hagen. As manager, where John McGraw had been a driver in the Twenties, Terry was a leader in the Thirties— by example on the playing field, and by being a good listener in the clubhouse. Part psychologist, part showman, Terry won three pennants and a World Series for the Giants, playing and managing some of the greatest teams in the history of baseball.

Why America's magical love affair with baseball? Even as one who has written volumes about baseball, I ask myself that question each time I begin a writing project or a new book on baseball crosses my desk. The thirst for baseball lore, whether fact, fiction, or fantasy, appears unquenchable.

I believe there are two main reasons why baseball occupies such a warm place in the hearts of American readers. The first is the constancy of baseball. Here is a quote from my novel *Shoeless Joe*, which became the movie *Field of Dreams*:

> I don't have to tell you that the one constant through all
> the years has been baseball. America has been erased
> like a blackboard, only to be rebuilt and then erased
> again. But baseball has marked time while America has
> rolled by like a procession of steamrollers. It is the same
> game that Moonlight Graham played in 1905. It is a liv-
> ing part of history, like calico dresses, stone crockery,
> and threshing crews eating at outdoor tables. It contin-
> ually reminds us of what once was, like an Indian-head
> penny in a handful of new coins.

The second reason is that baseball is particularly conducive
to storytelling because of the open-endedness of the game. There
is theoretically no limit to the distance that a great hitter could hit
the ball—or to how far a speedy outfielder could run to retrieve
it. This open-endedness makes for myth and for larger-than-life
characters, which is what great baseball writing is all about. In my
novel, *The Iowa Baseball Confederacy*, I have a game that goes on
for over 2,600 innings and an outfielder who runs from Iowa to
New Mexico in pursuit of a fly ball.

Baseball held a special place in the hearts of the Depression-
era America that Bill Terry knew, for, in spite of the poverty
brought on by national financial collapse and by the vagaries of
nature, people still believed in the American Dream. They
believed it was possible for the poorest boy in America to grow up
to be President or to play major-league baseball. Baseball was one
of the few shining stars left in the Depression sky. It was a beacon
of hope for an impoverished nation.

Other sports—football, hockey, basketball—are all twice-
enclosed, first by time limits, then by rigid playing boundaries.
Thankfully, there is no time limit on a baseball game, and, on the true
baseball field there is no outfield fence, only horizon, and the foul
lines diverge forever, eventually taking in a good part of the universe.

WHEN THE GIANTS WERE GIANTS

PROLOGUE

Bill Terry died on January 9, 1989, but he got second baseball billing in almost every paper because Johnny Bench and Carl
Yastrzemski were elected to the Baseball Hall of Fame on the same
day. Even the *Memphis Commercial-Appeal* was guilty. The one
exception that I could find was the *Florida Times-Union*, which
ran a page one obit; still, that's a Jacksonville paper, and they may
have given him the extra attention because of his importance as a
local tycoon. When the news came over the TV, I was by chance
in New York, the city where Terry had played and managed, and
I decided to go to a couple of sports bars to see if anyone was lifting a glass in his honor.

I went to Rusty Staub's place and asked if they had heard, but
the bartender didn't know Terry's name. I figured I'd have better
luck when I found another place called The Polo Grounds, but
the joint should have been called The Garden, since a Rangers
game was playing on the two huge TV screens; and here the bartender thought Bill Terry was a *football* Giant.

I decided to head back to Jersey, and I started thinking about
my last visit to Jacksonville, in August. Terry had seemed weak,
but certainly healthy. He walked me to the door, as he always did,
and wished me safe home. I remembered he looked at the little
paunch I was developing and patted it, laughing and saying,
"what's *this?*"

At that time I had both a couple of days before I had to head
back and an offer of free lodging with friends in Bradenton Beach,
so after I left Bill Terry's house I headed over to the other coast. I
didn't get there until well after dark, and my friends said we'd
have to hurry if we wanted any food. We drove to a restaurant on
the beach. The place had a spotlight outside, where a couple of
very energetic, very tan kids, high-schoolers, were tossing a ball
back and forth in the sand. I was exhilarated after my day with

Terry and full of talk; I told his stories about the loathed Dodgers, about how his minor-league manager would wait up in the hotel to make sure his kids hadn't gone drinking, about how he met and courted his wife, about how, not long after the turn of the century, he and the other kids watched Atlanta Cracker ballgames while they lounged in the big trees outside the park. Finally I realized I'd better give my audience a breather, so I shut up and turned to look outside again. They had turned off the spotlight. The kids were gone, and now all you could see was the dark ocean, flecked as it is at night with surf.

I turned back to the table and started working more seriously on the food; I was pretty much out of stories anyway, and unaware then that I'd heard my last one from this remarkable man. Still, I'd heard a good deal, enough to get a pretty good picture of Memphis Bill Terry.

Every fan of golden-era baseball knows who Bill Terry was. He was the hard-headed businessman who told the great John McGraw he'd only play for the Giants if he could make more money than Standard Oil was paying him, the multi-millionaire who was happiest selling cars at the Buick dealership he owned. In the era of the great Yankee teams led by the flamboyant Ruth, he was the *other* number 3—the star and, later, manager of the less raucous squad that played on the other side of the Harlem River. He was the brutal guy who humiliated the then-bumbling Brooklyn Dodgers. He treated the writers who publicized him like dirt: men like the lady-killing Richards Vidmer, the classics-lover John Kieran, the dewy-eyed Granny Rice or the acerbic Westbrook Pegler. Bill Terry was, unlike them, a cool and impersonal fellow, a man who played like a machine—a precision machine, it's true, but one with little interest in the game. In other words, he didn't thank us for our love.

But is this image really accurate? Partly, it is—Terry guarded his emotions carefully, was frugal if not mercenary, and certainly viewed baseball as a business as well as a sport. But it's only partly accurate, because, in Bill Terry's case, there was a vast discrepancy between image and individual.

My first encounter with Terry was over the phone. I'd written him a letter, explaining that I'd collected an anthology of my father's baseball columns and that I was looking for anecdotes from people who knew him. Terry knew him, all right. As Red Barber has said, my father, Joe Williams, was the writer primarily responsible for creating the image of Terry as hostile, cold, and arrogant, in part because Terry wouldn't give out his home phone number. I figured I wouldn't get a response, but that it was worth a try. Then late one afternoon the phone rang, and my daughter answered it.

"It's for you," she said.

"Who is it?"

She wasn't sure she had the name right. "It's some guy named...Bill Terry?" she said.

I wasted very little time getting to the phone. "Mr. Terry! Hello!" I yelled.

The tough customer on the other end said he'd had a real problem finding my number and that he'd just about given up when his housekeeper talked him into trying one more time. He obviously saw the irony in the fact that he was talking with me, since he was laughing very genially.

His phone call led directly to my first visit to Jacksonville, in January of 1987. This aloof and reclusive superstar told me to call him when I got in. He wasn't unlisted, he said; he was in the book.

Terry lived in a house he'd built for his late wife on the last lot at the end of an attractive residential street, directly across from his country club. It was a one-story, two-bedroom house, unpretentious but very comfortable. He was a little stooped and used a cane, and when he opened the door for me he did a little, startled take, smiled, and said, "My, you're a big one!" Then he offered a hand much bigger than mine, and we shook.

He was proud of the house he'd built for his wife, and he showed me through it: I saw the paintings she had done (she was an accomplished artist), and I saw photos of their kids. He said they'd been married 68 years, and that she'd lived in that house one year and one day. He pointed to the golf course across the way and told me how much pleasure it had given him when she sat outside on sunny days and he could hear her laughing at the duffers. There was reason to laugh, since he told me they "hit the porch, hit the screens, hit the garage—they even hit one in the kitchen window." Then he took me to lunch.

He drove. He pointed out all the features on his car, which was, of course, a Buick—a Skylark, I think. By now I was pretty sure I was not dealing with the fearful ogre of baseball myth, so I accused him of trying to make a sale. He laughed.

We pulled into a handicapped spot by the front door that was always reserved for him and walked into the club. Assorted members said, "Hi, Bill," and he acknowledged them without stopping to talk. He took me to a table for two, also always reserved for him, overlooking the river. He had a salad, I ordered some seafood, and when I got a beer he asked for a glass of white wine. After one more round, I felt bold enough to make my big confession.

"Mr. Terry," I said, "I don't know how to tell you this, but when I was a kid, I was a Brooklyn fan."

Bill Terry stopped eating. He put his fork down and glared at me across the table, deadpan and mischievous. "I *knew* there was some reason I couldn't stand your father," he said.

I made several more trips to Jacksonville to see him between January and August of 1988, and each one was a delight. We talked about going to a spring game together, though it never materialized; I passed on the good feelings of Ted Williams (accepted) and Leo Durocher (distrusted); he advised me to find a place that sold fried baby catfish, which delicacy I located at last in Orange Park, at Whitey's Fish Camp; once, on a particularly beautiful day, he looked out his big front window and said, "Boy, I'd love to go outside and throw!"—so, it seems, even pragmatic multi-millionaires are entitled to have a lot of little boy in them.

On my last visit he talked to me about his life and career, and much of what he said had very little to do with real estate, cotton trading, Standard Oil, or General Motors. He'd tell terrific stories which took him back more than half a century, often adding, "I surely never will forget it." He told me about how he met "my girl" when he was eighteen, and it was not a story marked by cold impersonality. I asked him to explain his famous insult, "Is Brooklyn still in the league?" and he laughed outright, plainly indicating that there was more good humor in that crack than he's ever been given credit for. In short, I found out that Bill Terry was anything but the callous, unemotional, mercenary machine he's been made out to be. This book is an effort to look at him objectively, to set the record straight, and, since I'm in a peculiarly ideal position to do so, to atone for the sins of the fathers.

PART I

"MEMPHIS BILL"

1

MR. McGRAW STOPS OVER IN MEMPHIS

*He could take kids out of the coal mines and out of the wheat
fields and make them play ball with the look of eagles.*
—Heywood Broun, on John McGraw

On a muggy Saturday morning in Tennessee in the spring of
1922, a short, round man in his late forties got out of bed in his
suite at the Peabody, Memphis's most elegant hotel. He put on a
robe and waited for the phone to ring. He was expecting a visitor,
and he knew he wouldn't be kept waiting. Nobody ever made him
wait. The short man was John McGraw, manager and co-owner of
the New York Giants, and the virtual personification of the game
of baseball.

Every spring after the Giants had closed their training camp,
they spent a couple of weeks barnstorming their way back north,
bringing in a little extra revenue and giving McGraw a chance to
scout the local talent en route. This was a fairly tiring jaunt, since
the team normally played one game in the day and then travelled
a good part of the night, so McGraw generally scheduled a couple
of consecutive nights in Memphis, where his team could play
some games against the local Southern Association club, the
Chicks, and get some rest. McGraw, who liked his creature com-
forts, always put the team up at the Peabody.

The Giants were the best team in baseball, the best team in modern baseball history; they were *the* franchise. They had won five pennants in the past eleven years, including one the year before, in 1921. They would win one in 1922, another the next year, and another in 1924. Then McGraw's record for pennants would be eight in fourteen years, and nobody else would come close until a different dynasty took over in New York.

On the Friday before the Giants were scheduled to play in Memphis, they travelled to meet the Chicks at Jackson, Mississippi, where, on a field soaked by a persistent rain, McGraw's team won, 7-2. The Giant star that day was future Hall-of-Fame first baseman George Kelly, who homered and singled and fielded beautifully. Kelly's immediate predecessor as McGraw's first baseman had been the brilliant but corrupt Hal Chase, who would soon be banished from baseball. The man who would eventually succeed Kelly is the subject of this book.

Now that the Giants were in Memphis, the city's *Commercial-Appeal* reported that they "looked like the world's champions they are," and Saturday promised to be an occasion: Judge Kenesaw Mountain Landis, the commissioner of Major League Baseball, was in town to throw out the first ball, and a big crowd was expected to congregate at the Chicks' Russwood Park to get a look at both the Giants and Judge Landis, the silver-haired, stiff-backed man who was already legendary as a trust-busting jurist and the man brought in to "save" baseball after the 1919 Black Sox scandal. Whatever his talents as a legal mind, however, the Judge had a lousy arm. The patrons that day would get to see his throw hit Johnny Rawlings, the Giant second baseman, in the back, which suggests that Rawlings was running for his life. The crowd would give Landis a big hand anyway.

All that, however, was still a few hours away. Right now McGraw was following up a tip. He had probably already talked to Tom Watkins, the owner of the Chicks, after the teams played in Jackson, since Watkins made it his business to scrutinize everybody who played ball in the Memphis area. He had certainly talked to Kid Elberfeld, who managed the Little Rock, Arkansas, team in the Texas League. McGraw and Elberfeld went back a long way. They had played against each other for a couple of years in the National League at the end of the century. In 1901, when they both jumped to the American League, they played against each other for a year and a half more, until midway through the 1902 season, when McGraw was hired to manage the Giants. McGraw always trusted the judgment of old-timers, and he certainly trusted Elberfeld's. Sometime after the Giants had broken camp in San Antonio, but before their train pulled into Memphis from Jackson late that Friday night, Elberfeld had contacted McGraw and told him an odd story.

There was, it seemed, a left-handed pitcher who'd had two good years with the Shreveport Gassers, also in the Texas League—a solid enough prospect for Elberfeld to buy out his contract when he took over as manager of Little Rock in 1918. The pitcher, however, told Elberfeld that he had a family to support, and he said that baseball, especially minor-league baseball, was getting too chancy as a career, what with the impending American involvement in the Great War. Looking back, Elberfeld had to admit the pitcher had been right, since in 1918 the minor leagues were in such a shambles that only one league finished the season. McGraw probably began to wonder why Elberfeld was going on like this about some pitcher who'd quit the game four years ago. But Elberfeld kept talking.

Elberfeld said that after this pitcher left baseball, he had started working for Standard Oil of Louisiana, which had an office in Memphis, and that for the past year or so he'd been the star of its company team. The team had played some games in August in Arkansas, where Elberfeld had seen the kid pitch. If anything, he looked even better than when he was with Shreveport—and he could hit. Elberfeld admitted he had tried one more time to convince him to play for Little Rock, offering him more money, but the pitcher had refused, saying that the long-range situation in the minors was still far from stable and that Standard Oil was treating him well. The pitcher said he would consider an offer from a big-league team, though, there being hardly any danger of a big-league squad folding. That, Elberfeld said, was why he was suggesting him to McGraw.

Had this recommendation not come from an old baseball man like Elberfeld, McGraw might have dismissed it, since it was unusual to hear such praise for a man who hadn't played a real league game in four years. The tip *had* come from Elberfeld, though, so McGraw asked the Giants' secretary to arrange a meeting. He was going to offer the young left-hander a job—at a low salary, of course, but it was still a job with the Giants. Now the phone in McGraw's Peabody suite rang; the man from the desk announced that someone was there to see him, and McGraw said to send him on up.

It's sad that nobody ever seems to be around to record the apparently trivial first encounters that turn out to be Great Moments. The young man who walked into McGraw's suite in the Peabody that Saturday morning—let the record show that it was April 1, 1922—was much bigger than McGraw. He was tall and muscular, well dressed, and entirely self-assured. Although his demeanor was mature and confident, he was only twenty-three. When they shook, McGraw noticed that his hands were unusually large, even for a six-footer. His grip was firm but not threatening, and he looked at John McGraw without glancing away. McGraw must have asked him to sit down, and he took off his hat—he always wore a hat—and did.

There are several versions of what happened next, most originating from the young man himself, who was, of course, Bill Terry. Terry would go on to record the thirteenth highest career batting average in baseball history, to gain a reputation as a deceptively fast runner and possibly the greatest of all first basemen in the field, to distinguish himself as the last National Leaguer to bat over .400 in a season, and to become a remarkable manager. But he was always, above all else in life, a family man. He already had one child, four-year-old Bill, Jr., and was devoted to his wife, who had been his childhood sweetheart—not that twenty-three is so far from childhood. He had even left the Baptist faith and joined the Episcopal Church because she was Episcopalian. He was a man of family and of sincere convictions, and those were his priorities at that moment, as they would be throughout his life. Sitting in the hotel suite with the great John McGraw, Terry was asked if he wanted to play for the best team in the history of modern baseball, a team that, in 1922, was at its absolute peak and had five future Hall-of-Famers among the first six players in the batting order: George Kelly, Frank Frisch, Dave Bancroft, Ross Youngs, and Casey Stengel. (The only one of the six players who wouldn't make it to the Hall was Heinie Groh, who had hit .331 the year before and was presently batting cleanup.)

Terry calmly asked McGraw how much he would be paid.

McGraw was startled. He answered by asking Terry how much he wanted. Terry named a figure that was at least equal to his Standard Oil paycheck, maybe a little higher. McGraw said it was too much. Terry politely declined the offer and got up to leave.

Some say McGraw was thunderstruck, and he probably was. Here was a courteous, dignified, soft-spoken, clean-cut young man, a man who carried himself like the Giants' legendary Christy Mathewson, being offered a chance to realize every boy's dream, and he was asking about a salary. McGraw explained the portentousness of the situation: *Don't you realize what I'm offering? A chance to play baseball in the Polo Grounds, with the New York Giants?* Terry did, of course, but he also knew what was most important to him. If he accepted the job at a cut in pay, he would make life a little harder for his wife and son. For Terry that made it a simple choice—no choice at all.

Since the several versions of this story all originate with

Terry himself, they differ only in detail. Here is his last account of what happened after he asked McGraw what his salary with the Giants would be: "And he asked me how much money I wanted. I said, 'I want a three-year contract. Eight hundred dollars a month to start.' 'Oh, I'm sorry, I can't do that,' he said. And I said, 'Well, no use us talking anymore,' and I said, 'Nice to see you,' and I took my hat."

In later years, Terry would gain a reputation as a tough bargainer—it started here—but he was never a haggler. Assuming the matter was closed, he took the elevator down to the lobby and started back to his home on Vance, a quiet, shady street about two miles away.

As Kid Elberfeld recognized, Terry had been very astute to quit organized ball when he did, just before the 1918 season. While the 1917 season had been relatively unaffected in the majors, the story had been different in the minors, where only twelve leagues had finished the year.

Terry had finished out the 1917 season with the Shreveport Gassers, but he read the papers, and through the fall and into the winter of that year, they were full of warnings. They reported that the minors might redistrict, with some teams disappearing in the process; that players would have to sign contracts with a clause that protected the owners (but not the players) should the war force a suspension of games; and that fewer games would be played in 1918. Ed Barrow, who would later become the Yankee general manager, was president of the International League then and he actually *wanted* to cancel his 1918 season; if he'd had his way, not even one minor league would have finished the year. Then the papers announced that only ten minor leagues would start the 1918 season (half the number of the year before), and finally they reported that salaries were going to be cut. Baseball in the minors had become a severely depressed industry, not a place for any conscientious head of a household, and Bill Terry certainly knew it. If Elberfeld had bought Terry's contract from Shreveport, no offense, but that was Elberfeld's hard luck.

So in early 1918, Terry started looking for profitable work. He got a stop-gap job assembling batteries, but this was essentially menial labor, so he kept looking and finally landed a job as a salesman with Standard Oil of Louisiana. Once on board, Terry volunteered to build the company team. His boss, Charles Scholder, told him to go ahead, and Terry quickly became the star and unofficial captain, developing a local following and becoming a popular figure in Memphis. The Standard Oil Polarines, named after a high-grade motor oil, played on Sundays and sometimes Saturdays, occasionally traveling as far as Knoxville to play in Tennessee tournaments. Terry would remain content to subordinate baseball to business for the next four years. He worked full-time for Standard through the spring of 1922, and it was a happy time for him. He was a young and ambitious man, affiliated with a major corporation that promised him a stable future; he was still playing a game that, despite what his detractors later said, he loved very much; and he was living in Memphis with a young wife and a baby son whom he loved even more. Terry had achieved his first great goal: he had created a stable home and family—something he had never known. To understand how important this was to him, it's best to take a look at the Terry family tree.

2

THE WILSONS ILLUSTRATE GEORGIA

I was interested in baseball. I was interested in playing it, from the time I was a little kid. I never will forget, my father decided I couldn't throw hard, so he got a mitt someplace, said, I want to see how hard you throw. Well, we went out in the back yard and he marked off the distance—and he couldn't catch me. I'd get warmed up and I'd turn the ball loose—Jiminy Christmas—I'd hit him all over. He said, you, I can't catch you.

He finally decided I could throw hard.

          —Bill Terry

Late in the afternoon of August 3, 1861, the owner-proprietor of William A. Kennedy's Boot and Shoemaker's on Decatur Road in Atlanta was feeling pleased. Not only was it a fine day, sunny and in the mid-eighties, but he had at last heard from his son, who had joined the Confederate Army shortly after Fort Sumter and was with it at the rout of the Unions at First Manassas. Since the battle had been fought two weeks earlier, Kennedy would not have been surprised to get a letter of a different kind and from a different and more official source. But he received word from his son instead, so he felt a sense of relief. His son was not only alive, but unhurt. He had also been part of a great victory for the South, and for the men of Georgia. His son's letter offered details about the exploits of the Georgian officers, Foreacre and Gartrell, and focused particularly on the gallant assault of Bartow's brigade, in which charge Bartow himself had been killed. Bartow had died, young Kennedy said, "to illustrate Georgia."

After reading the letter, Kennedy went to sit at the window in the front of his shop, so that he could share the good news with anybody who passed by. Pretty soon, a man in his thirties came along the road from the east, riding a mule toward town. Kennedy hailed him, and the man stopped and tied his mule to a post. He was Tom Terry, who ran the city's only sawmill. (Most of the wooden homes in antebellum Atlanta had been built with planks from Terry's mill.) Kennedy recited his son's letter to Terry, through the open window, and Terry, presumably, was pleased to see the shoemaker so elated. Meanwhile, two men had come up to the store from the other direction. They had spent the entire Saturday in town, and they were drunk. They had polished off a bottle of cheap champagne, then gone into a bar and replenished it with even cheaper rye. The bottle thus restored was by now only half-full.

This was the father-and-son team of John and James Wilson. John's nephew, Walton, a patriot like Kennedy's son, had enlisted as soon as the war started. Walton worked for Tom Terry and lived on his spread, and Terry had generously promised to provide food and shelter for Walton's wife and kids for the duration of the war. His selfless gesture suggests that Tom Terry was as well-respected by the small Atlanta community as the dissolute Wilsons were not. John and James therefore, discovered in envy two good reasons to hate Terry's guts—Terry's own generous nature and his recognition of a like spirit in their nephew, Walton. In fact, they had cursed and threatened Terry publicly many times in the past, usually after imagining injuries to their family name. Now John Wilson called Tom Terry out, asking him to step away from Kennedy's window and into the street.

Terry said he didn't want any trouble, but he was not a man to shrink in fear. He took a stirrup from his saddle-horn, putting his hand through it to make a brass knuckle, and walked out into the dust of Decatur Road. John was much older than Terry, and far from sober, so Terry probably felt relatively safe, despite the presence of John's son. Still, John was able to punch Terry in the right eye. Terry countered by hitting Wilson *pere* with the stirrup, drawing blood and giving James Wilson an excuse to join in vengefully. James, who had maneuvered himself behind Terry, hit him very hard behind the ear with the champagne bottle. Terry, of course, never saw it coming. After he fell, the father jumped on him, punching him furiously and repeatedly as he lay stunned in the dirt.

Kennedy ran out of his store and pulled John Wilson off of Terry, and the two drunks, satisfied, stumbled up Decatur Road. But it was too late. Although Terry was able to stand up and walk to Kennedy's porch, once even mustering the strength to try to go after the Wilsons, he was finished. He fell into a chair, and Kennedy gave him a glass of water. Terry, growing more and more incoherent, said, "I want to go home," then nothing more. Three doctors worked on him through the night, but he died a little after two in the morning on August 4.

The Wilsons were convicted—John for manslaughter and James for murder—and James was condemned to death. The Georgia Supreme Court in Milledgeville, however, granted a stay, and both men were still in Milledgeville prison when, in 1864, Sherman's army threatened Atlanta. Then the Confederacy granted all of the prisoners in every jail in Georgia their liberty, contingent upon their promise to join the cause and fight, and the doors to the cells were opened. Not surprisingly, the names of John and James Wilson failed to appear on the Confederate military rolls for this period. The Wilsons, of whom nothing further was ever heard, had "illustrated Georgia" according to their own particular lights.

Tom Terry left behind a wife and four sons. His wife, Mary Jane, was the daughter of James Thurman, an Atlanta blacksmith and wheelwright. There is also the sometimes reported, but unsubstantiated, possibility that Tom Terry himself was the uncle of the great British actress, Ellen Terry. If true, that would make Bill Terry a distant cousin of a later and even more famous actor, Sir John Gielgud. One of Tom's sons, Jasper, was less than two months old when his father was killed, and he lived only a week past his second birthday. A second son, Sylvester, was four; he died in 1872 at age fifteen. Newton, born on Christmas day in 1858, was two at the time of the murder, while William, the oldest son, was almost seven. William was the only one of the kids who would have had a clear memory of his father. William was Bill Terry's grandfather.

It must have been tough to be the oldest son in a family so pointlessly and suddenly devastated by two near-sociopaths. Young William probably tried to take charge immediately, to comfort the mother and become the man of the house; maybe he had to play this role again less than two years later when Jasper died. There's little doubt, at least, that when he married Ella Heath in Atlanta in June of 1875, he was hoping his luck would change for the better.

It did. Still, at the start, his career was unremarkable. His marriage went largely unnoticed, and the paper even got his name wrong, identifying him as "Mr. N. M. Terry." To give him his due, he was only twenty; nonetheless, someone should have remembered that his father had been a prominent businessman. It took him more than thirty years to leave his mark, but by 1907 the Atlanta city directory listed William M. Terry as one of the "Makers of Atlanta," and it printed his picture a page away from that of a local hero, progressive Governor-elect Hoke Smith. In 1907, Terry was, among other important things, chairman of the Board of Police Commissioners, and the directory praised him for the job he did under that hat, citing his "clear judgment and impartial rulings" and calling him a "prominent worker for the good of the city."

William M. Terry had made a decided success of himself in Atlanta, picking up where his murdered father had been forced to leave off. In addition to being a police commissioner, he was the owner of a thriving wholesale grocery business (located on Decatur near Piedmont, not four blocks from where Kennedy's shoe store had been), he served as a city alderman under two separate mayors, and he owned and presided over a bank of his own making, the Decatur Street Bank. In all of these accomplishments, possibly even in the name he chose for his bank, there is the flavor of a man using his own life to compensate for what his father was unable to finish.

Since William M. Terry had not had an undisturbed and tranquil home life, he sought to create one now. He bought a big house at 236 North Boulevard before the turn of the century and he lived there until 1921. He may have hoped this would provide his children with the sense of stability that had been yanked from his life at such an early age, or he may have simply wanted to recapture that feeling of security for himself.

Of William's four children, three were girls, and they all married promptly. Lena Terry became Mrs. Richard Ewing, wife of the head man at the Ewing Realty Co., and Ella Mae Terry married Emory Quarles, who died young, possibly in the war, leaving Ella Mae to wed again. Her second husband was Milton Lysle, who became the commissioner of the Memphis, Tennessee, Freight Bureau. Lena and Ella Mae had ended up in "good" marriages, certainly, but the most significant match was probably made by their sister, Grace Terry. She became the wife of "Big Jim" Ison, founder of the Ison Finance Co. in Atlanta. "Big Jim" got his nickname when he played baseball for Georgia Tech, where he set a number of records.

His best year there was 1904, when he had twelve consecutive base hits and a phenomenal season's average of .750. In one exhibition against the professional Cleveland Naps, Ison got three of the four hits allowed by Addie Joss, all for extra bases. Joss, a Hall-of-Famer who pitched a perfect game in 1908, has the second-lowest earned run average in major-league history, 1.88. Nap

Lajoie, the famed Cleveland manager after whom the team had been named, (his .422 average in 1901 is the second-highest for a season in this century) was playing second base in that game, and he was so impressed with Ison that he tried to get him to quit college and try out for the Naps. Ison resisted the temptation and stayed in school, although he did switch briefly to second base, admitting later that this was an act of hero-worship in deference to Lajoie. His normal position was first base.

William T. Terry was William M.'s only son; born in 1878, he married Bertha Blackman in October 1897 in the Fifth Baptist Church in Atlanta. Unlike his father, though, William T. could never make a success of himself. For the first four years of his marriage, he lived in his father's house at 236 North Boulevard. He got his own place for the next two years and moved to a new address on Decatur for the two years after that. He changed houses in 1905 and came back home in 1906. He was still there in 1907, when his father was honored as a "Maker of Atlanta," but he moved again in 1908, again the year after that, and again the year after that. By 1910, his father had created and become the first president of the Decatur Street Bank, but William T., although he had worked all those years in the family grain business, was still listed in the city directory as a "clerk."

William T. Terry was also unlike his father (and his grandfather, for that matter) in another way: he had only one child, only one witness to his various failures and to the eventual collapse of his marriage. That child, born on October 30, 1898, was William Harold "Bill" Terry.

Bill Terry's youth was certainly unsettled. As a child, he was taken along as his parents meandered from house to house, often punctuating their progress with the humiliating need to move back to 236 North Boulevard. Bill Terry was three when the family first moved, and it's doubtful that it affected him much then. But he was five the next time they packed up, then seven, eight, ten, eleven, and twelve. Tension in the family must have been building. By 1910, the young Terry was finding reasons to get out of the house. In the afternoons, he'd go to Ponce de Leon Park to watch the Crackers, Atlanta's Southern Association team. He and the other local kids had a favorite player, an outfielder who could hit pretty well, Roy Moran. Moran was traded to the Chattanooga Lookouts in May of 1911, and he made it to the majors in 1912, playing five games for the Washington Senators. But before all of that, he had a long career with the Crackers. "He was a good ballplayer, we thought," Terry remembered, "stupid as he was."

Terry couldn't afford to pay to get in to the Cracker games, though, any more than the other kids could, so they'd all climb the trees outside the wooden outfield fence and watch from there, lounging during the warm afternoons. When Terry described the setting, I said it was a very nice picture, reminiscent of the fans who nowadays bring lawn chairs up to the roofs behind Chicago's Wrigley Field. He didn't say much in response. "Much nicer," was all he said.

The summer of 1911 was probably an unhappy time for Terry. Not only did Moran leave Atlanta—not a small loss for the twelve-year-old—but it seems to have been the year of the first crisis in his parents' marriage and the initial moment of disillusioning truth for the young Terry. There is no record of an address for either of Terry's parents in Atlanta in 1911, and since Terry said he was thirteen when he left home to work as a laborer—he turned thirteen in October—this may have been the year they first separated. In any event, he dropped out of Highland Park grammar school to find a job.

The Highland Park School had a good principal, however, and Terry never did forget her. Her name was Hattie Cola Spears, and she was, he said, "a very fine lady." It was likely that her influence prompted him to go back to school, probably in the fall of 1912, and he probably graduated the following spring. He didn't go on to high school, though; in 1913, by the time he was fifteen, he was working in the railroad yard in Atlanta, heaving flour sacks onto trucks. He was a big kid, stronger and older-looking than his years, and he doubtless never told anyone there how young he really was.

If Terry's parents tried separation in 1911, there was an attempt at reconciliation the following year, an attempt the young Terry may have encouraged. William T. was still working for his father at the grain store, and he printed his name together with Bertha's in the Atlanta directory again, but this time they were joined by a third member, W. H., who was listed as a "bookkeeper." This was the only time Bill Terry's name appeared in the directory next to those of his parents. They were all living at the same address, but it was, once again, a new one. Terry's parents (but not Terry) would be listed at another new address in 1913, and in 1914 they would move back to 236 North Boulevard, possibly exhausted by their efforts and defeated by their failures. By 1915, only William T. Terry would be listed as living at his father's house; this time, it seemed, his wife had left for good.

In the meantime, Bill Terry tried to lead his own life. More and more, he must have felt that he couldn't rely on anyone but himself. He must have also seen the necessity of hard work and been determined to carve a comfortable life for himself by dint of just that. The importance of hard work so impressed itself on Bill Terry that it stayed with him from the time he quit school and left home to work at hard labor at age thirteen, to his last day in his office at his Jacksonville, Florida, Buick dealership at age ninety. He had seen firsthand how love and lives could be wrecked by a lack of money, so money became for him a defense, a shield—a means to security of the emotional even more than the financial sort. When his parents separated for the last time, he wasn't yet fifteen; nonetheless, it became obvious to him that he'd have to take matters into his own already capable hands. It's unlikely that he spent much time at home after 1912. He was either out working, planning to work, or—and only partly because there eventually turned out to be money in it—playing baseball.

3

IN WHICH BILL TERRY MOVES TO TENNESSEE

Mr. Garry Herrmann, Owner
Cincinnati Baseball Club
Dear Sir:
I am writing you in regard to a left hand pitcher I have on my club,
who I am sure will make you a good man. His name is Bill Terry, 6
ft. 2", weighs 185 lbs. coming 21 years of age. He is fast on his feet,
has a cracking good fast ball and plenty of nerve.
If any of your scouts are in this vicinity, and if you are interested I
would be glad to pitch him on their arrival.
Yours truly,
Harry Matthews, Manager
Newnan, Ga.

Terry played his first recorded baseball games in Atlanta in 1912, for Grace Methodist in the Baraca Sunday School League. It's possible his grandfather, a co-founder of Grace Methodist, encouraged him in this pursuit, but if he was on the Grace squad when it opened its season in late April, he didn't get to play. He still hadn't gotten into a game by the first of June, when a seventh straight loss made Grace's undisputed hold on the Baraca League cellar even more secure. The team was 0-7 on the season, so the Methodist manager tried to shake things up. On June 8, he started thirteen-year-old Bill Terry at second base.

Terry's baseball debut was unimpressive, and Grace continued its losing ways. In an attempt to start winning, the desperate Methodist manager gave Terry, who had a strong arm, a chance to pitch. He struck out two batters, but he was wild, losing that first start, 8-0. Nonetheless, the game was significant in that Terry looked as though he might be successful as a pitcher. Subsequent managers thought so, too, and they kept him on the mound for nearly a decade.

By 1913, when an older and huskier Terry was making money loading trucks, he had graduated to the Grammar School League, which had games throughout the week. In later years, he recalled having played some games for the Boulevard Stars of Atlanta in that league early in the season, although he doesn't appear in their boxscores. He did play for the Edgewood Avenue squad, taking part in an exciting playoff series against Formwalt that Edgewood lost. Terry and his young buddies had to settle for the second-place trophy, a pennant. Formwalt, on the other hand, earned a pennant *and* a silver cup.

Around this time, a veteran catcher named Harry "Matty" Matthews, who had seen Terry play, told Atlanta Crackers' manager Billy Smith about him. Smith gave Terry a tryout, then signed him to his first pro contract. Terry didn't get into any Crackers games, but he did spend much of the 1914 season working out in Ponce de Leon Park with the team he'd watched from the trees beyond the outfield fence. After the season ended, Terry got what he thought would be his big break. The new manager of the major-league St. Louis Browns, Branch Rickey, somehow had heard about this very promising kid, and he invited Terry to come to the Browns' training camp in Sarasota the following spring. Terry was so excited he bought a Saratoga trunk, poor though he was, although he didn't have enough clothes to fill it. Then the Browns had a change of heart and retracted their offer. Maybe they had discovered that Terry was only fifteen. It's likely he was crushed, but at least he was still affiliated with the Cracker organization.

Despite all these tantalizing hints and nibbles from pro teams, 1914, the last year his parents lived together, was not a terrific time for the fifteen-year-old. But his emotional luck would soon change. Sometime between the fall of 1914 and the following spring, Terry "met somebody," a girl who was just as smart and open and forthright as he was, and he fell in love with her as swiftly and as decisively as he did most things. I asked him how they met, and Terry looked back three-fourths of a century to that moment. "We didn't have much money in those days," he remembered.

> And this boy came up and told me he had a date with this girl, and he said, 'I don't have money to get over there on the streetcar. Come on, go with me, pay my way there.' I said, 'I'll do that,' and we went. He had a locket for her. She got the locket. 'Now,' she said to him, 'you can go.' 'Well,' I said, 'What about me?' I said, 'You want me to go too?' 'Well,' she said, 'I didn't say anything about you. If you want to stay, you can stay awhile. That's up to you.' And I said, 'I'll stay awhile.' And that was it. I didn't have any money, and she knew that; but we kept dating, and we never did quit. Her name was Elvena Virginia Sneed, very lovely. A lovely lady. I never will forget.

I asked Terry when he proposed to her.

"Oh, it didn't take too long," he said. "But I was very much in love with her. Stayed that way. For seventy-one years."

Elvena Sneed was a confident, strong-willed girl and, as such, she was ideal for Bill Terry. They met the year his parents' marriage was ending, and the timing seems significant—there's the sense of a man jumping from a sinking ship to the deck of a sturdy one. Terry's unhesitant judgments were frequently right, and nowhere did that knack for making a quick and accurate decision serve him better than when he met Elvena. At that time, he was living in nesting-box fashion with his parents, who were living with his grandparents. Hope for his parents' reconciliation was virtually gone. Terry, who had previously spent a good deal of time out of the house either working or playing ball, now had an even better reason to stay away from home: he was genuinely in love. It takes no seer to guess that he called on Elvena as often as possible. The Sneeds lived at 11 Saint Charles Avenue, about a dozen blocks from his grandfather's house, and Terry probably didn't hesitate to walk that distance even when he didn't have enough money to take the trolley that went up North Boulevard.

Whether he walked or rode, though, he had to pass Ponce de Leon Park to get there. The field would appear on the right side of the road as he travelled north, with the seats in the third-base grandstand directly across the street from him, and the trees and outfield wall coming into view a little later, after he crossed Ponce de Leon Avenue.

He had just finished a "season" that had provided nothing, but had promised everything—Billy Smith had hired him for the Crackers and Rickey's Browns had shown big league interest. He mapped out a future for Elvena. He told her a career in baseball was a strong possibility, citing the tangible encouragement he'd already been given and noting the comfortable life of the successful player. Always confident but never vain, he told her he was good enough to succeed and said that by playing ball, he could make a good life for her. At some point during this time he proposed. As he said, "it didn't take too long."

In the spring of 1915, Terry showed up at Ponce de Leon again. This time, Billy Smith farmed him out to Dothan in the Georgia State League, but he pitched terribly. He got into only two games, walking ten men in one of them, and his earned run average was over fifteen. He later placed some of the blame on his manager, an infielder who told him how to pitch, with the result that he got wilder than ever. "I couldn't get the ball over the plate," he said, after following the infielder-manager's instructions. "Don't think he liked me, anyway."

Then in June, Terry received good news: Matty Matthews, the man who had recommended him to Billy Smith in the first place, was now managing Newnan in the Class D Georgia-Alabama League. It was an era when formal contractual obligations meant less than they later would, when players sometimes were shuffled back and forth between teams almost as though they were trading cards. Matthews was able to convince Smith to get the Dothan skipper to unconditionally release Terry to Newnan. Terry had a few days until he had to report, enabling him to return to Atlanta to help Elvena celebrate her graduation from high school. "That's where I was, Dothan, Alabama, when they gave me my release," Terry told me. "And boy, was I tickled—tickled to get home because that wife of mine, who was just my girlfriend then, was graduating. And I got home in time to see her."

When he arrived in Newnan, tall and skinny and four months shy of his seventeenth birthday, nobody tried to change him. And this time, he pitched well. The lesson, like most others, was not lost on Bill Terry; as a manager, he would seldom try to change a player's style. Early in 1933, when he was managing the Giants, John Drebinger of *The New York Times* asked him how he was going to coach the erratic right-hander, Roy Parmelee, and Terry remembered his Dothan manager. "They tried to make me turn around before I made each pitch, with the result that I couldn't pitch at all," he said, adding that at Newnan, he "was allowed to pitch any way I liked, and I won nine straight games." Okay, Drebinger said, but what would Terry do with Parmelee? "If he can win games for us, I don't care if he pitches standing on his ear," Terry replied.

Terry's memory glamorized his achievement, but not by much. In the course of Newnan's very short season (hardly more than a month), he was 8-1. Even so, he was overshadowed by the team's star, Jack Nabors. In fact, Terry's first start came on June 17, the day after Nabors pitched thirteen innings of no-hit ball, something the *Atlanta Constitution* called "a world's record in organized baseball." That game was even reported in *The New York Times*. But Terry didn't stay in the background for long. He started to win regularly and convincingly. Finally, on June 30, Terry's moment of pitching glory arrived.

He remembered it with great pleasure, saying how much it meant to him as a kid of sixteen, and how happy he was to find that Archie Sneed, his future father-in-law, was very impressed.

Terry no-hit the Anniston club, winning 2-0. That story didn't make *The New York Times*, and the *Constitution*'s praise was a bit faint—under the headline, "Atlanta Boy Hurls No-hit for Newnan," the newspaper reported that "sensational fielding by Newnan robbed Anniston of several hits." Still, that may have been a fair account since Terry himself told me that "the last guy up hit a line drive into right field, and I knew it was a no-hitter, you know, and it *scared* me; but the right-fielder came up with it, anyway."

Some credit for Terry's success should certainly be given to Matty Matthews, an influence Terry never forgot (Matthews ended up as a jailer in Covington, Kentucky, and whenever the Giants played at Cincinnati, Terry would cross the river for a visit).

Terry remembered Matthews very fondly. He owned a bar in Atlanta; Terry and the other young players would go in every night, and Matthews would give them a pitcher of Coke on the house. "We used to kid with him like we wanted something," Terry remembered, although all they wanted was the Coke. "See," he said, "I was only sixteen." But their kidding made the manager a little nervous, and one night on the road when Terry and his friends stayed out late, Matty waited up: "We had four fellows and we could sing pretty good," Terry said. "I never will forget we were in Anniston, and we went to the fair. And we came in, back to the hotel, and there was a stairway to the second floor, and as you turn—he was sitting across the stair, and he wanted to see what we looked like. And we didn't touch a drop. And we sang, just walking around, and looking at things at the fairground, and didn't even think about drinking anything. It was a pretty nice group we had."

Most importantly, Matthews taught Terry how to pitch with control, or at least he tried. On the day Terry reported to Newnan, Matthews, who knew how wild he had been at Dothan, met him at the train station. Matthews was the team's catcher, and he had his chest protector with him. He walked with Terry to a drug store in town, bought a bottle of ink, and slapped the protector on the counter. Terry asked what was going on, and Matthews simply said, "You'll find out." Then he used the ink to make a spot right in the middle of the protector. "Now I'll tell you what I want," he told Terry, "no matter which way I stand, I want you to throw at that ink spot. We're going to get you so that you can pitch to a spot." Matthews' lesson speaks for itself—in half a season, Terry was transformed from a truly awful pitcher to one good enough to throw a no-hitter.

On July 7, 1916, Matthews wrote a letter recommending Terry to Garry Herrmann, owner of the Cincinnati Reds, embellishing on Terry's record (he said he'd won twelve, but he'd only won seven) and age (he said he was 21 when he was only 17). Matthews may have thought Terry's youth was keeping him from a shot at the big time. Later, commentators suggested Terry really was several years older than he claimed, but the Atlanta papers listed him as being seventeen in 1916, long before anybody knew who he was, so this isn't likely. In any event, Herrmann dispatched no scouts to Newnan, where Terry stayed and pitched again the following year.

Meanwhile, Archie Sneed, Elvena's father, who had worked for a stove manufacturing company based in Tennessee, was transferred to Memphis. The move probably pleased his wife, who came from a prominent Memphis family. (Her father had donated money to build the Hebe fountain, which still stands in Court Square.) The teenage Terry must have been devastated. He had met Elvena at fifteen, and he was not about to let her go. When he spoke of being in love with her "for seventy-one years," he meant the period extending from their wedding day to the day we talked in 1987, more than three years after her death. At the time she moved to Memphis, though, he had no money. He must have promised to follow her as soon as he could, and then set about finding a way to earn enough to do so.

Then, midway through the summer of 1916, Terry had a

piece of luck. After the Georgia-Alabama season finished on July 21, Matthews sold four of his stars to clubs in higher leagues—contending clubs with more conventional summer seasons to finish. The left fielder, Don Flynn, who was leading the league in hitting, went to Waco, and Matthews's second-best pitcher, R. Y. Watkins, was bequeathed to Beaumont, both of the Texas League. Mackie, the second baseman, went to Macon in the Sally League. Bill Terry was sold to Shreveport, another team in the Texas League. At last he had a use for his trunk. He packed it with whatever he had, probably still not much, said goodbye to his father and his grandparents, and left Atlanta for the last time. Not only was Shreveport going to be far away from a number of bitter memories, it was a lot closer to the new residence of Elvena Virginia Sneed.

On the same July day that Terry played his last game for Newnan, the *Shreveport Times* announced his impending arrival in a box on its sports page. The headline said he would arrive in Shreveport on Monday, July 24. "Terry has been with the Newman [sic] club two seasons and has been one of the most successful pitchers in the league," the paper reported, adding that "the Gassers have been without a left-hander during the last two months of the season," so "the acquisition of Terry is expected to materially strengthen the pitching department." Shreveport was in a fight for the league title, and, on Sunday, the paper was more specific about the team's new man, admitting that Shreveport manager Syd Smith had bought him as insurance for "the final dash," and adding that Terry's arrival meant that it was the Gassers' intention "to fight it out with all comers to the last trench." As it turned out, Shreveport's hopes were justified. Although it took him the better part of a week to report (he may have stopped off in Memphis first to see Elvena), by the end of August, Terry had become a local star.

Take August 24, for instance, when he was prominently mentioned in the *Shreveport Times* three times. The paper reported that he'd shut out Beaumont, 1-0, in "one of the niftiest duels ever witnessed here," Beaumont being "helpless throughout before the left-handed efforts of Bill Terry." A regular feature, "Sport Dope," added a couple of paragraphs, saying that "Bill Terry threatens to become as celebrated in Texas League circles as Beaumont's right field fence," which fence was notoriously short. Best of all, there was a third item, one that generated a little extra cash for minor-leaguers making slave wages: a full-page ad, sponsored by several local merchants and featuring endorsements by Gasser stars. In the ad, Terry is being used to sell Hupmobiles, and the accompanying photo is probably the first picture of him to appear in public print. Considering his achievements up to that time, he looked incredibly young, like a boy. Over his picture was a nickname some public relations person thought suitable—"Spitfire"—and below it is this text:

IT'S A "TWO-TO-ONE" BET WHEN
TERRY'S GOING TO PITCH
Ladeeeeeeeezzzz 'nd Gentleeem'n!
Batreeeeeez fur today—fur de home club, TERRY and SMITH. Fur de udder club—

But what does it matter? Hasn't he said enough already? Do we care who must assume the burden of the loss for the other club?

It's another chalk-up on the "won" side for the Gassers when his umps shouts those reassuring words of safe—"TERRY and SMITH."

THEY ALL BOW LOW
WHEN "SPITFIRE"
TAKES THE MOUND

Possessor of cunning, cleverness, steady control, a wise head on a pair of young shoulders, and a world of baffling "stuff," Spitfire Terry makes deadly .300 sluggers look like "rank" beginners.

Here's to Spitfire! May the Lord be with us and send
him back to us next year!

Terry and the Gassers continued to do well in 1916. They
lost the pennant to Waco, but only on the last day of the season.
The Shreveport fans were pleased enough to honor the team with
a Players' Day at which manager-catcher Syd Smith was given a
huge gilt wishbone covered with flowers. There was a purple
baseball pennant inside the wishbone, and it said, "Greater than
the Texas Pennant—You Have Won the Hearts of the Shreveport
People."

Now, for the first time, Terry did not go back to Atlanta.
Instead, he went to Memphis, to the Sneed home at 1032 Forrest.
It's very likely that he stayed there; Elvena's father admired Terry
both as a ballplayer and as a man, and if he had any doubts as to
Terry's intentions with respect to his daughter, they would have
been erased by this announcement in the November 21 edition of
the Memphis *Commercial-Appeal*. Under "Marriage Licenses,"
these were the first names to appear: "W. H. Terry and Evelina
Virginia Sneed." Once again, a Terry was too unimportant to
require the typesetter to be alert. The correct name was *Elvena*, of
course, not Evelina.

The Terrys' wedding, certainly small and possibly even a civil
ceremony, went unnoticed in the press, and only the bride's family attended. Terry's parents stayed away. When Terry spoke of
them to me, he made a sad slip. He told me he didn't expect them
to show up and implied that he had little contact with them after
that. "The only thing I did," he said, "I buried both of 'em, give
'em a good funeral. I went down, both times, to Georgia, and gave
'em a good wedding—a good funeral, I mean."

However, there was little point in looking back, and Terry
was never one for self-pity. Since Archie's house was hardly the
place for a honeymoon, and since Elvena had always wanted to
see New Orleans, they went there. He knew he could add a little

money to his savings if he played ball in the New Orleans winter league—for "twelve, fifteen dollars" a game, he told me—and he knew he was now sufficiently well-known in Louisiana to get that kind of work. So late in the fall of 1916, the Terrys headed south.

It's unclear which team Terry played for that winter, but he does appear on the roster of the Gaslights when they took on a team of all-stars on February 25, 1917. A glance at the lineups for this game serves as proof that the mid-winter leagues were anything but amateurish. The all-star team had, among other players, Jim Bagby, a 16-game winner for the Cleveland Indians in 1916 who would win 23 the following year and who would cap his career with a league-leading 31 victories in 1920. The first baseman for Terry's Gaslights was another Indian, Chick Gandil, an unsavory man who would gain fame of a different sort when he was shown to be a ringleader of the eight Chicago White Sox players who conspired to fix the 1919 World Series. At any rate, when the Indians opened their New Orleans training camp in March, Bagby and Gandil had to report. The winter-league season was over, and so was Terry's honeymoon. Terry had to get back to his regular job. He went to his own training camp, which was in Shreveport, and left Elvena temporarily behind.

By the time Elvena arrived in Shreveport, two weeks before the season opened and before paychecks of any size started coming in, Terry was penniless. He had rented a cheap room in a seedy hotel, so they had shelter, but there was no more money for food. He took Elvena to a cafeteria, spent his remaining change on breakfast, and explained the situation. She had believed him when he had said there was a promising future in baseball, so had her father, and now he felt he had let them down, badly. He was too proud to ask Archie for a handout, at least if he could help it, and he certainly didn't want to ask anybody in Atlanta for help. Elvena's engagement ring was no "rock"—it had cost him only forty-five dollars—but it could be pawned, allowing them to eat for the next two weeks. Terry promised his wife he would never ask her for money again. He told her he was more determined than ever to give her a comfortable life, and he said he'd make a million dollars for her someday. She may have taken this statement as an exaggeration. If she did, she didn't fully know her husband yet.

They got fifteen dollars for the ring, enough for two weeks of food, and, after he was paid, he bought the ring back immediately. Still, there's no discounting the haunting effect this episode had on Terry. As late as 1938, in an effort to explain himself to the press, he emphasized the incident in an article in *The Saturday Evening Post*. He was right in recognizing its importance. If anything explains what made Bill Terry tick it is this incident. It demonstrates that the real importance of money in Terry's life had much more to do with love than greed.

Terry did not have a great year for Shreveport in 1917. He alternated between fine games and terrible ones, and, since his hitting wasn't spectacular, Smith had little inclination to try him in the outfield on a regular basis. So Smith kept him in the rotation, hoping for solid, low-scoring games and occasionally using him as a pinch-hitter. The fans had no party for the 1917 Gassers, who finished in the cellar. After the dismal season ended, Terry packed up and went home to Memphis. He and his wife probably stayed with her family, at the old address on Forrest or the new one at 56 North Evergreen; they were still listed as living with the Sneeds on North Evergreen two years later. When Terry's own father had come back home, as he had done repeatedly, it always seemed more a matter of economic necessity than of choice. Terry himself seemed to have chosen to live with his in-laws partly from economic convenience, but also because of a desire for a cohesive and functional family environment. His wife didn't appear to mind, and when she told him she was pregnant, he probably thought it was an even better idea.

Although his season had been mediocre, baseball professionals had by no means given up on Terry. In late September,

Norman "Kid" Elberfeld, who had quit as manager of Chattanooga in the Southern Association, took over as manager of another Southern Association outfit, the Little Rock Travelers, and started looking for fresh talent. The Travelers, like the Gassers, had finished last in 1917, and Elberfeld was supposed to do something about it. Elberfeld could see beyond a player's statistics. In short, he was a good scout, and he felt Terry was a lot better than he looked on paper. So he contacted Syd Smith—after all, Shreveport needed a shakeup, too—and, in the spring of 1918, he bought out Terry's contract.

Terry flat-out refused to be bought. He knew the minors would be in dire straits in 1918. If he was going to work for a lousy salary, he'd at least work for a lousy salary that was secure, and, since his wife was expecting, he couldn't in good conscience consider enlisting in the military. So early in 1918, he gave up baseball, stayed in Memphis, and took an interim job with the Storage Battery Service and Sales Company. Terry was paid $18.50 per week to make batteries for Fred Bauer, who was the company's president, general manager, and just about everything else. Since he did the same thing every day, he became very good at this mindless work. After several months, Bauer began to offer bonuses, based on the number of batteries an employee produced, and Terry benefited from this new policy; while he didn't quite clean up, his energy and industry netted him a little more money to take home. After a while, though, Fred Bauer, Jr., decided to throw his weight around. He started telling his father's employees, including Terry, how to do their jobs. Terry, who worked all day and into the night, became fed up. He quit.

It's uncertain whether he tracked down his job with Standard Oil before he quit or after, but it's likely he wouldn't have left without knowing he had something else lined up, since he now had an infant son to feed. Standard had a big office in Memphis, with about three-hundred and fifty employees working in and around the city, and Terry would continue to work with the company, in various capacities, for the next couple of decades. At the height of his fame as a ballplayer and manager, Terry would be Standard Oil's public-relations man, touring in the off-season with a road show that featured Guy Lombardo and his dance orchestra, the Royal Canadians.

Corporations before World War I fielded semipro teams for a variety of reasons, such as workers' solidarity and public relations, but after the country became involved in the war, the teams also served to display the patriotism of the companies. The names of the leagues themselves began to reflect the country's jingoistic mood—the Red Cross League, the Old Glory League and Uncle Sam's League. Since it didn't seem wise for a corporate giant to drag its patriotic heels, Standard Oil of Louisiana decided it had better play ball. A year after Terry joined the company, he organized the Standard Oil Polarines. As noted, they played on weekends, sometimes even taking overnight jaunts to compete in state tournaments. Although Terry founded the team, he didn't play for it right away; on the day of the Polarines' debut on June 15, Terry was the umpire, impartially watching them lose a doubleheader. The Polarines continued through 1919, winning a few games, losing a few more, and in general stirring up very little excitement on the Memphis scene. But they did play well enough to be rewarded with uniforms. Terry's boss, Charles Scholder, asked him to get some, and to get good ones. Terry did, and everybody was happy: "Boy, we looked like something else!" he told me years afterward. Later, he would design outfits for another team. Whenever the contemporary San Francisco Giants play at home, they wear white uniforms, accented with black and orange. Bill Terry devised that color scheme, back in the spring of 1933.

After such a miserable start, something had to be done with the Polarines, and Terry's name now started appearing regularly in the box scores. He was also managing the club. It's important to note that during the Polarines' 1920 season, although he did sometimes pitch, Terry was usually found at first base. Terry always said that playing first was his own idea, not McGraw's or anyone else's, and the Polarine records support this claim. When he was at Newnan, Matthews pitched him; when he was with Shreveport, Smith pitched him, used him as a pinch-hitter, and played him in the outfield; and a few years later, at Toledo, Roger Bresnahan would start by pitching. But when he had the chance to call his own shots with the Polarines, Terry chose to play first base.

Still, Terry the player *was* a pretty good pitcher, and Terry the manager couldn't ignore that fact, so occasionally he would start himself on the mound. The most interesting game he pitched for the Polarines was one he lost to the Ploughs, 4-0, on July 25, 1920. Terry was wild, as he often was, and he walked two batters and hit one in the second inning. Combined with two errors, that gave the Ploughs all four of their runs—but, the Ploughs got no hits at all. So here's a question for trivia experts: which Hall-of-Fame .400 hitter also pitched two no-hitters in the bush leagues?

For some reason—was it that game?—Terry abandoned his formula in 1921 and started pitching himself fairly regularly. It was not a great decision. His wildness remained, and, on several occasions, he was thoroughly whacked by the opposition. Still, his decision to pitch more frequently was about to work to his benefit—surely a matter of luck, not foresight.

In August, Terry had arranged for his two-week vacation, and the company consented to let the rest of the Polarines take off the same two weeks. Terry set up a number of games with other teams. There would be admission fees for the games, and now the men would get paid for playing ball. Terry himself, as manager and bursar, would clear six-hundred dollars on the deal. When the trip started, Terry was pitching unusually well. While the tour was scarcely covered by the press, an account of at least one game got into the *Commercial-Appeal*. Under the headline, "BILL TERRY IN FORM," it described a "beautiful game" at Helena, Arkansas, on August 28. "Big Bill Terry, on the mound for the Polarines, was master all the way, striking out fourteen Helena batters," the account read. "For the first five innings not a Helena man reached first." Terry's control was uncharacteristically great; he didn't walk a single batter.

The importance of this game rests in the fact that it took place in Arkansas, not very far from Little Rock, where the Travelers played under Kid Elberfeld. It's clear that Elberfeld saw Terry play sometime in 1921, and it may well have been in Helena. If Elberfeld didn't see that particular game, he probably heard about it, and he must have watched Terry do something equally impressive. One account even has the Polarines playing a game against the Travelers, and beating them. However it came about, Elberfeld saw Terry. He also saw two more things: a chance to do a favor for his old friend, John McGraw, the next time he saw him and an opportunity to recoup the loss his club had sustained when they bought Terry from Shreveport in 1918. Elberfeld would tell McGraw about Terry, since McGraw was his pal, but if McGraw decided he wanted Terry, he'd have to pay Elberfeld for his contract.

Terry knew Elberfeld, obviously, so there's no doubt that when they met that summer in Arkansas, they talked. This must have been when Elberfeld again asked Terry to come to Little Rock, and Terry again turned him down. Terry probably had no specific inkling of what Elberfeld was planning to do the following spring, although Terry *had* told him he'd consider a job in the majors.

Terry went on with his life. He and Elvena moved into their own place, an apartment not far from the Sneeds, then to another apartment on the Sneeds' block, only a couple of doors away. By 1922, they were living in a cozy house on Vance Street, renting part of it to an accountant who had incorporated himself and appeared in the book as the head of his own company. The Memphis directory also indicated a change in Terry's status at Standard Oil—by 1922, even though he remained a low man on the corporate ladder, he had risen from "clerk" to "salesman." So, on that warm April Saturday when Terry went downtown to meet with John McGraw at the Peabody, he was holding more cards than the Giants boss imagined.

PART II

THE LAST YEARS OF
THE LITTLE NAPOLEON

4

JOHN McGRAW'S NEW MAN: 1922–1923

*When he joined the ball club as a pitcher, he said some-
thing about his hitting, and I said, "Are you a good
hitter?" He said, "If you stay on the club, you'll see."*
—Bob Wright, Toledo pitcher

There is some dispute regarding what Terry thought after he
left McGraw's hotel suite. Some accounts contend that he really
did think this had been his last offer, his last chance to play baseball for profit and fun. This view seems reasonable because he
kept managing and playing for the Polarines as if nothing significant had happened. On April 16, two weeks after he walked out
of the Peabody, he played right field in their season opener, and
he singled and scored. Another view is that he was pretty sure
McGraw would call again, that McGraw had even said as much to
him in the Peabody. This might also explain why he kept playing—as a way of remaining visible in case McGraw decided to re-
consult Tom Watkins of the Chicks or any of his other Memphis
contacts. The only certainty is that Terry wouldn't play for
McGraw unless McGraw met his price. He did this not because he
was a greedy or a vain man, but because he was a family man.

It's also difficult to imagine exactly what McGraw was thinking. Again, there are a couple of possibilities. It may be that he

was playing a waiting game, seeing whether Terry would buckle and call him first; it may be that he was taking some time to make sure he thought Terry was worth the investment. Whatever his reasons, there was a month-long delay before Terry heard from the Giants again. Finally, somebody from the Giants called, probably their secretary, Jim Tierney, and told Terry that McGraw had decided to meet his price at eight hundred dollars per month. "And he said, 'Mr. McGraw wants you to come join the club, and come on up now; he'll pay you what you want,'" Terry told me. "I said, 'All right,' so I went up and joined the club in Philadelphia." Terry made his first trip to New York City in early May. He went to Harlem, to the Giants' home field at the Polo Grounds and began working out for the first time on what was then the most famous diamond in baseball—with the greatest team the sport had yet known.

After a day or two, the Giants went on the road, taking Terry with them. McGraw wanted to see him work out with the team a little more before he committed himself formally. "And I stayed with the club 'till we got to St. Louis," Terry told me. "McGraw called me in and said, 'Well, you're going to stay with us; we like the way you're hitting, and we want you to stay with us.' 'Oh,' I said, 'great.' So I called my wife. I was all excited about it."

So it was done: McGraw promised Terry a contract at eight hundred dollars per month, and they shook hands on it. McGraw arranged to pay Elberfeld seven hundred and fifty dollars for the privilege to so promise. He also threw in a pitcher named McLoughlin to keep the Kid happy, and, on May 10, 1922, Bill Terry officially became a New York Giant.

For a day. On May 11, Roger Bresnahan, McGraw's former catcher, stormed into St. Louis. He owned the Mud Hens, the Toledo, Ohio club in the American Association. As a double-A minor league before the triple-A era, the Association was the highest training level for a player before he cracked the majors. The Mud Hens would become famous, although not until much later, as the team Corporal Klinger would live and die by on the television series "M*A*S*H." The Hens were having a miserable and embarrassing season, and Bresnahan was determined to clean house. Bresnahan wanted McGraw to sell him some young players. He was unloading his manager, Fred Luderus, and six other players, including a couple of infielders and a couple of pitchers. Did McGraw have anybody he wanted to deal? Bresnahan was particularly interested in left-handed pitchers since his two aces, Hugh Bedient and Bob Wright, were both righties.

McGraw said he'd give him Terry, along with two other young guys, but only on the condition that they officially remained Giants property. Bresnahan agreed, then McGraw talked to Terry. "Next day, next day he called me in—we were still in St. Louis," Terry told me. "And he said, 'You know, we got a situation in Toledo.' He said, 'Would you mind going out there and helping them out?' And I said, 'Same money?' He said, 'Yes.' I said, 'Sure, I'll go over there.'

Terry wasn't cheap, just careful with a buck, and with good reason. In the era of the miserly Charles Comiskey, the White Sox owner whose poorly paid players fixed the 1919 World Series, there was nothing mercenary about making certain your new boss hadn't found a way to cut your salary unfairly. At any rate, on May 12, Bresnahan cleaned house with a vengeance. He fired Luderus and six other players. He even sold the Toledo ballpark.

Bob Wright, who stayed on the Toledo staff as a right-handed pitcher, remembered those days. "Oh, it was great," he told me. "Toledo was a great baseball town. It's not a great *big* town, but during that summer, when we're out playing, we'd make that town our home. Yes, that's your home for the season." And that home was about to get an important new resident.

"Lefty" Terry, along with Ike Boone and Bill Black, joined the reshuffled Mud Hens when they were on the road in St. Paul. All three players would eventually get to the majors, and Boone would actually play two games for McGraw's Giants before the year concluded. Next to Terry's major league career, Boone's (eight years, four teams, more than three hundred games, a .319 overall average) would be the most successful. Boone, in fact, is sometimes remembered as the greatest minor-league hitter of all time; the problem was that his fielding was abysmal.

Terry didn't get into a game until the team got back to Toledo. Bob Wright, who had thrown four innings in two games for the Chicago Cubs in 1915 and, seven years later, was still trying to get back to the majors, was ninety-nine years old when he recalled that the morning of Terry's first game in Toledo was a Sunday. He remembered Terry doing something very much in character. "Sunday morning come about, the first Sunday he was there," he told me. "There was a church, I think Baptist denomination, right near to us. Sunday morning he says, 'Let's go to church.' And I said, 'Well, I don't know,' and he said, 'Let's go.' And we *did*. And after that, we went to church every Sunday. We were church-going people, understand, but that's at *home*. You're in Toledo, playing baseball, going there in the spring of the year, leaving in the fall, you don't think of church. Well, we started, and after that, I kept going on Sunday morning."

After services that day, the players went to Swayne Field. Joe Giard started on the mound for the Hens, but he was wild, and, after he gave up two runs in the first inning, George "Possum" Whitted, who'd replaced Luderus as manager, put in Terry. Terry's control wasn't all that great, either. He walked three batters, hit another, and eventually took the loss, but the Toledo *News-Bee* still applauded his performance. "Bill Terry, the new southpaw from the Giants, shows unmistakeable class," the paper reported.

Bresnahan and Whitted, still without a quality left-hander, kept pitching Terry. Bob Wright, however, wasn't sure that was such a good idea. "He didn't *look* like a pitcher," Wright said. "He looked a little awkward in his delivery." Nonetheless, he was fast and he had a decent curveball, so he stayed in the rotation. More importantly, he was hitting better than ever, and often with power. Wright figured Terry couldn't remain a pitcher forever. "When he joined the ballclub as a pitcher, he said something about his hitting, and I said, 'Are you a good hitter?' He says, 'If you stay on the club, you'll see.' You know, he was a sarcastic, determined fellow. He only pitched a few games, and they put him on first base, working out there, and they never took him off."

Soon the laconic Terry began replacing his few words with more concrete action, and he started hitting home runs—long ones. He was a natural left-handed pull hitter with a good deal of power, and it was becoming impossible to ignore these attributes, so on Saturday, July 15, 1922, Terry started at first base.

Who made the decision to put him there? It was either Whitted or Bresnahan. But even if they were acting on advice McGraw had given them, Terry, who had played first regularly with the Polarines, probably had something to do with the decision. He pitched a couple of more times after switching to first base, though he probably shouldn't have. He gave up seven runs in a loss to Milwaukee on July 19 and eight in another loss to St. Paul on July 23. The *News-Bee* printed a story that suggested the fans at the park might wish to substitute "Back to first!" for "Take him out!" if Terry pitched.

At Indianapolis on September 8, Terry was at first when the Hens faced a tough new pitcher, Fred Fitzsimmons, and lost to him; Terry, though, was 2-for-4. On September 12 at Louisville, he hit a homer, then connected for one more at Minneapolis on September 17 in the first game of a doubleheader. In the second game, he had a double and two singles. In the next series, in St. Paul, he got hot. On September 21, he was 2-for-5, with a triple and a double; the next day, 4-for-5, all singles; and the following day, a double in two at-bats. On September 24, the Toledo *News-Bee* reported this: "Terry hit a home run over the right-center-field fence in the ninth. He was the second player to perform this feat, Reb Russell being the first."

For the record, Russell was an exceptional hitter who did not have Terry's luck. He was, however, a good enough pitcher to make the big leagues, where he spent seven unexceptional seasons as a left-hander for the White Sox. They dropped him in 1919, and he played the next three years for Indianapolis in the American Association, hitting so well that by 1922, he made a comeback with the Pittsburgh Pirates as a thirty-three-year-old outfielder. He hit his first major-league home run with the Pirates, followed by eleven more in sixty games, for a slugging average of .668. As late as 1927, pushing forty and back at Indianapolis, he led the American Association in hitting with a .385 average. So it was not faint praise for Terry to have his hitting compared to Russell's.

In any event, the St. Paul series was not an easy act for Terry to follow, and his offensive production diminished during the rest of the season; he hit no more home runs and went 7-for-21, a .333 pace. Toledo remembered what he'd done, however, and, before the season ended, the *News-Bee's* Dick Meade made these comments: "Bill Terry is slated for the first-sack situation in 1923 and will make a first-class regular. He certainly can hit 'em and should be one of the home run stars next summer."

And so, in 1922, Terry finally started getting paid for his offense, not his defense. In June, he had been primarily a pitcher; in July, he was making his transition; by September, he was not only the regular first baseman, he was a "home run star" as well.

There was a significant change in the Memphis directory after Terry's first year in Toledo. In 1922, it had listed him as "W H TERRY slsmn Standard Oil Co"; in 1923, he became "W H TERRY ball player." He began to get national attention, too, when *The Sporting News* mentioned him for the first time.

When the 1923 Toledo season opened on April 19, Terry picked up pretty much where he'd left off. In the first four games, he was 6-for-16 (.375), with two doubles and two homers. On April 22, in the fourth game of the year, an infielder named Fred

Lindstrom made his first appearance in the Hen starting lineup. Terry went 3-for-4 that day, with a double and a homer, while Lindstrom went hitless in three tries. Bresnahan decided Lindstrom was too inexperienced, and he told Whitted to bench him. So Lindstrom sat out a few games, and Terry kept hitting, with a homer on April 27 and a triple on April 30. The game on April 30 was the last one of the first homestand of the season, and Whitted told Bresnahan he wanted to start Lindstrom again. Lindstrom did much better this time, getting three singles in three at-bats. Lindstrom would later join Terry both on McGraw's Giants and in the Hall of Fame, become Terry's good friend, and play a significant role in his later career.

Then, on May 5, in a game at Louisville, disaster visited the Hens. Terry, who the *News-Bee* was now calling "corking Terry," the "ponderous pounder," a "batter extraordinary," and even "Sir William," broke an ankle sliding into second. Initially, the papers thought the loss of "one of the greatest hitters the American Association has ever known" would mean the Toledo season was over, but Terry healed quickly. He returned on June 17, playing first until the eighth inning, when he was called in to replace a relief pitcher who had already allowed nine runs. Terry put a stop to the onslaught. However, what may be the most ominously interesting aspect of that inning was that a good deal of the trouble had been caused by a young infielder who, the *News-Bee* said, "got [the pitcher] into one thing after another with errors of omission." That infielder was young Freddy Lindstrom, who would play a similar role when the Giants reached the World Series one year later.

But Terry was back, and he was batting well again. On June 29, he hit a shot longer than any previous homer in the Indianapolis park, and the *News-Bee* said it was the first time anyone had cleared the scoreboard in a regulation game, although Babe Ruth had done it once in batting practice before an exhibition. In fact, Terry was more a slugger in his Toledo days than he would be again. As Ted Williams, who also played minor-league ball at Swayne Field, told me, they were still talking about him years later:

> Well, you know, first time I played in Toledo, first night I hit, at Al Benton, he struck me out three times. Jesus Christ, the lights were lousy and he looked like he was *that* high—right on top of me. And I struck out three times. Next day, I faced Dizzy Trout, and he could throw the shit out of the ball. First time up, however, I hit one. Well, when I come around, they said only Bill Terry hit one out there, over—there was a little dugout in right center, and I hit it over there, you know. When I got there to Toledo, they said only Bill Terry had hit one out there. The son of a bitch was some kind of hitter.

It may seem puzzling that a player such as Terry who could hit so well for power chose not to go for the fences more often during the rest of his career. Those who point to Terry's love of the dollar as his biggest motivator would probably note that there *was* an additional incentive for him to hit the ball long when he played in Toledo. A local restaurant gave a five-dollar coupon to any player whose drive hit its sign which was on the fence in right center. Terry, who could hit for accuracy as well as distance, nailed that sign four or five times in a single week, prompting the restaurant to take it down. "But they paid off," Terry added, laughing.

Terry had now become expert at pitching and hitting. He was also fast enough to steal, and his fielding was naturally good, although his arm may still have been a little erratic. (He reportedly beaned a Toledo coach with an errant throw on one occasion.) Terry had managed the semipro Polarines, too—another baseball skill that would be important for him later—and, on August 1, he was named the new manager of the floundering Hens.

Terry started his term by splitting a doubleheader. He lost the first game, despite his homer and an error by Minneapolis' Hughey Critz, an infielder who would later work for Terry on the Giants. The Toledo pitcher that day was Pat Malone, then twenty, who would go on to have a fine career with the Cubs and the Yankees, and who would pitch against Terry's Giants while with those teams. In the second game, the new manager went 4-for-5 with a double and a triple, helping himself considerably as he won, 5-3. The *News-Bee* reported this:

TERRY STARTS LEADERSHIP WITH A WIN

Bill Terry is the new manager. He's a youngster, a conscientious youngster whose husky shoulders have suddenly been loaded with considerable responsibility in view of the fact that from now on he must deliver to a fickle public regardless of his obstacles.

Bill wants to make good. He's the youngest leader on the circuit. He's got a tremendous job. His ambitions are the same as yours, Mr. salesman, lawyer, business man.

During Terry's tenure as the Toledo manager, his team played several games against the Louisville Colonels, who were managed by Joe McCarthy. When Terry managed the Giants in the 1930s, McCarthy would be his opposite number across the Harlem River in Yankee Stadium, and they would meet in eleven World Series games. In 1923, they opposed each other five times, and Terry, the new manager, fared very poorly indeed. His Hens lost to McCarthy's team all five times, including defeats of 15-2 and 10-1. The Colonels scored forty-two runs in these games, while Terry's Toledo team got only nine. Terry wasn't much help at the plate, either; although he did go 3-for-4 in one game, his team still lost, 7-3, and he was 0-for-4 in the 15-2 blowout.

On September 16, after more than six weeks at the Mud Hen helm, the *News-Bee* reported Terry was "called away by the death of his grandfather." It was actually his paternal grandmother who'd died. He never did get back to Toledo, although he hit .377 that year and nearly won the American Association batting title. After the funeral, he was called up to the major leagues.

He went straight from Atlanta to Cincinnati, and for the second and final time, he became a New York Giant. On September 24, in the eighth inning of a game between the Giants and the Reds at Crosley Field, John McGraw sent Bill Terry up to bat for the pitcher, Rosy Ryan. He grounded to third baseman Babe Pinelli (later a famous umpire), who forced out Freddie Maguire at the plate. It was Terry's first appearance in a major-league game.

Terry played in two more regulation games in 1923. On October 1 at the Polo Grounds, starting at first base and batting seventh, he got his first major-league hit, a single off of Boston's Jesse Barnes. Barnes had also issued him his first walk, and after the Giants' Jack Bentley followed that with a triple, Terry scored his first run. In the last regular game of the season, across the river in Brooklyn, Terry was held hitless by "Dutch" Henry to finish his short first season at 1-for-7. He had not been up long enough to be eligible for the World Series, which was won by the Yanks despite the efforts of an outfielder who was easily the Giants' most valuable player, Casey Stengel. Although Terry had very little opportunity to get to know Stengel during that week when they were both on the Giants roster, he later remembered him as only "a fair hitter," but "a good hustler." He told me that, in the dugout and clubhouse, "he was always talking, but nobody paid attention."

5

A WIN FOR THE BIG TRAIN: 1924

There's only one way to time Johnson's fastball.
When you see the arm start forward—swing.
—Birdie McCree

The Giants' 1924 season really began with the arrival of their manager at spring camp, which was being conducted in Sarasota, Florida, for the first time. When John McGraw showed up on March 3—he literally cruised into town on the yacht of circus owner John Ringling—he immediately started behaving like McGraw. His first directive was that sunny Florida and the abundance of courses notwithstanding, nobody was going to play golf. "There isn't any question about it," the boss said with absolute finality, "the baseball stroke and the golf stroke are vastly different, and the mastering of one spoils the other." The next day he spent an hour or so providing lessons in sliding (it was one of his fetishes) to—*The New York Times* reported—"Bill Terry, the Toledo Terror." Although Terry admitted he'd never been a very good slider after he broke his ankle in 1923, McGraw thought he performed adequately, or at least better than another pupil, Giants star Frank Frisch, whom McGraw pronounced "good only on one side."

McGraw tried out another young player from Memphis that

spring, Joe Bradshaw, and it's tempting to speculate that the player was in Sarasota at least partly on Terry's recommendation, since he had been one of the pitchers Terry managed on the Polarines. *The New York Times* reported that McGraw said, "he looks about ready for fast company, although I'll know more after looking at him a couple of times again." Bradshaw did survive the first cuts, lasting long enough to pitch four innings against the Chicks, back home in Memphis. The *Times* reported that "Bradshaw's return to his old haunts as a big leaguer was a complete success." Shortly thereafter, though, McGraw looked at him once more, decided he knew enough, and when the team left Tennessee Bradshaw wasn't with them.

A little before that, McGraw had come to a decision that probably helped Terry and the other rookies. He decided to dissolve the Yannigans, the Giants' second-string squad that normally took a separate barnstorming route north. Instead, he kept all his rookies with his regulars. Standing in the lobby of the Hotel Miramar in Sarasota, watching a torrential downpour wash out his practice and embarrass the local chamber of commerce, the *Times* reported that McGraw said the exhibition schedule looked pretty tiring. He wanted to have his recruits on hand to spell his regulars. "Besides," he said, "I want some of the youngsters under my observation on the trip northward. Some of them look pretty good to me." This meant that from now on those youngsters would get to play with experienced pros, as well as continue to get the benefit of McGraw's tutelage after the team broke camp.

On March 29, McGraw cut several more rookies, but Terry, Freddie Lindstrom and Hack Wilson survived, although the veterans on the club gave them the traditional cold shoulder. "How little those fellows did to help us take their jobs," Lindstrom later recalled. It seems a young player could learn competitiveness as well as strategy and mechanics by playing with the big boys. He could learn a little amateur psychology, too; Terry later claimed some of the credit for keeping the thirsty Wilson relatively sober in 1924, Hack's only full year as a Giant. Whether or not the slightly older Terry's monitoring had anything to do with Wilson's sobriety, Hack did well that year and the clubhouse man didn't have to keep a bathtub full of icewater waiting for him before the games, as would be the case later in his career with Chicago. Like Frisch, Wilson made the cover of *Baseball Magazine*, and the *Times* called him the "sensational find" of the season.

Now the roster was settled, and the Giants headed north. On April 3, they played the Chicks in Memphis, and Terry's pinch-hit single in the fifth inning was doubtless well-received by the Polarines and the other hometown fans in the stands at Russwood Park. A minute later, though, they must have had the daylights scared out of them; Billy Southworth hit a ground ball to first, Terry took off for second, and the Chicks first baseman, trying for a double play, nailed Terry in the back of the head with his throw. Terry fell down, briefly unconscious, but after he got up and sat on second base for a while, he "resumed play," *The New York Times* said, "amid great applause."

Terry played very little in the first half of the regular season, although he did have a couple of good games in May. On May 17, he went 2-for-4 with a double and his first big-league homer; five days later, he went 2-for-4 again, with another homer. On June 14, however, he was reminded that getting the first-base job was going to be difficult. "Long" George Kelly, the regular first base-man, hit three homers that day and batted in all eight of the Giants' runs.

Considering the large presence of Kelly, Terry was lucky to play forty-two games at first in 1924, especially since it turned out to be Kelly's greatest year—he averaged a career-high .324 and led the league with 136 runs batted in. One reason Terry started as many games as he did was that McGraw lacked left-handed hit-ters. Kelly would play against left-handed pitching, while Terry stayed on the bench until a right-hander came in (he led the league in pinch-hit at-bats that year). Against righties, McGraw would sometimes move Kelly to second or center, allowing Terry to take over at first. This platooning continued into the World Series and in fact was the reason behind a clever strategic move by the Washington Senators in the seventh game.

The World Series of 1924 belonged to Walter Johnson. Johnson was one of America's most popular sports heroes, a long-armed prairie boy who pitched for the Senators for his entire 21-year career. He was one of the greatest pitchers of all time, and one of the kindest men. If the Detroit Tigers' Ty Cobb was the meanest player and the Yankees' Babe Ruth was the most flamboyant, then the "Big Train" was the nicest guy. Along with Ruth and Cobb, he was one of the first five men elected to the Hall of Fame and one of only two pitchers, the other being McGraw's own Christy Mathewson. He ended up winning more games (416) than any pitcher except Cy Young, who won 511, and he is the only man to pitch more than one hundred shutouts (in fact, he had 110). Even taking "Cyclone" Young into consideration, Johnson was the first pitcher made famous by a phenomenal fastball, setting the stage for later purveyors of "heat" like Bob Feller and Nolan Ryan. Still, Johnson had never won a World Series game, so fans, players, and even umpires were rooting for him in 1924.

The Series opened in Washington, and game one was terrific. Johnson pitched twelve innings and struck out twelve, but was finally beaten by great fielding and only one run. Terry, playing first because Johnson was a right-hander, connected for his first World Series hit in the second inning and another one, a home run into the left-field bleachers, in the fourth. In the sixth, he fouled out to Muddy Ruel.

In the eighth, Johnson walked Terry to get to Hack Wilson. In the eleventh, with the score tied 2-2, centerfielder Earl McNeely made a good play on Terry's fly ball. Then, in the twelfth, Ross Youngs singled in a run with the bases loaded, and Billy Southworth came home on Kelly's sacrifice. Terry loaded the bases again with a two-out single, but Wilson flied to Goslin to end the threat with the Giants leading, 4-2.

The Senators hit for Johnson, sending up substitute catcher Ernest "Mule" Shirley. Shirley had only appeared in thirty games in 1924, but he was Washington's best pinch-hitter. He got all the way to second when Giant shortstop Travis Jackson dropped his high pop-up, and he eventually scored on player-manager Bucky Harris's single to center. When Harris got to third on a single by rightfielder Sam Rice, Rice tried to stretch it into a double and was thrown out at second. This meant that there were two out with a man on third, the Giants ahead 4-3, and the Senators' leftfielder, future Hall-of-Famer Leon "Goose" Goslin, at bat. Now Kelly, who had just been moved to second base for defensive reasons, made a great barehanded play and threw to Terry, who also caught the ball barehanded, for the out and the victory.

That final play of the first game of the 1924 Series exemplifies the timeless dispute over the importance of managers. Does moving Kelly to second base show McGraw's genius or just dumb luck? Kelly was called "Long" George (also "Highpockets") because he travelled fast on very long legs and he was also a great fielder with a strong arm. (The *Times* said his throw "almost knocked Terry over.") Terry had a much longer-than-average stretch, a terrific "spread," and Goslin was out by a step. As late as 1942, when Terry was asked to name the greatest fielding play he ever saw, he said it was that throw by Kelly. If McGraw had kept the shorter Frisch on second base, and depended on Frisch's less-spectacular arm, the Senators might have tied the game. Then they could easily have gone on to win because the next man up was Joe Judge, their hottest batter in the Series.

In any event, in his first appearance in a World Series game, Bill Terry had looked very good in the field, gone 3-for-5 at the plate with a long home run, and been walked with a man on third so that Johnson could pitch instead to the dangerous Wilson, who in a future year would set the major-league record for most runs batted in a season.

The next day the fans filled Griffith Stadium again and watched Terry pitch batting practice. That was all they would see of him, since McGraw started Kelly at first base and kept him there for nine innings. The game was another great one, with the Senators winning by one in the bottom of the ninth. President Calvin Coolidge, a Senators fan, listened to the game on the radio on his yacht, the *Mayflower*, and undoubtedly felt a silent pleasure when Roger Peckinpaugh singled home Joe Judge from second to end the contest. Walter Johnson looked on from the Washington dugout and smiled broadly, forgetting his own loss of the previous day. Giants fans, on the other hand, wondered why McGraw hadn't walked Peckinpaugh, putting him on an empty first base, in order to pitch to the slower-footed catcher, Muddy Ruel, and set up the double play.

The *Times* was unambiguous in its account, which ran under this headline: "MISTAKE BY McGRAW LETS IN WINNING RUN." Frisch, the team captain, had argued for the walk, but McGraw had overruled him. This was to be McGraw's last Series, and he had arrived at a strategic decision that made no real sense. It clearly was not a judgment he had made impulsively, since he had deliberately rejected the sound advice of one of his more knowledgeable players. Frisch may well have been astonished at his manager's refusal to listen to common sense. More importantly, this may have been the moment when John J. McGraw, the great third baseman of the 1890s and the greatest manager in baseball through the teens and early 1920s, finally got too old and lost touch with his players.

In 1924, however, McGraw was still viewed as a genius, even by papers that called him on his obvious errors. A writer from the *Times*, commenting that "it is hardly fair for a team to have more than one first baseman," asked him who he would play in the next game, the opener at the Polo Grounds. Firpo Marberry was scheduled to pitch for the Senators. Marberry, in his first full season, had been used primarily in relief, and he'd led the league in saves. Since Marberry was right-handed, McGraw said he'd go with the same line-up he'd used against Johnson in game one, with Kelly in center and Terry on first. In the clubhouse before the game, a horseshoe of flowers arrived for McGraw, but he wouldn't let anybody take it onto the field. "That's the worst jinx in baseball," he said, and his team went out and won, 5-4.

Terry didn't start game four, and the Giants lost. He started game five, getting a triple that was the longest inside-the-park hit of the Series, to help his team beat Johnson again. Terry was on the bench in game six, a loss. They had won all three games Terry started and lost all three he didn't. It would be reasonable to assume the superstitious McGraw would have noticed that fact, but he apparently didn't. Now it all came down to the final game in Washington.

On that last day, Bucky Harris surprised everybody by starting Curly Ogden, who was not a member of the Senators' regular pitching rotation. Ogden was a right-hander, so McGraw pursued his usual (and very public) strategy, playing Kelly in center and his hottest hitter, Terry, at first. Ogden, however, pitched to only two batters—Harris had actually intended him to face only one, but he looked good—before he was replaced by George Mogridge, a dozen-year veteran and the second man on his staff. Mogridge was a lefty, but McGraw was stuck with the lineup he used against right-handed pitching.

Terry, the real target of Harris' gambit, did not do well against Mogridge. He grounded out to Harris on the first pitch in the second inning and struck out in the fourth, so it may be hard to fault McGraw for finally lifting him for a right-handed hitter, Irish Meusel, when the Giants rallied in the sixth. But as soon as Terry was removed, even before Meusel took his cuts, Harris put in the right-handed Marberry. For the remainder of his life, Terry thought Harris won the World Series by conning McGraw into pulling him. Since Marberry himself was eventually relieved by Walter Johnson, and Terry had been hitting Johnson particularly well, Terry might have been right. At least one of the New York writers, Joe Vila of the *Sun*, thought so. Under the headline "HOW YOUNG HARRIS OUTWITTED MCGRAW," Vila theorized that Ogden had started because Harris knew McGraw *always* played Terry against right-handers, and *never* against lefties. While it's true that McGraw surprised Harris by keeping Terry in the lineup for two at-bats, it's also true that as soon as McGraw pinch-hit for him, Harris brought in Marberry.

But the game was far from over; Harris' strategy wouldn't bear fruit for another six innings. In City Hall Park in downtown Manhattan, the crowd watching the game on the *Evening World*'s automatic scoreboard had steadily grown, and by the seventh inning, it numbered about ten thousand. When somebody got a hit, a bat-shaped piece of white cardboard swung; when runners advanced or scored, white cardboard discs moved along basepaths or crossed a plate. Walter Johnson's national popularity was so great that this New York crowd was rooting for Washington. After the Giants scored in the sixth, the fans actually groaned.

Meusel, hitting in Terry's slot in the order, came up again in the seventh inning. He hit a feeble grounder to Marberry, who tagged him for the third out. In their half of the eighth, the Senators got to the Giants' starter, Virgil Barnes. With two out and the bases loaded, Bucky Harris hit a bad-hop single over Lindstrom's head, the first of the game's two so-called "pebble plays." Two runs came in, tying the score at 3-3, and McGraw brought Art Nehf in for Barnes. The *Times* reported that the crowd at the park "cheered and cheered," and back in New York, the people watching the *World*'s scoreboard did the same, making a roar that could be heard "from Park Row to Broadway," a roar that frightened some of the horses under the sixty-odd mounted cops stationed there for the occasion.

Marberry had pitched very well, allowing two hits and no earned runs in three complete innings, but Harris pulled him in the ninth, anyway. He had warmed up Johnson once before, in the three-run Giant sixth; now he brought him in with the score tied to pitch the ninth. The papers reported that when he walked through the outfield to the mound, he received the greatest ovation of his career, and the *Times* commented that "from that moment on, the Giants were a beaten team."

Still, the game had to be finished. Frisch put a scare into Johnson in the ninth with a long triple, but Johnson got out of that inning and retired the side in order in the tenth. In the eleventh, with Groh on second and one out, Frisch came up again. Johnson struck him out, walked Youngs to get to Kelly, then struck out Kelly. The papers said that even Coolidge hollered.

The game and this great Series finally ended in the bottom of the twelfth, when Earl McNeely hit a ground ball directly at Freddie Lindstrom. The ball bounced over his head, bringing Muddy Ruel in to score, giving Washington a 4-3 victory. Johnson finally had his first Series win and his Senators were world champions—all because of the famous Series-winning "pebble play." Legend insists that it was an easy out, that, at the last instant, the ball hit something in the infield and caromed out of Lindstrom's reach. Still, not every reporter covering the game thought the hop was *that* bad, and even Terry, watching from the visitors' dugout on the third-base side, was unconvinced. He obviously felt that, although the ball took a difficult bounce, Lindstrom might have made the play. When I asked him about it, he didn't seem to want to say anything negative. "Too bad," he said after a long pause. "I hated to see that happen to Freddie. He was quite a ballplayer."

And what about McGraw's decision to play the percentages and lift Terry for Meusel, when everybody knew Johnson was waiting in the bullpen? "I could hit Walter just like I owned him," Terry told me. "I don't know why, but every time I'd hit one it'd be harder than the other one; poor Walter. But the old man decides he's going to be smart. He put Meusel in, and Meusel and those other right-handed hitters we had, well, they just couldn't hit Walter at all." Apparently, Frisch wasn't the only Giant who thought McGraw helped lose the 1924 Series.

After the seventh game, the city of Washington indulged in what might have been the most enthusiastic celebration of a Series win in history. Even Billy Evans wept when Johnson finally won it—Billy Evans, the umpire. The party started, of course, at the park, where the fans stampeded the players. The *Times* reported that McNeely "was thumped and pummeled and hugged and reached the bench a very crushed young man." Downtown, thousands of people soon filled the streets, blowing horns, shaking rattlers, throwing confetti and crumpled paper out of windows, and even firing pistols, making a racket that outdid any New Year's Eve celebration. Local theaters were forced to cancel performances because the patrons couldn't hear the actors' lines. An impromptu motorcade, klaxons blaring, was formed on Pennsylvania Avenue; soon there were at least a thousand cars, forcing the trolleys to stop running. By morning, the confetti and paper thrown from offices was several inches deep in the streets. Not until Charles Lindbergh's solo flight from New York to Paris three years later would the country indulge in such an impromptu celebration in Washington.

The Giants packed their bags and went home. There's little doubt that Terry felt good for Johnson—once, when I asked if Johnson was as nice as the myth had made him out to be, Terry said immediately and with warmth, "Oh, he was, he really was." But Terry also had learned a couple of things. He was personally nettled, since Harris' effort to get him out of game seven had worked. And he now knew that McGraw was fallible.

Nonetheless, Terry could only be satisfied with his own performance—errorless fielding, the highest batting average (.429) of any player on either team in the Series, and the distinction of being the batter whom the great Johnson least wanted to face. Although he played in only 77 games in 1924 and his overall average was a melancholy .239, there had been one particularly encouraging sign: he seemed to be very good in the clutch. Not only had he led all batters in the Series, he'd also been a particularly dangerous pinch-hitter during the regular season, with an average (.422) only seven points lower than his post-season mark. But he didn't hang around to bask in either Washington or New York; there was no practical point in doing so. He went back to Memphis—to his home and family and winter job with Standard Oil.

6

SUMMERS OF DISCONTENT: 1925–1927

*Terry, you can ask for more money in the winter and
do less in the summer than any ballplayer I know.*
—John McGraw

Two of the better-known "sports writers" at the 1924 Series were Babe Ruth and Ty Cobb. Cobb would play only two more years for the Tigers before joining Connie Mack's Philadelphia Athletics in 1927, the year Ruth hit sixty home runs. Cobb had already been eclipsed as baseball's biggest hero by the flamboyant Ruth, and he didn't like it. On the day the 1924 Series started in Washington, Ruth barged into Coolidge's box to shake hands with the President. Despite a Secret Service regulation that clearly forbade anybody in the park from entering the box, an exception was made for the Babe. When he arrived at the foot of the temporary press seats and started jawing with the writers, he created five minutes of pedestrian gridlock in the stadium aisles. And when he went down to the Senators' dugout a little later and posed with several players, the *Times* reported that "dozens of cameras were worked overtime." Meanwhile, Cobb was already in the press section, working on notes for a column that would later be ghost written by a real journalist, and being interviewed by only a few reporters. Cobb's era was over, and the era of Ruth (and of Coolidge) was in full swing. Even in 1925, when Cobb outhit a slumping Ruth by nearly 90 points, the Babe was the center of baseball attention, a god whose lapses were more absorbing than the triumphs of the titan he'd deposed.

There were reasons for this trend, of course, and they can be traced to a new national mood that began at the end of the war in 1918 and probably became fully established in the wake of Coolidge's landslide presidential victory one month after the 1924 Series. Cobb's era had been one in which hard work was rewarded, and Cobb fit in well. It's been said that for Cobb, baseball was as competitive a jungle as the world of American business. When defending himself against charges of fixing a game, Cobb said, "My conscience is clear," because "all I have thought of was to win, every year, every month, every day, every hour." In a magazine piece that came out at the height of Cobb's career, another writer referred to business itself as a game, adding that "in this game there is no 'luck'—you have the fun of taking chances but the sobriety of guaranteed certainties."

By now, however, the game was becoming less business-like and more fun. Like the country itself after the Volstead Act inaugurated Prohibition in 1919, it seemed a lot less sober. The country was entering what one 1924 writer called "The Age of Play." The greatest significance of this age, he said, was that the U.S. turned its back on "unceasing industry" as an admirable quality, recognizing that "unremitting toil is not necessarily a law of human destiny." In democracy, the writer concluded, "the people are king—et le roi s'amuse."

This was no country for Ty Cobb. Dour, hostile, and wanting nothing at all out of this world but to defeat everybody else in it, Cobb was a king who found very little to laugh at. It was a time for a different kind of hero—a lovable swaggerer and braggart who usually made good on his boasts, a profligate and frequenter of speakeasies who was unfazed by any hangover, alcoholic or sexual. Ruth's two greatest years were certainly 1920 and 1921, his first ones in New York, but he didn't really begin to symbolize the age until the mid-1920s, roughly the period between the election of Coolidge in 1924 and the great stock market crash of 1929—or, in baseball time, the seasons of 1925 through 1929. During this period, Cobb, like Ruth's teammate, Lou Gehrig, who joined the Yankees in 1923, was often overlooked. Cobb was not a showman, and his work ethic was not just outdated, it was vehemently rejected. Walter Hagen, one of the greatest golfers of the era, is a good example of this freewheeling spirit. He sometimes arrived at tournaments still wearing last night's tuxedo, and he allegedly once chipped over a high stand of trees to reach the green in one on a par-five dogleg. He wasn't scorned for such stunts, he was lionized instead. Terry, who lacked this kind of color, was mostly ignored by journalists, suffering a fate similar to Cobb's. The important difference is that Cobb was on his way out of the game, while Terry had plenty of time to wait. When this brief "Age of Play" was over and the country's mood turned quite serious again, a mature Bill Terry would become a role model for a harsher era.

McGraw's players had won the pennant in 1924, which had pleased him; then they had lost the Series, which had not. The player who had outhit everybody else on both teams in the Series was also the man who might have won it for McGraw, had McGraw not played the percentages and taken him out of the decisive game. This year, McGraw figured he'd better play Bill Terry more often. The solution was to move George Kelly, who could play virtually any position well, to second and to start Terry at first.

Terry played the entire 1925 season as the starting first baseman, using his speed and range to lead the league in chances. He played his position so well that he missed having the top fielding average in the National League by only a fraction of a percentage point (Both he and Boston Brave first baseman Dick Burrus had numbers that rounded off to .990). He had grumbled about his status on the team over the winter and held out in the spring. Although he now had the excuse of an additional mouth to feed—Marjorie, his only daughter, had been born—he probably held out simply because he felt he could get McGraw to pay him more money. Burleigh Grimes, who played with Terry in 1927, was succinct about it: "Bill Terry," he said. "*Smart* guy. Used to hold out all the time."

Even though both Grimes and Hal Schumacher remembered Terry as an annual holdout, that wasn't true. Still, once Terry saw that holding out was a viable way to put economic pressure on his boss, he wasted no time in doing so. His first holdout came in 1925; granted, he'd had a terrific World Series, but he had only started as a regular for half of the season. At first, it might have seemed that Terry felt protected because the Giants' other first baseman, George Kelly, was also a holdout. Before long, however, Kelly signed, as did the team's acknowledged star, Frankie Frisch. In fact, Terry was the last unsigned Giant in 1925, "the last of the rebels," according to *The New York Times*. And when a reporter for the paper asked him to elaborate his position, Terry said: "I'll go back home and go to work before I'll play at those figures."

Another *Times* reporter suggested that work was a "terrible alternative" to playing first, but Terry ignored him. He did finally sign, of course, and although nobody was told the final figure, the fact that he would hold out on several more occasions suggests the Giants had thrown at least a little more into the kitty.

In 1926, he held out again, and so too, did Kelly. Kelly, once again, caved in first. Terry was the "lone truant," as Harry Cross called him in the *Times*. Later on, McGraw told Cross that he'd received a wire from Terry, but hadn't answered it because, Cross said, "a submission to Terry's financial demands would probably be too great a strain on the bond market." From Terry's perspective, matters were made worse because George Kelly was having a great spring, routinely having multiple-hit games and including extra-base hits in that tally.

Still, Terry knew how much he was worth and that, despite how he felt about the game, he didn't need baseball to make a living. He had already begun to buy, improve, and then rent homes, and this aspect of Terry's Memphis life was well enough known in New York for Harry Cross to make reference:

> Mr. Terry, it would appear, during the past year has developed into an affluent Memphis landlord. He has numerous domiciles for which he exacts rent each month. The arrangements between Landlord Terry and his tenants, so the story goes, is such that Mr. Terry can, without any suffering on his part, assume a somewhat independent attitude in relation to baseball. He doesn't have to make base hits to keep the wolf from the door.
>
> Of course, there is another side to the case. The side of the Memphis tenants. If Terry doesn't come to an agreeable financial arrangment with the Giants, some of the holders of the Terry leases fear that they may have to bear the brunt of the misunderstanding. So it is easy to see that the Terry case involves many more than simply the player and the Giants.
>
> After Terry's telegram was deciphered it became known that Memphis Bill wants a two-year contract. It would require no detective to see that the proposition presumably was inspired by the tenants, who see in the arrangement a means of keeping their landlord quiet and peaceful for at least that period.

Cross' piece was printed on March 22. On April 1, James B. Harrison wrote a story for the same paper in which he said he'd heard that "Big Bad Bill Terry" might relent and join the team. Two days later, the Giants played a game in Memphis, as they always did on their spring tour. It had been during that barnstorming segment that Terry had first been approached by McGraw, and now was a perfect time for McGraw and Terry to negotiate again. However, as the *Times* reported on two successive days, it didn't quite work out that way:

> "I have called McGraw's room several times and knocked at his door several times," said William, "and as long as I get no answer I assume he doesn't want to see me. The next move must come from the New York club. I have told them what my terms are and if they are not ready to do business I suppose it means that I will stay in Memphis and forget the idea of playing baseball."

In fact, Terry had tried to reach McGraw in his suite at the Peabody, but McGraw had elected to not be there, particularly since several other Giants, all of whom he thought to be Terry, had knocked at his door on the same day. McGraw figured that if Terry was that eager he'd be back, and that he could stew awhile, and the *Times* quoted him:

> "I did not come to Memphis to talk with Terry," said McGraw. "The time for him to do the talking was at Sarasota. It's too late now. The case is solidly in the hands of President Stoneham. Terry must make his peace with Stoneham."

There was serious stonewalling on both sides, and Terry was not in the lineup on opening day, April 13, missing the inauguration of the new and improved Polo Grounds. In fact, he didn't report until April 26, nearly seven weeks after everybody else on the club had signed. *The New York Times* reminded its readers that any player who hadn't come to some agreement with his club before the season was more than ten days old would be automatically suspended, adding that Terry had "communicated with Manager McGraw" on April 23, at the last legal instant. As usual, the salary wasn't disclosed, only the *Times* said that "the call of the game was so strong on Bill that he decided he couldn't stay away any longer."

What happened in 1926? Did Terry simply lose the battle of wits, and did McGraw end up compromising not at all? Whatever the case, Terry ended his holdout and he didn't try one again until 1930, after his wonderful 1929 season. In the spring of 1930, Rud Rennie of the *New York Herald-Tribune* called Terry the "most determined" of the eight Giants who wanted better contracts. Rennie pointed out that Terry had a reasonable argument, since he had been "the best first baseman in either league last year." This time, though, Terry defected early, in mid-February, before many of his seven teammates. When the issue was settled, the Giant front office (predictably) insisted he'd signed at their original figure; Terry (more believably) insisted the contract he'd signed and returned was their third offer. Still, as Richards Vidmer pointed out in the *Tribune*, it didn't really make a lot of difference. "It doesn't really matter whether Terry signed the first, second or third contract," Vidmer wrote, "as long as he is signed. Without him the Giants would have no more authority than a lance corporal."

In 1931, Terry would hold out again, even though, according to McGraw, the team had raised his pay from $18,000 to $22,500. McGraw had reason to increase his pay, of course; Terry had just batted .401 for the season, something that has only been done once since then, by Ted Williams in 1941. Terry wasn't to be the last player to settle in 1931—he was second to a relatively insignificant Giant named Joe Genewich—and this is probably because McGraw, for a change, decided to recognize and reward what he had accomplished. McGraw had offered Terry $22,500, and Terry had demanded $25,000; John Drebinger of *The New York Times* figured they compromised. The following spring turned out to be Terry's last as only a player, an employee with no administrative connection, and it was a special case anyway, since the Depression had given the owners the power to cut salaries drastically, which meant that everybody held out. In Bill Terry's case, suffice it to say that he always held out when he either thought it was economically sensible or when he was convinced he deserved more money, and that in the only two years he didn't, 1928 and 1929, he may have had reason either to think that he was being properly paid or that a boycott would not work.

In 1925, Terry was still unsigned when the exhibition games started, but he was in uniform and hit the first Giants home run of the spring in Sarasota, described by the *Times* as "a prodigious drive that rode high and far on the wings of a strong and chilly wind that was sweeping in from the bay." Then, on March 12, he finally signed a contract. While he didn't have one of his greatest years, he managed to bat over .300, as he did in every season he played regularly for the Giants. There was a new baseball publication in 1925, a noble experiment that offered columns by well-known writers such as Damon Runyon and Fred Lieb. The *Weekly Baseball Guide* lasted only one season, a year the publication covered well, and it gave special notice to Terry. It zeroed in on him early in May, reporting that the Giants were "fortunate" to have a young first baseman who "can hit and field almost equally well" and paying special attention to a triple he'd hit at the Polo Grounds. Considering the fun-house dimensions of that stadium, it may have been the longest big-league triple ever:

> The three-base hit which Terry made in Sunday's game, May 10, with the Cubs and which sent up a buzzing among the fans that has not died away, traveled 462 feet on the fly. Arnold Statz, Cub centerfielder, who went in pursuit of the ball, but couldn't get close enough to it to even make a jump for it, pointed out the approximate spot where it struck to Eddie Brannick before yesterday's game, and Eddie and his trusty band, armed with a tape measure, got on the job. The result: a finding that the ball had scarred the turf 462 feet— count 'em, 462—from the home plate.

The measurement made by Brannick and his intrepid men had been requested by National League President John Heydler, and the calculations were filed in the league office.

Further accounts in the *Weekly Baseball Guide* suggested that both Terry's fielding and hitting improved perceptibly in 1925, that it was a year of important maturation for him on the field. On June 1, Sam Hall said in the *Guide* that Terry was not at all bad at first, although he was "no Kelly," adding that he "fields fairly well." As a batter, Hall said, "he can murder right-handed pitching," although he made no reference to Terry's ability to hit lefties. Only a month and a half later, though, Hall changed his mind. By then, Terry was ranked with Frisch and Kelly as a defensive star, and his fielding was "superb." Hall admitted that although Terry used to have trouble hitting lefties, "it must be said for Terry that as a rule the left-handers do not bother him overmuch."

The Giants never had much of a shot at a pennant in 1925, though. Hack Wilson, the previous year's hot prospect faltered; maybe Terry got fed up with acting as his nursemaid. Wilson got into only 62 games, and he was hitting only .239 when he was sent to Toledo. Fred Lindstrom hit .287, not very good for him; the next year he'd embark on a string of six straight .300-plus seasons. Nor was the pitching exceptional, with nothing more than a fifteen-game winner on the staff. So, on August 8, McGraw brought up a young left-hander named Fred Fitzsimmons from Indianapolis.

Fitzsimmons had been around awhile (it will be remembered that he beat Terry's Mud Hens in 1922 when he was pitching for Indianapolis), but he was still inexperienced. Later, when Fitzsimmons recalled the year he came up to the majors, he recalled how rough McGraw could be on players. Just after he joined the Giants, they lost a game, and Fitzsimmons went back to the clubhouse along with everybody else. He figured it was time to get dressed and go home. He started taking off his uniform, but when he dropped one of his spiked shoes on the floor and was startled by the noise, he realized there was a dead silence in the locker room. Freddie Lindstrom nudged him.

"Sit still, kid," Lindstrom said as McGraw walked in.

McGraw was already showered and changed, wearing his suit jacket. He rolled up his sleeves and started in on the team. For two hours, in Fitzsimmons' words, "he cast doubts on each man's ancestry, intelligence and guts, and he never repeated himself." Fitzsimmons asked Kelly if the outburst had been unusual.

"Get used to it, kid," Kelly said. "This is the way it's going to be from here on in."

Time was beginning to pass McGraw by. It was less and less possible to run a team effectively by bullying the men on it. When Thomas Boswell wrote recently about managerial archetypes, he cited McGraw as the first and best example of the hard driver, the dictatorial boss characterized by intensity, emotion, passion, and an obsessive desire to win. McGraw's players, though, were beginning to think that what had once been passionate intensity was now frustration, anger, and injustice. As Fitzsimmons said, "McGraw's abuse antagonized so many men that their refusal to play for him eventually forced his resignation."

Fitzsimmons had little impact on the team in 1925. Terry batted .313 for the season, and his work at first was solid enough to make McGraw feel comfortable about having moved Kelly to second. Still, McGraw didn't like to lose. His response, as always, was to chop heads. It was reported in the *Times* that he tried to trade Terry for, among others, right-handed pitcher Dolf Luque, another player he was always actively seeking. He had already sent Hack Wilson back to Toledo, bringing up another outfielder, Earl Webb, in his place. Webb had a few good years with the Red Sox and the Cubs (he ended his career with a .306 average), including one in which he hit 67 doubles, a record that still stands, but his tenure with the Giants consisted of no hits in three at-bats. Later, when Webb was in Chicago, he played with the man he'd replaced on the Giants, Hack Wilson. McGraw had not bothered to keep Wilson under Giant contract in 1925. Chicago (and history) gathered up Wilson the following year. Letting Wilson slip away was one of McGraw's low points as a judge of baseball players.

Notwithstanding such lapses, McGraw always kept his eye for talent. A kid who tried out for the New Orleans Pelicans was turned down, not because he wasn't good enough but because he was too young. He was only fifteen, younger than Terry had been when Harry Matthews lied to the Reds about Terry's age, and a couple of years younger than McGraw himself had been when, in 1890, McGraw had not admitted to the Olean club in upstate New York that he was seventeen. The kid actually cried when he was turned down, causing the Pelican owner to take pity. He suggested a tryout with a local semi-pro outfit run by a rich Louisianan named Harry Williams. Williams signed him, and the kid, Mel Ott, did well.

Williams was a friend of McGraw's, a lucky break for all concerned, and he advised McGraw to take a look at Ott. McGraw sent Ott a postcard telling him to report to the Polo Grounds in September. Ott had been playing for uniformed teams since he was ten; he was a prodigy, which is probably why he was able to get his father to convince his mother he'd be all right travelling alone. He packed his straw suitcase and boarded a train.

When Ott arrived in New York, it took him two hours to figure out the subway system and how to get to the ballpark. When he finally made it there, he found out the Giants were on the road. Since he was only fifteen and was small for a ballplayer, it took him some time to convince Giants' team secretary Jim Tierney that he'd really been called in by McGraw. Eventually Tierney, satisfied that Ott was authentic, gave him money for a downtown hotel and told him which "el" to take there.

Ott had never been on an elevated train. He was terrified the train was going to lurch off the track and into the street below. In addition, he had spent very few nights away from his home in

Gretna, Louisiana, and when he arrived at his hotel, he locked himself in his room and piled all the furniture he could move in front of the door. But he *had* played baseball before, and when McGraw came back to town and saw how talented Ott was, he offered him a contract on the spot. There were only a few games left, and Ott wasn't placed on the roster, but he received four hundred dollars to work out with the team for the rest of the season. Although he never played in a game, 1925 was Mel Ott's first year as a paid member of the Giants, and he watched them finish second, eight and a half games behind the Pirates, losing their first pennant in five years. At spring camp the following March, McGraw wrote Giants' principal owner Charles Stoneham a letter containing a run-down on the team. "Ott is a standout with me," he said. "Ott is the best-looking young player at the bat, in my time with the club."

The national boom continued in 1926. The country had an uncontrollable appetite, a need to consume. Coolidge summed up this trend in the euphemistic language of a politician: "The uncivilized make little progress because they have few desires," he said. "The inhabitants of our country are stimulated to new wants in all directions."

Cobb didn't "desire" anything but to win. Terry didn't "want" anything but to provide well for himself and the people he loved. But Ruth—ah, Ruth was another story. *His* appetite, whether for home runs, hot dogs, women, steaks, or beer, was immense. No public figure of any kind in the mid-1920s better symbolized the mercantile gluttony of the American people. After a sub-par year in 1925, Ruth had a great season in 1926, and the idol was restored, the god re-born, the prodigal son come back home. In the face of drama such as this, who could develop much interest in the Giants or the business-like craftsman who was about to take over permanently at first base?

McGraw seemed to have forgotten Terry's performances in

the past two seasons, because, in 1926, he used him only as a pinch-hitter and as Kelly's understudy. The little manager may have been sidetracked by his personal problems, which were substantial in 1925 and 1926. He'd put a lot of money into a housing development in Bradenton, Florida, called Pennant Park, the streets of which had been named after former Giant stars, but two disastrous hurricanes had wiped out the investment. Instead of making him a lot of money, Pennant Park put McGraw a hundred thousand dollars in the hole. There may have also been medical reasons for his moodiness. McGraw hated doctors, and when his wife, Blanche, finally dragged him to one in 1932, it was too late—he had less than two years to live. It's not inconceivable that his debilitating uremia had begun to affect him as early as the mid-1920s. Whatever the reasons, he had become a sour and distracted man. The sportswriter Bill Corum remembered a scene that spring in McGraw's room in the Sarasota Terrace Hotel. The short, chubby manager was sitting on his bed, still in his silk pajamas, holding court with reporters; specifically, he was "castigating" Terry for holding out. During the tirade, he kept trying to cross his legs, but the top one kept slipping off. The World's Bozeman Bulger interrupted the manager and asked if he'd like some sandpaper to put behind his knee. "Won't take but a minute to get it," he said. McGraw exploded, told them all to go to hell to find their stories, and threw them out of the room. They could hear him still yelling behind the slammed door.

Meanwhile, Terry had been getting great pre-season reviews. A February article in *Baseball Magazine* said he was "a born hitter," "a really great hitter, so good that he cannot be spared." The article said George Kelly had been "the greatest first baseman of his league," but that he wasn't anymore. The story was titled, "The Man Who Shoved George Kelly Off First Base."

Terry probably figured this article would help him at contract time, but if McGraw saw it, it could have made him even more rigid—McGraw was not a man to bow to journalistic influence. At any rate, Terry held out, didn't report until the season was more than a week old, and probably received little or no extra money for his effort.

It's surprising that Terry didn't see that this bickering was impractical for everybody involved. While the growing ill-will between the two men seems to have been mostly a result of McGraw's calcifying temperament, Terry probably took McGraw too seriously. A looser personality might have been able to laugh off McGraw's peevishness and come to terms of some kind before the season was a week old. It's as though neither man was in the proper decade: McGraw belonged in the feisty pre-World War I era of Irish saloons, the time of the rough-riding Teddy Roosevelt, while Terry was better suited for the teamwork and self-sacrifice of the Franklin Delano Roosevelt years. Neither seemed entirely comfortable in the 1920s.

In any case, McGraw hid in his suite in Memphis, and Terry walked off in a huff, thus missing a week of work, which did not sit well with the field boss. It seems possible that McGraw, never one for positive reinforcement, started Kelly at first all year because he didn't want either *Baseball Magazine* or Terry telling him what to do, and because Kelly both made it to camp and was in uniform for opening day. After all, in at least one case—that of Edd Roush, in 1930—McGraw would react to a holdout by actually *lowering* his offer. In addition to being manager, McGraw was one of the club's three owners, although, like his friend, Francis J. McQuade, he only owned seventy shares. (The real power was Charles Stoneham, who held thirteen hundred shares.) And although McGraw was still viewed as a mastermind (on May 7, both Stoneham and McQuade agreed with McGraw that he should be re-hired as manager for three more years), the players were beginning to sense that he might have become a detriment to the team, which would finish in the second division in 1926, only four games in front of the despised Brooklyns of McGraw's former Baltimore teammate, the lovable if uninspired Wilbert

"Uncle Robbie" Robinson. The Giants had not finished so far back since 1915.

Before the season ended, though, there was a major flareup that epitomized what was wrong—a flare up that would have serious ramifications for the Giants for years to come. Late in the season, while on the road in St. Louis, the problems with McGraw grew critical, and the players' dissatisfaction became a public matter for the first time after he confronted the team captain, Frank "Charlie" Frisch. A year earlier, the *Weekly Baseball Guide* had commented on the "iron fist methods" of "Czar McGraw," saying that "missing a signal" resulted in an automatic $25 fine and concluding that "the players have been assailed with epithets that they would not take from any man in the world were they fist free to resist." Now, in August 1926, Frisch, who had a bad cold and was exhausted by the St. Louis heat, missed a crucial signal, allowing a run. In the dugout, he was blistered by McGraw, who liked to call the German-American infielder "krauthead." Infuriated, Frisch decided to quit the team. *The New York Times* reported that Frisch was seen eating breakfast at the Chase Hotel the next morning, apparently "angry about something." About eleven, he got into a cab with his luggage and went to the train station. He had been rooming with George Kelly, and they had been hanging out with Terry and his roommate, Irish Meusel; the three had gone with Frisch to a speakeasy the night before, so they knew what he was up to. They saw off Frisch that morning, then went to Sportsman's Park to play the Cardinals. In fact, all three were as fed up with McGraw as Frisch was, and Terry laughed when he told me how they supported him unanimously when he took off: "Frisch never would've gone, but Kelly, Meusel and myself went with him to the train," he said. "Moral support." I asked if Terry was sure Frisch wouldn't have left if his friends hadn't gone to the station with him. "I don't believe he would," Terry replied.

McGraw's pattern was to place blame, never take it, so he put on a mask of moderate rationality with reporters. He told a reporter from *The New York Times* that Frisch "had never done a thing like this before. Indeed, he has been very easy to get along with." But then McGraw said that Frisch was "the only man on the team" who had missed that signal. In fact, McGraw said, he had flubbed another play in the previous game. McGraw added that he didn't know whether Frisch was unhappy about being moved to third base, but that he was going to stay there because Lindstrom was "a higher-class ballplayer" who was going to keep Charlie's old job on second, that "this has happened many times this year." McGraw went on to say that as team captain, "Frisch never satisfied me, but I kept him there, hoping he would make the grade," and "I am manager of this team, and as long as I remain manager I shall run it in the way I think best," and on and on, most counter-productively, most loftily.

Now the cat was out of the bag, and the reporters felt free to admit what they had known for some time about McGraw's relations with his players, and especially with Frisch. The *Times* said the disputes between Charlie and his manager had been going on for a couple of years, and, during those disputes, "neither party minced words." The "Giant players," the *Times* reported, "said that McGraw was free with his criticisms of Frisch from the bench." The *Times* probably understated the case greatly.

The bottom line was that McGraw's authority had been challenged. Meanwhile, Frisch publicly claimed he was ailing and summoned a doctor to verify that he suffered from both a cold and a charleyhorse. McGraw, typically, gave no ground. He said some nice things about Frisch and insisted he would be fair with him, but he sounded, as always, like an unjustly wounded parent.

A week passed, and Frisch continued, with the support of Dr. James B. MacGrath, to call in sick. In fact, he never reported for work as a Giant again. On October 2, a trade of Frisch for Edd Roush was reported to be in the works, but it apparently fell through. On December 20, Frisch *was* traded, but for Rogers

Hornsby, whose bluntness with Cardinal owner Sam Breadon had landed him in similarly hot water in St. Louis.

On paper, the Hornsby trade looked like a good deal for the Giants, even considering the loss of Frisch. Bob Feller told me Hornsby "was the toughest hitter I ever pitched to. I pitched to him in '36. I think he was no doubt, by far, the greatest right-handed hitter that ever lived, maybe the greatest hitter that ever lived." The problem was that in Hornsby, the Giants were getting a man even less willing to toe the managerial line than Frisch had been, as well as a man who himself didn't mind acting a little like Napoleon if given the chance. Plus, it's important to remember that Frisch had not wanted to jump, he had been pushed. On ceremonial occasions in later years, even though by then Frisch had become inseparably associated with the Cardinals and their "Gas House Gang," he always preferred the Giant uniform.

The year 1926 hadn't been a great one for Terry, either. His grandfather, the "Maker of Atlanta," died in January, and Terry had his worst season on the field since his spectacular debut in the 1924 Series. He played part-time, never got into a rhythm, and ended up batting only .289, with a fairly measly forty-three runs batted in and five homers. Until his last year, when he was hurt too often to play regularly, he would never again appear in fewer than 120 games; and, no matter what the conditions, his average would never again slip below .310.

7

THE GROWTH OF A GREAT PLAYER: 1927–1929

I used to kid Terry to beat all hell, while he sat on the bench,
waiting to take my place. I wouldn't go out of the lineup. I didn't
make the mistake that Wally Pipp did.
—"Long" George Kelly

In 1927, the American decade was as prosperous as it would get, and everybody was sure it would stay that way. President Coolidge was in office, and he had already proclaimed that "the chief business of the American people is business." The national love affair with the hero also reached its peak in 1927, when Lindbergh made it into Le Bourget. And the corollary, the popularity of sport, the fascination of a culture at play with distinctive players, also continued: Boxer Jack Dempsey lost his re-match with Gene Tunney, golfer Bobby Jones won the U. S. Open for the third straight year, Grantland Rice created a new platform for heroes when he picked the first all-star football team for *Collier's*—and there were the Yankees and Babe Ruth.

A number of authorities claim the Yankee teams of the 1930s, the same ones the Giants would run up against, were better than the 1927 Yanks; but these same experts usually rate the 1927 team a pretty close second. It won more games (110) than any other Yankee team, and its winning percentage was a hefty

.714. Once again, the Yankees were the team of the era, the club that best reflected the national psyche. If asked to name the most memorable baseball event of 1927, is anyone *not* going to say it was Ruth's sixty home runs? And the second-place team the Yankees beat by nineteen games, Connie Mack's A's, was very strong indeed: in the regular lineup, only Max Bishop, the second baseman, batted under .300, and, in the outfield, Al Simmons and Cobb hit .392 and .357, respectively. But nobody remembers Cobb's .357 average, although it was a point higher than Ruth's. Ruth was the model of hero that the time demanded.

The Giants also had a decent season, which, again thanks to Ruth and the Yankees, went relatively unnoticed. Hornsby signed his contract in January, and both he and McGraw said they were pleased with their new association. Hornsby said it was "great to be in New York," that one of his ambitions had always been to be a Giant and that he was "mighty glad to be with John McGraw." McGraw responded by giving him Frisch's old job as team captain. Neither of these two amiable fellows could be accused of being irascible or bad-tempered.

On January 10, McGraw acquired Burleigh Grimes from Brooklyn and George Harper, a good-hitting outfielder, from the Phillies. Then, on February 9, he made another important trade. He finally got Edd Roush, giving up the older of his two talented first basemen, George Kelly, to acquire him. The Giants had actually tried to give up Terry for Roush—in October Charles Stoneham wrote Reds owner Garry Herrmann a letter to this effect—but the Reds were firm, and the Giants finally relented, sending them "Long" George. Although McGraw had put him back on first in 1926, Kelly always felt Terry would take his job, even though the two remained good friends. "I used to kid Terry to beat all hell, while he sat on the bench, waiting to take my place" Kelly said. "I wouldn't go out of the lineup. I didn't make the mistake that Wally Pipp did."

True, he didn't make the famous mistake of the Yankees'

Pipp, who got sick for a day and was replaced by Lou Gehrig for the next fifteen years, but he probably did leave just in time. In any case, the implication for Terry's career was obvious—no more platooning, pinch-hitting, or being an understudy at the manager's whim. Terry was the Giants' first baseman now. He could be his own man with less fear of being benched should he get on McGraw's bad side.

In mid-February, another revised Giant team headed for Sarasota. Terry arrived on March 3, completing the remarkable starting infield of Terry, Rogers Hornsby, Travis Jackson, and Fred Lindstrom. This may have been the only infield ever to be composed entirely of Hall-of-Famers and to also include two .400 hitters. Cobb was at the March 3 practice, and he predicted the Giants would have an easy time of it, and so would his A's. The *Times* quoted him as saying, "Nothing would please me better than to fight out a World's Series with McGraw." In fact, the World Series he contemplated *would* have been something: Mack against McGraw, Cobb versus Hornsby. For good measure, throw in Al Simmons, Eddie Collins, Jimmy Dykes, Mickey Cochrane, Jimmy Foxx, Zack Wheat and Lefty Grove for the A's. For the Giants, in addition to that Hall-of-Fame infield, the lineup included Edd Roush, Mel Ott, Burleigh Grimes and Fred Fitzsimmons.

McGraw, however, was becoming increasingly surly and remote. More and more articles, while pointing out that his career had been long and glorious, hinted that it must be nearing its end. One, by Billy Southworth, was bluntly titled, "McGraw, the Mussolini of Managers." On June 15, the *Times* reported that Hornsby was possibly be being considered as McGraw's successor. McGraw quickly denied the rumor, but since Hornsby ran things (or tried to) with his *own* mailed fist on the many occasions McGraw was away on other team business, this report may have started the manager thinking. Worse, a celebration of McGraw's twenty-five years as manager of the Giants was scheduled for July 19 at the Polo Grounds. It looked as though it might be time for the sapphire ring and the hearty handclasp.

The season opened with a flourish with a three-game series in Philadelphia. The famous yachtsman and perennial America's Cup bridesmaid, Sir Thomas Lipton, was at the first game, part of a sellout crowd that had somehow been crammed into tiny Baker Bowl. As one Phillies fan said, a little cryptically, "Yes, sir, this park is filled to capacity—and then some." Terry, who'd had a great spring, clinched a win with a grand slam in the fifth. Richards Vidmer reported in *The New York Times* that he "knocked the ball out of the park, Hal Carlson out of the box and the game into a state of security with one mighty blow." Nor did the team let up, sweeping the Phils in three, then holding on to first place until May 21, the day Lindbergh landed in Paris. A homer by the Pirates' Pie Traynor beat them in the twelfth that day, finally dropping them back to second in the standings.

In early June, the Pirates were still in front. The Giants were in third place, five-and-a-half games back, when they took a free day to play an exhibition against Casey Stengel's Toledo team. Roger Bresnahan, now one of McGraw's coaches, acted as the substitute manager; of course, the old Toledo boss was well received. Before the game, the Mud Hen fans gave Bresnahan a shotgun and a bird dog. Terry's homecoming was a good one, too; he hit a homer so far that it cleared the telegraph wires beyond the right-field fence. Stengel started himself in right field (in 1927, he was still only thirty-six), and toward the end of the game, he put in a twenty-year-old fireballing right-hander. The pitcher, Roy Parmelee, who would later play for Terry, gave up three runs in the seventh, but then he settled down and shut out the Giants in the last two innings.

The team kept hitting well, but offense wasn't the problem in 1927. The Giants were only playing .500 ball halfway through the season, when McGraw had his day at the Polo Grounds. It was a major event, as most of these celebrations were in the pre-television era—a kind of one-shot state fair, with bands, presentations, and dignitaries. The biggest dignitary on "McGraw Day" was Commander Richard Byrd (he wasn't an admiral yet), who showed up in spotless whites after speeding up Broadway in a motorcade with New York's "official greeter," Grover Whalen, and its mayor, Jimmy Walker. When they got to the Polo Grounds, they were introduced to the crowd by Joe Humphries, the boxing announcer, and Commissioner Landis joined them in their box. The grandstand was decorated with brightly colored festoons of bunting in the colors of both the state and of the nation, along with plaques honoring McGraw. Byrd left in the fifth inning, although he promised to stay in the city one more day; he didn't want to miss the Dempsey-Jack Sharkey fight. McGraw was forced to stay through the bottom of the ninth, leaving only after an 8-5 loss to the Cubs. In 1927, the Giants had too good a team not to be in the pennant race, but they could only come close. They finished two games back, in third, behind the Pirates and the second-place Cards.

Everybody connected with the Giants was frustrated, particularly the man who was supposed to have made the difference, Rogers Hornsby. Since Hornsby was as temperamental as McGraw and since, when Mac was away, he tried to exercise his authority as team captain to "push and drive" the players, those players began to dislike Hornsby almost as much as they did their actual boss. Further, McGraw may have become suspicious of Hornsby's managerial aspirations. In any event, although Hornsby never realized (or never admitted) that he'd made McGraw's "list"—he felt some remarks he'd made to team secretary Jim Tierney in a cab had got back to Charles Stoneham—Hornsby was wrong. Terry told me that it all came out after the morning game of a doubleheader in Boston.

"One of the players on the Boston club hit a brand-new ball straight up and it came right down in Hornsby's spot. And it was hard to see. And Hornsby said, 'You take it, Bill.' And I said, '*You* take it, it's in your spot; I can't see it.' And the ball hit him on the top of the head. And we lost the ball game, 8 to 7. And we had sandwiches set out between games, and McGraw made a smart-aleck remark, and then Hornsby cussed him out. And we sat there, didn't eat anything, not at all. Hornsby started hollering at me first, before he and McGraw started up. And, boy, then Hornsby really cussed *him* out. He was mad then. I don't blame him. He was out that same year."

Freddy Lindstrom told Bob Broeg of the *St. Louis Post-Dispatch* about the fight. According to Lindstrom, all McGraw said was, "I guess I'll have to take out insurance on your head, Rog," although that sounds very mild indeed for McGraw. Lindstrom continued: "McGraw might have been the manager, but no one made fun of Hornsby. Before Rog finished blistering the boss with his language, I had to wind up pulling the men apart."

Terry also said that despite what Hornsby had said to the press, Hornsby "was against being on the Giants to start with. Because he didn't like McGraw; he didn't like him, and he wasn't the type of fellow McGraw could handle anyway." Terry added that, when he himself was managing, he "would've liked to have him," that he could have handled Hornsby as a player with "no trouble, no trouble. No trouble at all." But McGraw, of course, was McGraw, and by January the brief era of Hornsby the Giant was over, when he was sent to Boston in one of the most notorious trades in the team's history.

The tension of working for a difficult manager never seemed to affect Terry's performance, at least as long as that manager played him. In 1927 he hit a career-high .326, quadrupled his previous years' home run total with 20, and batted in 121 runs to boot. As always, however, he put the game behind him in the winter, as one Henry P. Edwards discovered in an interview that is preserved in typescript at the National Baseball Library:

I would call Bill Terry the National League's most industrious player in the winter months. In the good old summer time, Bill just drifts along, loafing around the hotels when on the road, playing cards some, going to a good show now and then and making sure he gets the necessary sleep. During his spare time in New York, he brings out his car (and it is always a good one) and takes out the family, Mrs. Terry, his nine-year-old son and three-year-old daughter.

If Bill's playing days should be terminated abruptly, Bill will not have to worry. Neither will his family for Bill has not been wasting his winter months. He likes hunting and fishing and nothing would delight him more than to spend the off-season in those two sports. But a man who builds a house every winter, owns a public garage and buys and sells real estate doesn't have much time to spend in knocking over quail and rabbits.

Bill lives in Memphis and, upon arriving home each fall, he drives around until he finds a vacant lot on which he knows he can build a cheap house which he either can sell or rent. He superintends the job himself, being his own architect and hiring day labor. When he hears of a piece of real estate that can be bought at a bargain, he buys and then unloads at a small profit. But, between building and real estating, he finds time to show up at the garage each day, play handball several days a week and golf occasionally, just to keep in condition.

Oh, yes, he dances now and then, Mrs. Terry insisting he put on the black and white front whenever the Memphis Shriners stage a ball. "But, dancing is no hobby," confesses Bill.

In his Memphis home on South Willett Street, Terry has plenty of books. "But," he says, "I am waiting until I am through with baseball before I start reading them.

Want to keep my batting eyes in good shape as long as I can and have come to the conclusion reading does not help them."

Hornsby may have helped Terry come to that last conclusion. Hornsby's conviction—that reading books or going to the movies harmed your vision—seemed reasonable at the time, however medically off-base it may have been. Hornsby's own eyesight wasn't particularly damaged by the tout sheets he consulted with some regularity, and presumably his ban on reading didn't extend to *The Morning Telegraph*. Maybe Terry, like most great hitters, listened at least briefly to any advice from a respected peer. Maybe, with such exceptional eyesight (like his admirer, Ted Williams, he said he could see the stitches on a pitched ball), he didn't want to take any chances. In any case, in 1928, Terry left his books in Memphis along with his growing family (a second son, Kenn, would be born that year); he probably figured it was hazardous enough simply reading the sports pages.

Hornsby's winter revolved around one of the most startling controversies in the history of the Giant ballclub. Even this lead paragraph of a page one story in the *Times* seems shocked:

> *January 11, 1928.* Rogers Hornsby, outstanding and highest salaried player in the National League, was traded last night by Manager John McGraw to the Boston Braves for two obscure players "for the best interests of the New York Giants."

How could the "outstanding" Hornsby be considered the equivalent of even *two* "obscure" players? The less charitable might even say they were more than obscure, they were second rate. One of them was Frank "Shanty" Hogan, a catcher known more for overeating than for defensive skills, although he could hit pretty well; the other was Jimmy Welsh, a so-so outfielder. Replacing the great Hornsby at second would be Andy Cohen, a near-rookie who had played 35 games for the Giants in 1926 but had been sent back down to the minors in 1927. The *Times* story later said: "Had the ceiling of the room fallen down upon the heads of the astounded baseball writers there could have been no greater consternation."

Hornsby, contacted in St. Louis, was also utterly surprised. He was, a reporter noticed, "obviously at a loss for words," and said he had just been trying to get McGraw on the phone to discuss hiring a new trainer. Neither McGraw nor Charles Stoneham could be reached, however, by Hornsby or anybody else. Like the press, Hornsby couldn't figure out the reason for the trade. He only said, "I do not know what the New York officials mean by saying I was traded for the best interests of the club," and it's not hard to imagine his tone of voice as he said it. Hornsby certainly made a lot of enemies; sportswriter Lee Allen once described him as "frank to the point of being cruel, and subtle as a belch." It appears that the trade was made solely and specifically to get rid of him. Hornsby would have had no regular contact with Stoneham at all unless the latter had chosen to promote him, so the trade was most likely McGraw's doing, and the precedent was the trade of Frisch. The scenario is certainly similar: a great player disputes the mighty McGraw, a manager with the further clout of a co-owner; a full season elapses, and the great player assumes a truce has been called (Hornsby had told the press he and McGraw were great pals); then the great player is traded during the winter, summarily and without being personally notified. And that's that. Maybe this was the plan: Stoneham, himself disenchanted with Hornsby and supporting McGraw's decision to fire him, would take the blame to spare the manager further conflict with his players; Jim Tierney would selectively "leak" laundered information to the press, and everyone would hope the press would buy the story.

In the tight, secretive, almost political atmosphere of the Giant front office, squabbling was always hidden from outsiders. In this instance, Stoneham, lying low, wasn't available for comment until two days after the Hornsby trade was announced, when he issued the prepared statement mentioned earlier. Not only wasn't McGraw available, he was in Havana, Cuba. When McGraw did resurface a short time later and a reporter asked him about the trade, he walked out of the room. From the beginning, the Giants had said very little. Now they were through talking.

> All your Welshes, Cohens and Hogans
> Won't begin to fill the brogans
> That Hornsby wore so well at second base
> —The Baseball Writers of America

The uproar following the Hornsby trade might have shaken a less confident man, but it seems to have had little effect on McGraw. A month later, he decided to deal his best pitcher, Burleigh Grimes, to the Pirates. In return, he got their fourth-best pitcher, Vic Aldridge. Aldridge *had* won fifteen games in 1927, but Grimes had won nineteen, with thirteen of those coming in succession toward the end of the season. Aldridge also had a significantly higher earned run average than Grimes. Years later, Grimes said that this horrible trade was just business, that there had been no bad blood between himself and McGraw. Few people would have believed that.

In the meantime, the season opened, and the Giants fielded their revised roster. On May 4, the *Times* reported that McGraw had refused the five-year contract offered by Stoneham, but that he had agreed to stay on as manager for two more seasons. It may be that McGraw was only offered a two-year contract to begin with, particularly considering the possibility that Stoneham later broke with McGraw. Suffice it to say, however, that this announcement seemed as carefully planned as most emanating from the Giants' front office. McGraw, nevertheless, continued to have his troubles, and on one May afternoon, after an 8-2 loss to the Cubs, he was hit by a roadster as he tried to cross the street outside Wrigley Field. He was knocked ten feet, and although no bones were broken he needed a couple of days to recuperate. Dick Bartell, a master of the malaprop (he likes to read baseball "antidotes") who was in his first season in the majors that year, told me about the accident. "Well, McGraw had a temperature, you know, and he'd take off—you know, at one time he just left the ballpark and walked across the street and got a broken leg—in Chicago. He got disgusted and he just walked out and left the clubhouse, went across and got hit by an automobile." Bartell implied that even this accident could be traced to McGraw's "temperature" tantrums and preoccupations.

While McGraw was looking less and less like a leader to be taken seriously, Terry was leading by example. On May 29, two weeks after McGraw's encounter with the roadster, Terry hit for the cycle against Brooklyn. John Drebinger of *The New York Times* called the game "a terrible slaughter of the innocents," and feared the disheartening effect it might have on the Giants' "transpontine rivals," the Dodgers (also known as the Robins, after their manager, Wilbert Robinson). Although Terry's double and his homer had both come with the bases loaded, he ended up with only six runs batted in, indicating that the double might very well have been a single had it been hit by a man of less speed or hustle.

The team stayed close all year. The acquisition of a pitcher named Carl Hubbell on July 13 didn't hurt matters, and Terry himself kept hustling, particularly when the games were vital. On August 19, the Giants took their third in a row from the Cardinals, 3-2, giving them the National League lead. Terry batted in two of the three Giant runs in the victory. Through mid-September, the Giants remained in the thick of the race, and a headline in the *Times* said Terry was a "Strong Factor" in the team's success. On September 20, the Giants split a doubleheader with the Cards—Terry went 4-for-7—and were two back. On

September 22, the Giants beat St. Louis. On that same day, ex-Giant Burleigh Grimes won his twenty-fifth game. (That year, Grimes' 25 led the league in wins, while Vic Aldridge was 4-7.) On September 23, the Giants beat the Reds in 14 innings, but the Cards also won. On September 25, both teams won again, and the Giants were one game back.

Two days later, the Giants could have taken a doubleheader from the Cubs to tie for first. In game one, Andy Reese tried to score from third, but he was blocked by Cub catcher Gabby Hartnett, who, reported the *Times*, "stood astride the baseline like a colossus." The paper added that "with a clear baseline, he would have scored easily with the tying run." Umpire Bill Klem refused to call interference, however, and the game was played under protest. The Cubs won by a single run. McGraw never forgave Klem or National League President John A. Heydler, who would not reverse Klem's decision despite a press photo that seemed to prove McGraw's point. The Giants won game two, but no ground had been gained. Though not mathematically eliminated, their season was over.

Still, they had been in it until the last couple of days of the season, and Terry himself did well, hitting .326 for the second straight year and again driving in more than 100 runs. Ott did well, too, and continued to play with a kid's enthusiasm. He knew McGraw demanded good base-running, and since he was never particularly adept in that department, he decided to get in some extra practice. At night, in his hotel room, he'd pile up pillows against one wall and take running slides into them. The thumps could be heard all over the building.

But the most important development of 1928 was the acquisition of Hubbell. *The New York Times* found the transaction to be worthy of a separate article, largely because of Hubbell's price tag:

GIANTS PURCHASE HUBBELL
Texas League Southpaw

Brings Record Price,
Reports Soon

July 13, 1928. The Giants today announced the purchase of Lefty Hubbell of the Beaumont club of the Texas League. The price was not announced, but John McGraw said the sum was the highest ever paid for a Texas League player.

Hubbell, who has had tryouts with the Detroit and Toronto clubs, will report in Chicago next week. He is 28 years old and was recommended by Scout Dick Kinsella.

Scout Dick Kinsella had gotten lucky. In fact, he hadn't been in Texas to scout players, he was there as a delegate to the Democratic National Convention. One afternoon, he decided to take the day off and go to a game, and he saw Hubbell win in eleven innings, 2-1. Kinsella headed directly to a phone and told McGraw he'd found another Art Nehf, referring to the old Giant lefty who had averaged twenty wins between 1920 and 1922. McGraw told him to "forget about that damn convention" and follow Hubbell. Kinsella did, and by July, Hubbell was pitching in New York.

Carl Hubbell started in the majors as though he'd always been there. In half a season in 1928, he won ten games, and his earned run average was 2.83. On May 8, 1929, he no-hit the Pirates. In the ninth inning, when two straight errors had put the first two men on base, bringing up the future Hall-of-Fame Waner brothers in succession, even an experienced pitcher might be forgiven a little fretting. Hubbell, however, got coolly back to work. He struck out Lloyd and then got Paul to ground out, as *The New York Times* reported:

> The senior Waner slashed the ball along the ground between the pitcher's box and first base. Like a flash Hubbell dived for the ball and scooped it cleanly.

Whirling and without waiting to recover balance, he
fired the ball to second base.

The Giants' sloppy fielding had already allowed a total of three
men to get on base on errors; Hubbell himself had walked only
one. Hubbell's own fielding, however, had been flawless, especially on that last, difficult play, a play that usually gave him trouble—so much so that McGraw had considered sending him back
to the minors for a little more work. Well, no longer. His no-hitter—one writer said Hubbell had pitched it with "monotonous
ease"—would be the last one ever by a New York Giant.

While the arrival of Hubbell and Ott completed the nucleus
of the great Giants teams of the 1930s, Terry was the team's star,
a great hitter who seemed able to do everything well. A good
example of his ability to combine power and precision came three
days after the no-hitter, the day Charles Stoneham presented
Hubbell with a watch in a ceremony before the game. Terry came
to bat with the bases loaded. Considering he was playing at the
Polo Grounds, where the right-field fence was only 257 feet away,
he thought he'd try for a grand slam. A foul ball, of course, wouldn't
be damaging, and since there was only one out, a long fly that
veered toward center would at least score the runner on third.
Besides, he thought the pitcher would give him a good pitch to hit.

The pitcher did. As the *Times* reported, "Terry crashed a
high pitch and hit the fifth row of the upper grandstand just
inside the foul line." Just fair; right where he wanted it. The
Giants went on to win, 6-0, and only one of the six runs wasn't
knocked in by Terry.

While Terry wouldn't become "the most hated man in
Brooklyn" until 1934, he couldn't have been very welcome in
Ebbets Field even in 1929, considering what he usually did to the
Brooklyn Robins' pitching, even when he couldn't help the Giants
win. On June 18, for example, the Giants dropped two games to
the Robins in Brooklyn, losing each game by only one run, but

Terry must have thrown a number of scares into the local fans. He went 9-for-10 with one homer.

With all of their talent, though, the Giants were erratic in 1929, never really in the race. The tail end of their season was interesting usually only when something quirky occurred, such as the August game when Terry, in an extremely uncharacteristic mental lapse, took his at-bat ahead of Ott instead of keeping to his proper place in the order. This was so unlike the cerebral Terry that even the umpires didn't notice the mistake. Terry couldn't help the Giants much at the end of 1929, but he continued to play the best ball of his life, to take the game seriously and to work at it diligently. Halfway through the summer, when the Giants were still in contention, the *Times* reported that he was "one of the main factors in the Giants' drive for the National League pennant," and "a dangerous man in a pinch" whose "skill in the field leaves nothing to be desired. Few, if any, first basemen are as adept as he in playing the position. This season, Terry has been playing even better ball than before." Terry was certainly doing just that, batting .372, stealing ten bases—his career high—and fielding well enough to win a Gold Glove, had the award been given in those days. His homer total reached double figures for the third straight year, and he had 226 hits, 103 runs, and 117 runs batted in, although even statistics like these weren't strong enough to take the pennant from Joe McCarthy's strong Cub team. The Cubs were led by the irascible ex-Giant Rogers Hornsby, who had come to them after one year in Boston. Hornsby, having his last great season, outhit even Terry in all of the above categories, and the Giants finished in third place, thirteen and a half games back.

Terry, who had already begun to distrust McGraw's judgment and who undoubtedly felt, along with most of the New York press, that the Hornsby trade had been a dumb one, knew he had pulled his own substantial weight in 1929; it wasn't hard to figure how the final standings might have changed if Hornsby's .380 average, 149 runs batted in, and league-leading 156 runs scored had been moved from Chicago back to New York.

Still, Terry was never one to complain about matters beyond his control. What he *could* control was his own performance, his own contribution. Looking at the Hornsby trade must have taught him a significant lesson: letting personal feelings dictate important decisions was simply bad business. At any rate, there was nothing more Terry could do for the Giants, so he went home. When he read the Memphis paper on October 17, he saw that Andy Cohen, McGraw's replacement for Hornsby, had been sent down to minor-league Newark after only two years in the majors. On October 30, his wife and three kids presumably wished him a happy birthday—he was 31—but when he looked at the paper *that* morning, there would have been little to celebrate. This was 1929; the bottom had just dropped out of the stock market. Although it would take quite awhile to sink in, both economically and psychologically, the good times were over. The Great Depression had begun.

8

THE BEST OF A BAD DEAL: 1930–1931

I grew up in San Diego, and the closest big league baseball at that time was played in St. Louis. Hell, that was two thousand miles away and pretty near seemed like the end of the world. But I did read the sports pages, and when I was at an impressionable age as can be, say twelve or thirteen, the names of certain big leaguers were in my mind. Hornsby and Ruth were over the hill, but Paul Waner was right at the top of his game. Lou Gehrig was certainly on top. But for some reason, Bill Terry's name was the name that hit me a little bit in a special way. I'd be playing, or just swinging a bat, and I'd say to myself, 'Bill Terry's up, last of the ninth, bases loaded, 3-and-2 count.' You know how kids announce their own games.
'Here's the pitch. Terry swings...'
—Ted Williams

Bill Terry may well have been an ideal hero for bad times. He had been poor when young, and he was a man determined to make a better life for his family than he'd had himself. He had energy and unusual intelligence. He was also fair, unselfish, determined, and he had a silent strength that could have been the envy of Randolph Scott. There is a resemblance between the actual Terry and the heroic characters Hollywood used to dramatize the depression, characters like Joel McRae's Sullivan, Gary Cooper's John Doe, or Henry Fonda's Tom Joad. These figures fought to survive in a bitter world, trying to shape the best possible life out of very little, using the only tools available to them, perseverance and hard work. Like Terry, they were traditional American heroes—self-reliant, strong, and ingenious. However, and again like Terry, they differed from the popular heroes of the teens and twenties in that they had a strong social awareness. They may have retained the old competitive urge to do better than anybody else, but they had a new and sympathetic understanding that bad times afflicted everybody, a new recognition that everybody was in the same boat.

The Depression took a while to catch up with baseball, which actually made a greater profit in 1930 than it had the previous year (a *much* greater profit, in fact—$1,965,000, as opposed to $1,336,000 in 1929). Terry held out, although he came to terms in mid-February, which was relatively early for him. Edd Roush held out, too—he was notorious for it—but this time he waited too long and pushed McGraw too far. Roush, like most of the players, had been dealt a cut in salary in his 1930 contract; the second contract he was offered had a larger cut than the first one. Roush never reported to the team, didn't play at all in 1930, and was sold back to Cincinnati the following season, his last. While it seems likely, considering the game's prosperity in 1930, that McGraw was simply using the coming Depression as an excuse, he sent a reasonably strong message to future holdouts throughout the majors.

Terry led the Giants hitters with a .380 average in spring training of 1930. Just before the season opened, *Baseball Magazine* ran an article by F. C. Lane called "The Terrible Terry," explaining in a subhead that the word terrible "carries no trace of criticism," referring instead to his talent and power at the plate. (A few years later, during his battles with the press, Terry himself would point out that the word "terrible" had acquired a more sinister connotation.) The remarks Lane attributed to Terry in the article illustrate what he was like and show how his unfrivolous and practical approach to the game was consistent with the "we'd-better-buckle-down-and-get-to-work" mood of the 1930s:

> It's serious business. I have worked hard all my life and I have a family to support. Back there in Memphis, Tennessee, which I have called home for fourteen years, there are three little Terrys. The oldest isn't so little either. He's a husky lad of eleven and hopes to be a first

baseman some day. I wish him luck.

And the off-season is no vacation to me either. I work for the Standard Oil Company of Louisiana. I've had a job with them for nine seasons. I'm strong and well able to work, and I need all the income I can get. Why should I take it easy just because I may have a few fairly big seasons in the major leagues?

Conditions on the Giant team are a little different than elsewhere. McGraw generally calls for the ball he wants you to hit. That bothers some fellows who seem to chafe under restrictions, but I'm used to McGraw's system now and I can't say that it hampers me any in my individual work. There's no doubt it works to the advantage of the team as a whole, and, after all, that's the only thing to be considered in baseball.

Terry was always up front and to the point, and his voice comes through even when diluted by a journalist. Here he states two vital parts of his credo: first, that his priority was supporting his family, and that baseball, if nothing else, was a good provider; and, second, that it wasn't necessary to sacrifice "individual work" in order to support "the team as a whole," even though that team was "the only thing to be considered."

After Terry's great spring, he began the season playing equally well, but as usual his heroics went unnoticed. Even after the season was half over, the sports writers weren't paying much attention. Take the July 26 game, when he went 3-for-5 with two doubles and an inside-the-park homer, but the headline in the *Times* simply said, "Giants Rout Brame and Upset Pirates." This was typical, both of Terry's performance and the coverage thereof; even the losing pitcher seemed more newsworthy.

By August, however, it had become clear F. C. Lane's doubts that Terry could improve on 1929 were misplaced, and reporters began noticing his remarkable year. The *Times* ran a headline proclaiming that Terry was "IN MIDST OF GREATEST SEASON" and, as the month wore on, he kept improving. Even so, he wasn't the only Giant hitter who was having a fine year. Ott, who would end up with 25 home runs, hit three of them in succession on the last day of the month. One of them cleared the roof of the Polo Grounds. Self-effacing though he was, Ott always received better press than Terry, and the account of the game the next day in the *Times* began with this headline: "OTT HITS 3 HOMERS AS GIANTS DIVIDE." John Drebinger's lead paragraph in the *Times* also lauded Mel: "Prodigious were the deeds performed at the Polo Grounds yesterday by Melvin Ott," he wrote, "the silent little man who patrols right field for John McGraw." There was no mention of the silent big man who was by now hitting well over .400.

The next day, September 1, Terry got four hits, including a double and a triple, helping the team move to within four games of the first-place Cubs. Nonetheless, the headlines went to Fred Lindstrom, who had wrenched his knee tripping over first, forcing him to leave the game. The day after that, Terry did even better, with four hits, including a double and a homer. The story in the *Times* did give him credit, in a subhead in lower-case type, but there was also this subhead, all in caps: "OTT GETS THREE DOUBLES." Next to that story, uncommented upon, was a box in which the year's leading hitters were listed. Terry was leading both leagues. On September 2, he was batting .411.

Terry didn't appear to care about the publicity. His toughest critic was himself, and he'd certainly given that critic little to complain about. He surely didn't need the writers to tell him what a good job he'd been doing. The next day, he simply kept it up, going 3-for-4 in the first game of a doubleheader against the Braves. This time, the papers had a good reason for ignoring him, though: McGraw had just signed a new five-year contract. Still, in the two-month period from July 8 to September 3, Terry had batted .446, and you'd think somebody would have said something.

Like the rest of the Giants, though, Terry was undoubtedly more interested in the pennant, still a possibility, than in personal statistics. Even though the Depression had yet to really take hold, it had certainly begun, and only the Republicans seemed optimistic that it wouldn't get much worse. If a team competed in the World Series, the players made bonus money that, in Terry's time, was proportionately much greater than it is today—they could actually double their salaries. Many of the Giants came from poor families and depressed areas of the country. Given what was at stake, the Giants were a team that was deadly serious about winning. When the third-place Giants began a series with the second-place Cardinals on September 10 at the Polo Grounds, they were still only four games behind the league-leading Cubs.

It was a bad time to turn cold. The Giants lost the first game, 5-4, after a four-run Cardinal eighth. In the second game, they lost 5-2 and disgusted everybody, the *Times'* Drebinger included, by leaving fourteen men on base, the highest total in the league that year. Drebinger bitterly suggested that a pennant for New York was always, like national prosperity, "just around the corner." And when they lost again the next day, the season *was* over.

September 28, the last day of the 1930 season, was memorable in a number of venues. In Boston's Fenway Park, Babe Ruth pitched for the next-to-last time in his career, and the first time since 1921, once again reminding the Red Sox that perhaps they shouldn't have traded him in 1919. The *Times* noted that he was still fast, and that he "used the same perfection of delivery that characterized his work of twelve years ago." His control was fine—he only walked two—and he went the distance in picking up the win. Meanwhile, in Sportsman's Park in St. Louis, a rookie Cardinal named Jay Dean pitched his first major-league game. He did even better than Ruth, beating Larry French and the Pirates 3-1 on a three-hitter.

Over in the Polo Grounds, the Giants had to beat Philadelphia in order to edge Brooklyn for an undisputed claim to third place. Terry was even with Lefty O'Doul's National League record of 254 hits for a single season, and he had five chances to break the mark. He walked his first time up, then batted out three straight times. His last at-bat came in the ninth, with a man on third base and one out and the Giants one run back. The score-board mistakenly showed that Brooklyn had already won. Terry hit a sacrifice fly to tie the game, and the Giants won it 5-3, in the tenth. Terry had not passed O'Doul, but the Giants did win both a tight game and third-place honors. He did get some recognition for his "individual work": besides tying the league record for most hits, he hit 23 homers, scored 139 runs, and batted in 129. He also finished the season with an average of .401, a mark that only Ted Williams would better in later years. Terry remains the last National League hitter to have topped .400.

In a baseball alphabet, Ogden Nash saved a letter for "Memphis" Bill: "T is for Terry," Nash wrote, "The Giant from Memphis / Whose 400 average / You can't overemphis." But was Terry's .401 an inflated figure? Much has been written about 1930, the greatest hitter's year in the game's history. The 1930 Giants infield, in fact, had the highest cumulative batting average of any infield in major-league history. Sports writer Red Smith believed that there just happened to be a glut of great hitters in those days. "Never since then have there been so many so good," he wrote, and in his list of examples, Bill Terry's name came up first. The great Hall-of-Fame hitter Johnny Mize argued that the Polo Grounds was a terrible park for averages, adding that Terry might have hit .500 someplace else. Still, there were plenty of incidents in 1930 to support the theory that there was a livelier ball. Big-league pitching suddenly and inexplicably collapsed. Hubbell, for example, had his worst-ever earned-run average, 3.76 (at least until 1942, when he was distinctly past his prime and recorded 3.95); Jimmy Foxx, the great slugger who once hit 58 home runs, hit one that year that was the first-ever hit over the left-field stands in Chicago's Comiskey Park. In another game that year, the Giants took a 14-1 lead into the fifth inning against the Cubs and almost blew it, holding on to win, 14-12 and on one road trip, the A's scored a total of ninety-seven runs in eight games. One writer summarized it this way:

> According to survivors, the fuel behind the hitting binge of 1930 was in the ball. The stitches were low, almost countersunk, which kept pitchers from getting a good grip. The insides had been gradually pepped up for a decade, and in 1930 they reached such superball resiliency that Ring Lardner called it "a leather-covered sphere stuffed with dynamite."

Contemporary statisticians, of course, have pounced on 1930, and while their intent has probably not been to discredit Terry, that's been the result. Terry's "Relative Batting Average," a statistic from the Society for American Baseball Research that attempts to account for year-to-year statistical fluctuations, would place him at about .350 for that year. (There's even one statistical wizard who determined that Wade Boggs, who led the Red Sox and the American League in hitting through most of the 1980s, would have hit .567 in 1930.)

The numerologists, however, seem to have missed at least two points in their concentration on the lively ball. One is the possibility, proposed by scientist Stephen Jay Gould, that defensive strategies of the game simply grew more sophisticated and effective after 1930; the other is that a more durable bat was used in baseball's earlier years. (Since averages dropped significantly after 1930 and night baseball was not played until 1935, night games do not seem to have been a factor here.) Terry had two favorite bats in 1930. He broke one in June, and used the other for the remainder of the season. He once mentioned this to Ty Cobb, and Cobb agreed that sturdier bats could have been a factor in 1930: "Maybe that's why there were higher averages in the old days. We had better wood. What does an average hitter use now each year…a couple of dozen bats." Bats in 1930 were also much heavier than they are now, as Terry pointed out in an interview with Red Barber:

> I asked Terry what had become of the .400 hitter. He began explaining.
>
> "One thing is that the batter of today is swinging differently, using a very light bat, around 31 ounces. Lou Gehrig and I used a 44-ounce bat. Babe Ruth's was 45 ounces. Even little fellows like Paul Waner were using a 42-ounce bat."

It's also worth noting that Terry had *not* used a heavy bat any earlier than 1929, and, in fact, 1930 may have been the year he switched. Before that, he said he used "a fairly light bat, with a long, thin handle." He added that after he switched, he began to choke up on the bat a little, producing fewer homers, but more hits. "I prefer to make the base hits," he said.

In any case, the best defense of Terry's hitting is both obvious and persuasive: a player who bats .350 or above is having a fine year by any standard; a player who outhits players such as Babe Herman, Chuck Klein, Lefty O'Doul, Fred Lindstrom, Paul Waner, Pie Traynor, Hack Wilson, Kiki Cuyler, Mel Ott, Frank Frisch, Chick Hafey, Harry Heilmann, and George Sisler is having a great one. Those skeptical of Terry's 1930 achievement should also consider this: he ranks higher on the all-time list for career average than any of those hitters except Heilmann. Heilmann, however, played most of his career in the teens and twenties, when higher averages, like the ones that seemed unusual in 1930, were the norm, and it is not out of the question that Terry was a better hitter than Harry, too. At least Hal Schumacher was genuinely impressed. "One year he hit—what was it, .401?" he said to me. "I don't care *how* you hit 'em—you have to hit 'em between 'em, or over 'em, or in front of 'em, I don't know which way. But, gee, .401…"

Regardless of history's verdict, Terry earned the respect of his contemporaries, even those not directly connected with the game. The great husky-voiced, melodramatic actress, Tallulah Bankhead, was a diehard Giants fan; once she complained that "Bill Terry used to get as many as 200 hits a season," although "an actress is lucky if she gets two in a lifetime." Terry garnered more pertinent praise in 1930, winning the writers' unofficial Most Valuable Player (MVP) award, in the last year it *was* unofficial. He beat out his former teammate Frisch in a fairly close race, while Hack Wilson, with 56 homers and 190 runs batted in, was third. Terry's counterpart as MVP in the American League was Washington's Joe Cronin; soon the two men would face each other in a World Series. What did Terry feel was his most important achievement in 1930, his .401 average, his 254 hits, or his MVP? "Probably .401," he said to me, "probably, as far as people are concerned."

It could have been the most important achievement as far as Terry was concerned, too, because he knew that salaries were measured by success in the categories most popular with the fans—strikeouts and wins for pitchers, home runs and average for hitters. Terry, as he well knew, was a star because he hit for average. "I want my basehits," he told John Drebinger of *The New York Times* toward the end of the year, "that's what I get paid off on." Then Drebinger followed up his interview with a brief sketch of Terry:

> If ever a young man attained perfection in his chosen field through the combined qualities of self-assurance, perserverance and a singular faculty for swiftly analyzing his own shortcomings it is William Harold Terry—Memphis Bill—who plays a marvelous game of baseball for the Giants in the Summer and conducts a thriving oil business for himself in the Winter to the end that young Mr. Terry is rapidly amassing a fine fortune.

Among ball players Terry is regarded as a shrewd and calculating fellow who knows what he is worth and possesses the assurance and intelligence to get it.

Baseball was still prosperous in 1930, and Terry was even more so. When baseball's situation began to change in 1931, Terry's did not. He continued to have the assurance and the shrewd intelligence to make the most of whatever was available to him in the tough decade to come. When he got back to Memphis in 1930, a couple of incidents involving the town's favorite son were reported in local papers, and they reveal the hard bargainer, the family man, and the sincere believer all at once. In the first incident, he won a lawsuit against the Greyhound Company after one of its buses forced his car off the highway. He was particularly incensed because Elvena and his three kids were with him, and he went for the throat; the company settled with him for more than ten thousand dollars. In the second, he got in hot water with the Memphis Trades and Labor Council for using non-union workers on a construction project. This may sound cheap, but the project involved fixing his church, St. Luke's, and the "mercenary" Terry was paying for the work out of his own pocket.

Nineteen-thirty was Terry's greatest season as a player—the year in which a twelve-year-old Ted Williams, swinging a bat alone, imagined himself to be Terry before a cheering crowd. By 1931, however, Terry was nearly thirty-three, his good years as a player were certainly numbered, and the solid businessman in him must have begun to think about preparing for the future, about finding opportunities for work after his life in baseball was finished.

"God, we had wonderful times in those days," Hal Schumacher told me.

They were building the George Washington Bridge, I remember sitting out, as a young kid, a lonely kid, when

I first came, 1931—sunset after coming back from the ballpark—and I'd look over across the river, and here was the George Washington Bridge being built, going to be finished in a couple of years, I've forgotten. It was great to look over on the other side, at the Palisades. That's when you could walk there at night and nobody would touch you. Really, New York was a wonderful spot. And *eating* places! And they were a dollar and a quarter, instead of a hundred and twenty-five dollars.

A lot of folks who wanted a meal couldn't even raise Schumacher's buck and a quarter. The Depression had hit with nearly its full force. In February, John Kieran of the *Times* noted the disbanding of the Sally League, drily commenting, "evidently the depression continues" and it appeared that the only way out of it would involve teamwork. McGraw had always achieved his successes as an isolated autocrat, but, in an era clamoring for compassion, the manager's players rebelled against a man who felt that showing any warmth was a weakness. As early as mid-1930, Fred Lindstrom was shouting at the manager, in the manner of Frisch and Hornsby. Terry, disgusted, blew up at him once, then declined further conversation with him for more than a year, although it never affected Terry's play. "I think," Terry told Bob Broeg, "that in that uncomfortable time, I tried even harder."

McGraw's first priority had become the preservation of his image as a leader; Terry's chief interest remained getting the job done well. "Doc" Marshall, who played shortstop for McGraw, told me that Terry wasn't interested in "star" status. "He just did the job, you know, he just did the job every day, and he was just another one of the players. And that's about the way I remember him. McGraw used to chew him out, just like he did the rest of us. He didn't have any favorites at all, McGraw didn't. And you can understand that, because he was a...he was just a crusty old man. And Terry didn't have to be given many instructions, either."

Marshall went on to give me a sketch of McGraw's Giants: "Lindstrom was more outspoken, though, than Terry was. He could be pretty outspoken, Lindstrom. Even Hubbell, Hubbell resisted McGraw's penchant for calling the signs up to the catcher, you know. And Hubbell was a mild sort of person."

If anybody was milder than Hubbell, it was Mel Ott. On top of that, Ott was McGraw's latest favorite, but even he couldn't escape the manager's wrath. Whenever another Giant would make a mistake, McGraw would turn on Ott: "Don't let me ever see you do a damn fool thing like that!" McGraw would scream. "You've got to learn to anticipate plays!"

If this was as close as McGraw could get to expressing affectionate concern for a player, and it probably was, maybe his two earlier surrogate sons, Christy Mathewson and Ross Youngs (both of whom died while McGraw was still at the top), were well out of it.

Mac was not going gentle into that good night. He was compulsively raging against his players and everyone else, but he was also becoming the last thing he'd ever wanted to be: a fat, little guy, sometimes ludicrous, sometimes only pathetic. By 1931, although he could still be brilliant, McGraw had changed in one very important way—he was tired. Shortly after McGraw's death, Frank Graham admitted in the *New York Sun* what everybody around Mac understood, but kept quiet: "I did not think I ever would see the day when he would lose the enthusiasm for the business of managing the Giants," Graham said, "but I did. That was about a year or so before he retired." By 1931, even though he had failed five straight times to win the pennant, McGraw had even grown lethargic when it came to cleaning house. He made a half-hearted effort to deal players before the season began, but gave up on the idea almost as soon as he'd started. He said the other teams insisted on getting either Travis Jackson or Fred Lindstrom, or they'd make no trade at all. McGraw said he wasn't going to put either of those players on the block, although that could have been an alibi for not spending more time at the bargaining table.

The Giants were now, in some ways, leaderless; there was hardly a player left who still had any respect for the "old man." But the job had to get done, and whatever the conditions were at the Giants' plant, the proletarians got to work. It's tempting to think that 1931 and 1932 were the years when the Giants, having rebelled against McGraw, learned how to do their jobs without his guidance. They pulled together as a group of tough-minded and hard-working individuals who functioned well, not because of McGraw, but despite him.

In 1931, Terry was a holdout again. He was the last major player to report to the Giant camp, the next-to-last overall, and he ended up with more money than the $22,500 McGraw had said was his final offer, although neither man ever revealed the exact figure. Terry was always given more leeway in these negotiations than other Giants—a mark of his worth to the team and possibly an indication that the front office knew *this* player could, unlike most others, find another good job. Terry, however, would have less success at holding out for higher salaries after 1931, the last year of unambiguous solvency for the major leagues as the Depression deepened.

Once he started playing, he showed McGraw he was worth the extra money; in San Antonio, in his first spring game, he hit what the *Times* called "two terrific hits"—one off the right-field wall, another off the scoreboard in center.

Terry particularly liked San Antonio—steaks were great there, he said—and his affection for the city may have showed in his performance. However, he couldn't have liked the game that was played in Houston on March 21. The Giants lost to the White Sox, 11-6, but, more importantly, they dropped what the *Times* called "the first nocturnal contest in major league history." Terry was vehement in his dislike of night ball; he once even took the time to publish a magazine article in *Collier's* attacking the practice. For as long as he could, he refused to let his team play night games in Cincinnati. "I told 'em I wasn't going to play night baseball, where you go out there and the ball is wet—just wasn't good," he said to me. "I just don't like to play night baseball. It's not a night game." Then he remembered Larry MacPhail, the Cincinnati general manager who ushered in night games in the majors in 1938, and how MacPhail reacted to his distaste for his pet project. "MacPhail got mad," Terry told me. "He said, 'We're playing night baseball next time around.' And I said, 'MacPhail, not me; we're not going to play.' And he called Mr. Stoneham, and Mr. Stoneham said, 'I'm sorry, I can't do anything about it. He's running the club. It's his prerogative.' I said, 'We draw enough people; we don't need to play any night baseball.' Yeah, we had quite an argument, MacPhail and I, about that; but it's all over now."

Terry's Giants were largely purists, defenders of baseball's arcadian faith, and his firm position on night baseball was reminiscent of a quieter comment Carl Hubbell made to Giants catcher Harry Danning a few weeks before Hubbell died in 1988. Danning asked Hubbell, who ended up poor, if he regretted not playing in the era of high salaries. "Harry," Hubbell said, "I'm just thankful I played all my games in the daytime and on grass."

That first night game was a one-shot novelty in 1931, though; the real problem had to do with the team's performance in the daytime. When McGraw told reporters his squad had a better chance at winning the pennant than in 1930, he may have been saying what he thought they wanted to hear because the Giants showed very little spark in 1931.

As frustration increased and age and physical decline crept up on him, McGraw grew even more sullen. In mid-July, he used some McGravian language on umpire Bob Clarke. Clarke, in turn, complained to National League President John Heydler, and Heydler suspended McGraw for three days. It was the first suspension in ten years for the manager the *Times* now called, in an interesting use of past tense, "once one of baseball's stormiest petrels." McGraw received the word of the suspension in the dugout, just before a game. He left in a rage and ran right into Heydler. McGraw, red with fury and out of control, cursed the league president; Heydler, more concerned than angry, tried to calm him down. McGraw was so upset he began to have difficulty catching his breath. After the manager stormed off, Heydler said he was afraid McGraw was "a sick man." Shortly after this incident, his wife Blanche finally persuaded him to go to the doctor. The doctor found that his kidneys were damaged beyond recovery.

Whatever the precise facts, McGraw *was* a sick man in 1931, a man, in fact, with only two and a half years to live who looked less and less like an irremovable institution. His team wasn't much fired up by the suspension and subsequent explosion. They dropped two games that day to the Cardinals.

In 1931, although the Giants were never really in the race, Terry continued to play well. In an exhibition benefiting the mayor's Committee on Unemployment, he won a foot race from home to first, making the thirty yards in 3.6 seconds, breaking the previous record of 3.8, which had been set by a sometime Giant named Jim Thorpe. In late September, in Hal Schumacher's first big-league start, Terry, as John Drebinger of the *Times* reported, "clipped three straight singles over second base," then, with the Giants safely ahead of the Cubs by eight runs, "craftily called it a day." The "craft" of which Drebinger accuses Terry here refers to the very tight race for the league batting title. Chick Hafey of St. Louis and Terry were neck-and-neck all month, and Drebinger implied that Terry came out of the game to ensure that a 3-for-3 did not become a 3-for-4.

Brooklyn got its revenge on Terry at Ebbets Field on September 27 in the last game of the regular season. Terry started the day less than a percentage point behind Hafey, but neither man performed well at the plate. Hafey went 2-for-8 in two games, and Terry was 1-for-4 in the first game of his doubleheader. In the second game, though, Terry got a hit during a six-run outburst and moved ahead of Hafey. Then, after three and a half innings, the game was called on account of darkness, thus invalidating Terry's hit and dropping him behind Hafey. Terry wound up batting .3486 to Hafey's .3489. The time was only 5:30 p.m., but it was unquestionably too dark to continue. Fresco Thompson, later an executive with the Dodgers, was playing shortstop for them then, and he set fire to a pile of scrap paper to suggest to the umps that it was the only means he had of seeing the ball. Certainly, strange things happened in Ebbets Field, particularly when the Giants were in town, but this sort of meteorological sorcery was probably unprecedented even there. Perhaps it was a sign of divine melancholy, since this was the last time McGraw and his old teammate "Uncle Robbie" Robinson faced each other as managers.

The Giants ended up thirteen games back, providing pennant-winning St. Louis with no contest at all. The disappointing season obscured the fact that a great team was gradually coalescing around Terry. He didn't win the batting title, but he led the league in both triples (20) and runs scored (121), while posting the third highest average of his career. His teammates were doing all right, too. Ott led the league in walks, as he would the next year, the first of six seasons in which he was the National League home run champion. Freddie Fitzsimmons won eighteen games and lost eleven. Hubbell won fourteen. In 1932, he would win eighteen and lose eleven, matching Fitzsimmons' record of the previous year. Although they would all need to hold on for one more year after that before truly coming together, the wait would turn out to be worthwhile.

9

DEPRESSION AT COOGAN'S BLUFF: 1932

I Said, 'I'll Take It.' —Bill Terry

The year 1932 didn't begin well—for the Giants or anybody else. The Depression was growing worse, and the players began to feel lucky to have work. Giant left fielder Joe Moore remembered the year this way: "Baseball was good to me," he told me, "because we played in a time, at the start of my career, when times were bad. I mean, you couldn't hardly get ahold of a dollar. People can't believe that unless they lived in that era. In New York, I saw street corner after street corner where they had soup kitchens, and the people waiting would be four abreast and the lines would run for several blocks."

Hard times now reached baseball to the extent that even the great Ruth agreed to take a cut of $23,000, nearly a third of the $75,000 he'd made in 1931. To understand how staggering this was, imagine how much money a superstar of today like Barry Bonds would lose if his salary was cut by one-third. Terry, told his salary was going to be reduced by forty percent, exploded. He said he was "thoroughly disgusted" and demanded that he be sold or traded. As columnist Rud Rennie said in the *New York Herald-Tribune*, "All Memphis was not large enough to contain Terry when he grasped the full import of this proposal." When he returned his unsigned contract to the team, a copy of Stoneham's written response to Terry was delivered to reporters so quickly, in a matter of hours, it's hard to avoid supposing that Terry's reaction was expected—that perhaps Stoneham had already written his reply by the time Terry exploded. After all, as Drebinger said, Terry holding out had become "something of an old story." In any case, Stoneham refused to consider trading Terry, basically telling him to sign with the Giants or quit baseball. In better times, Terry probably would have left the ballpark for a more profitable arena in the private sector, but he didn't have that luxury now, so he stayed. At least he had the satisfaction of knowing that everybody was being similarly penalized. The *Times* ran this headline: "SALARY LISTS OF MAJOR LEAGUES TO BE CUT $1,000,000 THIS YEAR."

Hack Wilson, who had made $33,000 with the Cubs, was stunned when the Cardinals offered him only $7,000. Even the tranquil Mel Ott complained in the *Times*, although he said his cut was not as great as Terry's. "In view of the fact that the Giants made money last season, I don't see how they expect a man to play ball for such salaries," he said. "I hope I have mine adjusted, but I certainly don't feel as if I deserve such a cut as they offered me this season." Much later, Hal Schumacher was able to laugh about the situation when he told Red Smith of the *Herald-Tribune* he was being paid so little anyway that he wasn't really affected. "If I'd taken a cut back in those days," Schumacher said, "I'd have been paying the club."

Was the Depression really responsible for these drastic cuts in pay? Yes. Major-league teams even cut their rosters from twenty-five to twenty-three men. But how could this be? Mel Ott, as honest as he was nice, said the Giants finished 1931 in the black. Baseball was nervous, certainly—the overall profit margin had tumbled to 2.3 percent from 16.4 percent the previous year—but it was still called a *profit* margin.

What baseball probably had in 1932 was an early example of collusion on the part of the owners. The players couldn't win: if they protested too much, they would surely lose the support of the man in the street, who was all too often actually *in* the street. In a contemporary column in the *New York Sun*, Joe Vila quoted one owner who remembered the players who had jumped to the Federal League, a maverick organization that signed many talented players from 1912 to 1915:

> Now it's our turn. For years I had a system to keep the players satisfied. I gave them everything I had and when they demanded more I invited them into my office and helped them look for it. But, after all, a club owner must live, too. I didn't lose any money last year, but I would lose it this year if I made out my salary list according to the players' ideas. Now my ideas will be carried out—and I don't feel badly about it, either, for although I have found it necessary to do a little slashing here and there and to refrain from granting unreasonable increases, I am sure none of my ball players will wind up in the bread line.

The tone of this anonymous owner was both vengeful and threatening; he obviously enjoyed backing his employees into a corner. The players surely couldn't complain about cuts to people who were already in the bread line. If they didn't keep their mouths shut, they'd probably have to join them there.

Whatever cries of foul came from the players, even genuine ones wouldn't be heard. It was certainly the beginning of the end for poor Hack Wilson—in 1932, he would lead the league only in strikeouts, and, halfway through 1934, he'd be released by Philadelphia. Wilson, a friendly man who drank like a bum, eventually became one. When he died in 1948, his body lay unidentified and unclaimed in a Baltimore morgue for three days.

The writer who saw most clearly what the owners were up to was Westbrook Pegler, then of the *New York Post*, a writer who later became quite conservative himself. Pegler didn't shy away from using a word like "conspiracy," and he identified Terry as one of the most prominent victims:

> The conspiracy is an old one, of course, but hitherto the conspiracy has been invoked only in individual cases. This year it is being used against the whole body of players. There has been no more insolent announcement by any employer in the entire course of the present depression than the one from Charles A. Stoneham, owner of the New York Giants, that if his first baseman, Bill Terry, does not accept the salary which he, Mr. Stoneham, offers him, he, Mr. Stoneham, will drive Terry out of baseball, which is Terry's profession. It would be quite all right of Mr. Stoneham to refuse to re-employ Mr. Terry, owing to a disagreement on the terms of hire, except for the fact that under the baseball conspiracy Terry cannot obtain a job with any other firm. This is the industry which has the effrontery to represent itself from time to time as the great, characteristic American sport.

This was pretty strong stuff, and fairly accurate, too, written four decades before Curt Flood challenged the reserve clause that made such collusion between owners possible. But, as Pegler angrily suggested, there wasn't a thing Terry or any other player could do about collusion in 1932. When Terry finally went to New Orleans to meet McGraw and sign a contract in February, some kind of compromise had been reached, but the traditionally close-mouthed front office gave no details. Was the rumor that McGraw himself paid Terry an extra thousand dollars true? Since

McGraw was a co-owner, did it matter? McGraw, contacted at the track on the New Orleans Fair Grounds by a reporter from the *States-Item*, grinned and said, "We never give out figures." He added, "We are both satisfied; I know I am." Another reporter from the same paper asked Terry if he was really satisfied. "Well, I guess so," he said. "Yes, quote me as saying I am satisfied." The different degrees of satisfaction implicit in these comments are very plain.

The Depression was now having its greatest impact on the country and, according to the owners, on the game. Baseball management felt the need to publicly announce that it would not reduce ticket prices. American League President Will Harridge pointed out rather irrelevantly in the *Times* that "during the boom period, baseball made no attempt to take advantage of easy money." John Heydler, Harridge's National League counterpart, argued that the cost of running a club had increased and that "about half the clubs in our league are finding it impossible to meet the enormous overhead." John Kieran wrote a tongue-in-cheek column for the *Times* in which he proposed that the experts wrestling with the nation's economic problems should help out in sports, too, particularly with respect to the Giants' holdouts:

> The Giants must feel that Freddie Lindstrom, Bill Terry and Fred Fitzsimmons are needed.
> "No money to pay the salaries they ask!" say the magnates. Why, it's elemental, as dear old Sherlock Holmes used to say. Issue bonds and the money will roll in.

Morale on the Giants was unquestionably poor. Add McGraw's irascibility to the players' financial reversals, and the result was, at best, uncomfortable. Terry said he was seriously looking beyond baseball again. During spring training, he groused to John Drebinger:

> "Just give me two more years of this and I'm through.

I am pretty well fixed, can easily get into some other business and if I can put in two more good years at a top salary, you can have it." He didn't mean the salary, of course, but the game of baseball itself.

Drebinger, however, didn't buy it. He pointed out that Terry very often had chances to make more money in other fields, opportunities he did not take. He concluded that, whatever his claims, "Bill Terry is heart and soul wrapped up in baseball."

In 1932, the Giants moved their training camp to Los Angeles, an area not lacking in diversions. It combined great weather, the uncritical adulation of the local Hollywood stars, unlimited access during prohibition to good beer, and even a visit to Jim Coffroth's plush Agua Caliente track, across the border in Mexico. The notorious horseplayer McGraw should have been in a great mood.

He wasn't. When the mayor of Santa Cruz cajoled the Giants into playing an exhibition in his town, he closed the schools, the banks, and the stores so that nobody would have to miss the game. McGraw was advertised as the big attraction, but he had a lengthy lunch and then ran into some old pals, not getting to the park until after the game had started. The fans had become apprehensive—maybe the great man wasn't going to show. As a result, the public address announcer was particularly relieved when he saw McGraw finally walk onto the field. He had trouble controlling his excitement, shouting "There he is! The famous Muggsy McGraw!"

In defense of this anonymous announcer who lived thousands of miles from New York, he wouldn't have known how deeply McGraw detested that nickname. It was like calling Richard Nixon, however naively, "Tricky Dick" to his face, or publicly referring to Charles III as "the Fat." McGraw, predictably, started cursing. Just as predictably, he found a scapegoat to curse, working over his pitcher, Roy "Tarzan" Parmelee, whose legendary wildness was worse than usual and who had already walked a number of the minor-league batters he was facing. Sportswriter Frank Graham, who was at that game, said, for McGraw, this overamplified embarrassment had taken all the pleasure out of the trip.

At this point, the players must have realized the pleasant spring hadn't changed anything. A couple of games later, in Oakland, Blanche McGraw called Fred Lindstrom over to her box near the dugout. McGraw himself was taking the day off, watching the action from the bleachers, and Blanche wanted to know if Lindstrom knew whether her husband was staying for all nine innings. He didn't hear her the first time, so she called him again, and when he came over she good-humoredly scolded him for not paying attention. "God," he's supposed to have said, "are *you* giving signs, *too*?" Lindstrom is also supposed to have said this with a smile, but, even if he did, there's no denying the underlying significance of the comment or the tension on the club that it revealed. The explosion in Santa Cruz had shown everybody that it was far too late to rehabilitate John McGraw.

The regular season began, and Drebinger predicted (accurately) good crowds on opening day, "despite the depression." The Giants, however, started the year dismally. McGraw, in his thirtieth season as the Giant manager, watched the team drop three straight games to the Phillies. The third loss was a wonder of ineptitude: the Giants made eight errors, including four in the ninth, to lose by one run. Terry hit a double, and his fielding was typically flawless, but Marshall accounted for three of the mistakes. This might have been the game after which one uncharitable writer is supposed to have compared Marshall to the "Ancient Mariner," because "he stoppeth one of three." Most remarkable, however, is not that a McGraw team had played so abysmally, but that the manager apparently sat quietly through the entire circus. There was no mention of him in any of the stories by the beat reporters covering the game. For all practical purposes, he seems to have been a defeated man; the fire had gone out of him at last.

The players must have known this, and the third game of the 1932 season might have been pivotal for them, too. For some time, they had been without a leader they could respect; now they no longer worried about the tempermental explosions of one they feared. When the Giants of this era spoke of McGraw later on, they seldom had kind words. Fred Lindstrom said that if one of McGraw's players made a mistake, McGraw would "tear him apart right in front of the team," but he added that "Terry and Ott, and Hubbell and Jackson and me, we were a different breed. We didn't need somebody hitting us over the head to keep us in shape. In fact, we wouldn't take it—at least Terry and I wouldn't." Terry's own comments were even more damning. He said McGraw was "the type of fellow who would call all the shots until you got in a spot, then he'd leave you on your own."

Whether or not anything was said or thought on the Giant bench or in the players' homes after that game, the club began to play well. Schumacher started the next game and shut out the Braves, 6-0. A few days later, Terry embarked on the best batting spurt of his career, hitting six home runs over a four-game stretch to tie the record held by Chuck Klein and Babe Ruth. When Hubbell beat Brooklyn a couple of days later, it looked like the season might be successful, after all. Roscoe McGowen, writing for the *Times*, said the Giants were "continuing their retarded climb toward the top of the league ladder."

No such luck. Lindstrom, who represented more than anybody the will of the team in opposition to McGraw, broke a bone in his foot. Fred Fitzsimmons carried him off the field like a baby. When he heard gamblers in the stands had offered 8-to-5 odds that he'd drop Lindstrom, Fitzsimmons said he was sorry he couldn't have gotten a piece of that action. The loss of its most defiant member, however, took the starch out of the team, and six weeks later, on June 1, the club stood dead last. The *Times'* John

Kieran wrote a column in which he said, very pointedly, "The players are there. This team belongs up in the race, and if it doesn't get there Congress should appoint some committee to investigate the mystery."

On June 2, a cloudy Thursday, they suited up to play a doubleheader with the Phils at home, but the games didn't get off because the weather was "threatening." After the games were postponed, McGraw called Terry into his office. They hadn't spoken for nearly two years. McGraw had the quirky habit of telling a visitor to stand facing his desk, his back to the open office door. Terry was told to do this, and did so. Over McGraw's desk were his only concessions to emotionalism, the two framed photos of his stricken favorites, Christy Mathewson and Ross Youngs. "He called me in," Terry told me, "and asked me, he says, 'How would you like to be manager of this club?' I said, "I'll take it.' 'Well,' he said, 'wait just a minute.' He said, 'you got to go upstairs and talk to Mr. Stoneham.' And he says, 'Suppose you go ahead and take a shower and get dressed and come on up.' I didn't say anything more to him, and, for the balance, Mr. Stoneham and I talked."

The versions of this story vary slightly, and the above is Terry's last telling of it. Still, one element remains constant: Terry accepts on the spot, without hesitation, surprising McGraw, who is puzzled that he needs no time at all to think about it. The ability to make this sort of assertive decision may have been Terry's most characteristic trait.

After McGraw told Terry to shower and join him in Stoneham's office, the three men met up there and sat down. Jim Tierney, the club secretary, joined them. Terry said he was accepting the job only on the condition that he would be the complete boss, and Stoneham assured him that would be the case. Then Terry, without missing a beat, said he wanted the trainer, "Doc" Knowles, fired. Stoneham said that was fine. This was a remarkable scene, because everybody present knew why Terry wanted to fire Knowles—he was not only the man responsible for enforcing curfew, he was also McGraw's spy in clubhouse and dugout—and because McGraw was sitting in the room, helpless to do anything about this last humiliation. McGraw, whose later public announcement contained a promise that he would remain with the team "as general adviser and counselor in business as well as baseball matters," had lost even Stoneham's confidence. His influence was not only diminished as he sat meekly in Stoneham's office that afternoon, it was gone. No matter what a discreet front office or a charitable press might later say, he had become a figurehead—a curiosity, a museum piece.

The Giants released no information to the press immediately, preferring to take their time with what they knew was a blockbuster story, but they did put a notice on the clubhouse bulletin board to let the players know. They intended to issue one of their carefully worded press releases later on, from their midtown office on 42nd Street. There was no reason to think the story would leak, since the doubleheader with the Phils had been rained out and none of the writers would see Terry taking over for McGraw on the field. Besides, what reporter would go all the way up to Harlem for no reason on a rainy day?

They didn't count on Tom Meany. Meany, the Giants writer for the *World-Telegram,* needed a story. He went up to the Polo Grounds, hoping to get an interview with some player who might be hanging around after the games had been officially called. He heard the rumor first from a hot-dog vendor, then saw the notice on the bulletin board. That afternoon, the *Telegram* printed the biggest scoop of Meany's career, and one of the biggest exclusives in baseball history. Even a historic batting feat by the Yankees' Lou Gehrig—four home runs in a single nine-inning game—got bumped off page one. The legendary McGraw was gone.

Later that day, the Giants office was forced to call in the other papers earlier than planned. The team gave them copies of McGraw's formal statement, which the writers took back to their typewriters, after which everybody eulogized McGraw. Joe Vila of the *New York Sun* said he was "the man who saved the National

League." Grantland Rice of the *Sun* said it was as though "the Leaning Tower of Pisa had fallen and the Seven Hills of Rome were in dust," but he went on to write an honest review of the McGraw era, concluding that the manager was "not to be judged by the last few years, when illness and misfortune and the passing of time had taken their toll." W. O. McGeehan of the *Tribune* mourned the retirement of "the spirit of the American game incarnate," and the *Post*'s Westbrook Pegler said that since "McGraw was the Giants, and the Giants were McGraw," it was "almost as though McGraw had died." He added that he was not unhappy to see either McGraw or his stooge Knowles go, referring to the former as a "sour and grouchy boss" and to the latter simply as a "snoop." He also wrote:

> Bill Terry had experience of this espionage. Not long ago, in St. Louis, one of the house detectives who infested the family circle of the ball club challenged Terry to account for his conduct when he came in at bedtime, which was 11:30 under McGraw's rule.
>
> "It's none of your business where I have been," Mr. Terry said. "But I don't mind your knowing that I was dining at the country club, and it might interest you to know that I am going again if I get another invitation." The house detective in this case was the club trainer, Doc Knowles.
>
> It seems incredible that a man as independent as McGraw, with McGraw's contempt for timidity, should have imposed on a body of men who were expected to hold their heads up and fight for ball games a set of conditions which would be an insult to a West Point cadet.

Terry restored sense to the club without abandoning structure. The curfew remained, but it was moved back to midnight, and if a player asked for an extension and had a good reason, he received it. What Pegler called "the inhalation of small beers" would be permitted, too, and the new boss even said he'd buy. Terry took over McGraw's office, but he didn't lurk inside like a crab; he opened the door wide and made no absurd rules regarding the proper posture to be adopted when in the presence. In fact, he told his teammates they'd be foolish to keep using the clubhouse pay phone, since they could use the one on his desk for free. Pegler said that less than a day after the previous occupant had left, "the carpet on the floor of McGraw's own office had begun to show the wear-and-tear of baseball spikes, and the mystery of the old man's office had been completely dispelled." The Giants, at last, were being treated like adults and professionals.

The most amusing fallout of Terry's sudden elevation was the reaction of the young Hal Schumacher. Schumacher was the last kid McGraw had scouted and hired, the final surrogate son. He was a student at St. Lawrence University in upstate New York, working his way through college by waiting on tables and doing hard labor with a road gang. It's remarkable that he had any time left to play ball, but he pitched for both the university and, in the summer, for a hosiery company's squad in his nearby hometown, Dolgeville. Dolgeville had also been the home of McGraw's friend and former teammate George Burns, which couldn't have hurt Schumacher's chances with the superstitious manager. Schumacher was a genuinely nice kid, an Ott type, and he was also a great pitcher, a tall right-hander with a superb sinker who immediately reminded McGraw of Christy Mathewson. McGraw added him to the staff in 1931, and Schumacher talked about his first start in training that spring. "I was the last man signed by McGraw," he told me.

> And McGraw, I think, did have a soft spot in his heart for me. I always tell the story about the first ball game, spring training, first year I was with the Giants—and pitched against the White Sox. The last two innings I struck out five of the six White Sox players, in the last

two innings. And when I came over and walked into the clubhouse, John McGraw came over. I was at the fountain, bending over to take a drink, and somebody patted me on the shoulder. Turned around—it was Mr. McGraw. He said, 'Schumacher, I want to congratulate you on your wonderful appearance you made in front of your Polo Grounds fans on your first appearance here.' And he turned around and walked away. Travis Jackson was standing right near—he turned around, and he said, 'Geez,' he said, 'the old man's gettin' soft.' This was the last year that he managed, because you know how tough he was on his ballplayers.

Since he knew he'd been one of the manager's pets and that McGraw and his successor hadn't even spoken for two years, Schumacher was understandably nervous about the change, particularly since he was now rooming with the new man. He told me the story:

About the second year I was still a rookie on the ball club, we came back from a western trip. And we came into the hotel, and I was standing by the desk to register. Suddenly somebody's patting me on the back, I turned around, it was Bill Terry. He said, 'Hey, kid.' He says, 'Would you like to room with me?' Oh, boy, I just puffed up with pride to be asked by Terry to room with him! It was wonderful! And so I roomed with him that night, and the very next day I went over to New Jersey, over to Hackensack, I had friends over there; and while there I learned that Terry had been picked as manager of the Giants! McGraw had been sick and ailing, and he couldn't carry it on anymore. Boy, I hustled back and I got out of that room in a hurry! When I came in there, there were Pathe News, and Fox News and all these others, and I couldn't get out of there fast enough! Nobody could accuse *me* of being partial with the manager! Oh, he got a big laugh out of that, whenever we talked about it!

Finally, after the newsreel photographers had followed Schumacher out of the hotel room, Terry threw himself down on the bed for a breather. "Honest," he said, "I haven't had time to sit down for a minute and say to myself: 'I am the manager of the Giants!'"

The new manager of the Giants, however, was not a man to waste much time either basking in the limelight or lounging on the bed; he had already fired Knowles, and the next day, making a typically quick decision, he brought Joe Moore up from the minor-league branch in Jersey City. Moore would be a star for the Giants for years, a fine lead-off man and probably the best National League left fielder of his era, but McGraw evidently couldn't, or wouldn't, recognize his ability. He thought Moore, who, at 150 pounds, was much lighter even than Ott, was too small. Terry's first professional move as manager illustrated both how fallible McGraw's judgment had become and how good Terry's could be. Moore said that he was always grateful for Terry's confidence in him in 1932, but he didn't neglect to add that as a player he proved that confidence was sound.

Terry's debut on that Saturday in 1932 was a great success. The club took two from the Phillies, 10-4 and 6-4, and it moved out of the cellar into seventh place. Terry had a lousy day, going 1-for-9, but since he was a man normally relaxed and always confident, it's unlikely he had the jitters on his first day as player-manager. Frank Graham of the *Sun* had asked him the day before whether he could handle both jobs. Could he manage and "still play first base and flatten the ball?"

"Don't make me laugh," Terry replied.

The Hollywood script here, of course, calls for a gradual rise through the ranks until the Giants win the pennant, but that kind of miracle was beyond Terry, at least in 1932. He did get them as high as sixth, where they eventually finished, and Charles Stoneham approved. As a player, Terry had had his usual solid year, batting .350 with 225 hits, 124 runs, 117 runs batted in, and 28 homers, the most he ever hit. But he had begun to become even more important to the club as its manager. Halfway through September, Terry was given a two-year contract extension under that cap. Now he felt completely comfortable to use the authority Stoneham had always promised him he had, and he started to move. On the day his new contract was announced, he said only four players couldn't be traded—Ott, Travis Jackson, Fred Lindstrom, and, for some reason, Shanty Hogan, the player of ordinary talent who had been part of the Hornsby trade. Terry may have wanted to protect him because Hogan was his only experienced catcher; in October, however, he traded for catcher Gus Mancuso, and Hogan's privileged and protected status suddenly changed. Although Mancuso had been only a bullpen catcher for the Cardinals, Terry felt this was the best trade he ever made. He knew Mancuso was particularly good at blocking the wayward pitch, and he wanted this skill because of Schumacher's sinker and, of course, Hubbell's screwball. Now Terry could get rid of Hogan—a player whose chief attribute was that he dearly loved to eat—and he sold him outright to the Braves in December.

Terry did trade one more man from his list of four, but this time he did it very reluctantly. He was fond of Freddie Lindstrom, who was even the tenor on his barbershop quartet. McGraw apparantly led Lindstrom to believe that he would be the next Giant manager, though Terry said Lindstrom had been misinformed. "Who made that decision to give you the job?" I asked Terry. "Stoneham," he said. "Sure."

"Do you think McGraw would have gone for Lindstrom then?" I asked.

"If it had been up to him it'd have been Lindstrom," Terry said. "Tierney thought so, too, that McGraw had the say. But he didn't."

While Lindstrom thought McGraw chose Terry over Stoneham's objections, Terry was particularly firm in insisting it was the other way around. Considering McGraw's obvious loss of influence and his visible decline, plus the strong possibility that McGraw was either encouraged or forced to quit, Terry's version seems more likely. It becomes even harder to disregard when you consider what Buddy Hassett said Lindstrom told him when they were both playing for Brooklyn: "Lindstrom always claimed that McGraw double-crossed him by giving the job to Terry," Hassett told me. "Lindstrom told me that Mr. McGraw had told him to work with Bill—Bill was holding out, and the story is, as I got it from Freddie, that McGraw told him if he could sign Bill, he had the job. Well, the next thing you know, Bill signed, but he signed as the manager," Hassett said, laughing. "It sort of shook Freddie up a little, I guess. The story as I had it was that he had the job if he could sign Terry, and then Freddie woke up, and Bill had the job."

Whatever the facts, Lindstrom, had been, as he saw it, not only passed over, but betrayed, and at the end of the season he said so to Terry. Terry and Lindstrom were good friends—on the day McGraw quit, Fred Lieb wrote in the *New York Post* that Lindstrom was Terry's "particular pal" on the club—and, despite rumors to the contrary, there were never any hard feelings between them. While he felt he'd been badly deceived, Lindstrom never thought Terry had anything to do with it. After the season Terry, who knew Lindstrom was unhappy, sought him out. Lindstrom, far from criticizing his manager, started explaining his feelings to his friend. Most accounts say Lindstrom immediately asked Terry to be traded, but that's not quite how Terry remembered the scene. "He didn't ask to be traded," Terry told me. "I called him in and told him, 'You know what the story is and I know you're not happy.' He said, 'I won't be happy.' I said, 'Where would you like to go? I'll try to trade you wherever you want to go.'"

"But he wasn't angry with you, was he?" I asked.

"No," Terry said. "And before he died, he said, 'I want you to take me out and kick me as hard as you can kick me.' And I said, 'What for, Freddie?' He said, 'You know what for—for letting me talk you into trading me!' I said, 'I didn't want you to stay if you weren't happy. But,' I said, 'if you'd've stayed here, we'd've won at least one more pennant, maybe another one—maybe two.' And he said, 'Look at the money I lost.'

The years Terry was talking about were 1934 and 1935, the two seasons Lindstrom spent with the Pirates and the only two in which the Giants lost the pennant between 1932 and 1938. Could Lindstrom have made the difference in those two years, giving the Giants five straight flags? Terry may have been right about 1934, at least, when the race was very close and Lindstrom had a much better year than his replacement in the Giant outfield, George Watkins. In trading Lindstrom, Terry acted in a manner that didn't make sense economically or strategically. In fact, right after the move, Dan Daniel of the *New York World-Telegram* pointed out that since the rest of the league figured "the Giants had to get rid of Lindstrom," his value as a trading asset "had fallen to a ridiculously low level." Like McGraw, Terry had seemed to allow his feelings to interfere with his business sense. Unlike McGraw, however, Terry had made the trade primarily out of friendship, not anger.

But the rest of Terry's changes would turn out to be most adequate. In addition to Moore in left and Mancuso behind the plate, he brought up John "Blondy" Ryan, a shortstop who made up for major-league inexperience with an enthusiasm bordering on the hyperthyroid, and, halfway through the 1933 season, he would trade to get Lefty O'Doul back from Brooklyn; O'Doul had beaten out Terry to lead the league for average in 1932. In 1933, Terry's canny trades would combine with great luck as several players reached their primes simultaneously. A *kind* of prosperity, at last, *was* just around the corner.

The pennant-winning 1923 New York Giants, the team on which Terry broke into the National League. Terry is second from right, top row. Among other future Hall of Famers in the photo are: front row, Frank Frisch and Ross Youngs, sixth and seventh from left; middle row, Hack Wilson and Casey Stengel, first and second from left; Hugh Jennings and John McGraw (in overcoat), fifth and sixth from left; Dave Bancroft, eighth from left; top row, Travis Jackson, fourth from left. *National Baseball Library, Cooperstown, N.Y.*

Action in 1924 World Series. Goose Goslin, of the Washington Senators, is out at first; Terry has taken the throw. *National Baseball Library, Cooperstown, N.Y.*

Spring training, San Antonio, Texas, 1929. Left to right: Fred Lindstrom, Travis Jackson, Andy Cohen, Andy Reese, Bill Terry. *National Baseball Library, Cooperstown, N.Y.*

Giant outfield candidates, Wrigley Field, Los Angeles, spring training, 1932. Left to right: Len Koenecke, Ethan Allen, Chick Fullis, Mel Ott, Joe Moore, Fred Leach, Fred Lindstrom. Of these seven outfielders, only Ott and Moore were on the 1933 world championship team. *National Baseball Library, Cooperstown, N.Y.*

Harpo Marx, foreground, with four New York Giants during spring training in Los Angeles, 1932. Left to right: Fred Lindstrom, coach Dave
Bancroft, Travis Jackson, Bill Terry. *National Baseball Library, Cooperstown, N.Y.*

Three hard-hitting Giants, 1933 or 1934: Bill Terry, Lefty O'Doul, Mel Ott. *United Press International*

Terry crossing the plate following his second home run on opening day
of the 1932 season at Baker Bowl, Philadelphia. *National Baseball Library,
Cooperstown, N.Y.*

Terry and John McGraw, 1932, after he replaced McGraw as manager of
the Giants. *National Baseball Library, Cooperstown, N.Y.*

Terry afield (above) and hitting fungoes (right) during spring training, 1933. *National Baseball Library, Cooperstown, N.Y.*

The three starting pitchers for the Giants in the 1933 World Series. Left to right: Hal Schumacher, Carl Hubbell, Fred Fitzsimmons. *National Baseball Library, Cooperstown, N.Y.*

The 1933 National League All-Star team. Left to right, front row: Pepper Martin, Lon Warneke, Tony Cuccinello; middle row: Bill Hallahan, Dick Bartell, Bill Terry, coach Bill McKechnie, manager John McGraw, coach Max Carey, Chick Hafey, Wally Berger, Lefty O'Doul, Chuck Klein; back row: Gabby Hartnett, Jimmy Wilson, Frank Frisch, Carl Hubbell, Bill Walker, Paul Waner, Woody English, Hal Schumacher, Pie Traynor, trainer Andy Lotshaw. *National Baseball Library, Cooperstown, N.Y.*

President Franklin D. Roosevelt tossing out the first ball at the second game of the 1936 World Series, Polo Grounds. Terry is at left and New York Yankee manager Joe McCarthy at right. *Associated Press*

World Series action, Polo Grounds, opening inning of sixth game, October 1936. With Joe Moore on third, Dick Bartell on second, and Hank Lieber on first, Mel Ott doubles to right field off the Yankees' Lefty Gomez, scoring two runs. The Yankees, however, won the game, 13-5, and took the Series. *National Baseball Library, Cooperstown, N.Y.*

The Giants' "Meal Ticket," Carl Hubbell, delivers a pitch during the 1936 World Series against the Yankees. *United Press International*

Outfielder Joe Moore crosses home plate at the Polo Grounds after homering to score Gus Mancuso and Alex Kampouris ahead of him, 1938. Dick Bartell, left, and the batboy offer congratulations. *Associated Press*

Three Giants who were named to the National League All-Star team in 1939. Left to right: Bill Jurges, Mel Ott, Harry Danning. *Associated Press*

Gus Mancuso, left, and Carl Hubbell, boarding a train for the Giants' 1943 spring training grounds in Lakewood, New Jersey. It was to be Hubbell's last season. *Associated Press*

Bill Terry and Joe DiMaggio at the old-timers' game at Yankee Stadium in
1954. Each hit a home run. *National Baseball Library, Cooperstown, N.Y.*

Bill Terry and Dizzy Dean, right, at the old timers' game, Yankee Stadium, 1960. *National Baseball Library, Cooperstown, N.Y.*

Six one-time New York Giants, as photographed during the 1950s. Left to right: Hal Schumacher, Bill Terry, Rogers Hornsby, Hank Gowdy, Dave Bancroft, Dick Bartell. *George I. Brown*

Four .400 hitters, later 1950s or early 1960s, Cooperstown. Left to right: Bill Terry, Ted Williams, Rogers Hornsby, George Sisler. *National Baseball Library, Cooperstown, N.Y.*

Terry with his family. Left to right: Mrs. Kenn Terry, holding Kenn, Jr.; Kenn Terry; Mrs. Bill Terry; Bill Terry; grandson Tim Miller; Terry's daughter, Marjorie Miller. *United Press International*

Terry packs his briefcase after resigning as president of the South Atlantic League, Atlanta, 1958. *United Press International*

PART III

A NEW DEAL AT
THE POLO GROUNDS

10

THE YEAR THE EARTH MOVED: 1933

I always think of the Giants in terms of 1933—and naturally, '36 and '37;
we won pennants then too—but to me the '33 season is the
New York Giants.
—Hal Schumacher

Economically, 1932 had been a disastrous year. The Depression, out of reasonable control like some fiscal malignancy, had created unemployment figures so high that they were grimly (and seriously) being compared to the casualty lists of the World War I battle at the Somme in France. Would 1933 be any better?

It was doubtful. The country was now entrenched in the Depression, and there were plenty of signs that a grim era was not only at hand, but would be around for a while. The flamboyant McGraw had been forced out of his job in June, 1932, and *Baseball Magazine* called his no-frills successor "a colossal anticlimax." In September, New York Mayor Jimmy Walker, who symbolized the carefree and prosperous 1920s as much as anybody, was himself forced out; even New York could no longer tolerate a night-owl songwriter who posed as a public servant. And just before Herbert Hoover was emphatically deposed by the electorate, he went to West Virginia for a dedication. After the traditional 21-gun salute, an old, unemployed man looked up at the President, who was still standing ceremonially erect, and said, "By gum, they *missed* him!" Even the taciturn Calvin Coolidge had confessed bewilderment at what had happened to the country over which he'd presided. On January 5, 1933, Coolidge had breakfast with his wife, spent the morning in his office, and drove back home at lunchtime. His wife took the car to go shopping and he went upstairs to shave. When she returned, she found him dead on the bathroom floor. He'd died as quietly as he lived.

In 1933, the players were again forced to take enormous salary cuts. Poverty, even starvation, was tangible and public. If the Giants drove to Wrigley Field along the elevated Michigan Avenue when they were in Chicago to play the Cubs, they had to be uncomfortably aware of the hundreds of homeless people one level down on Wacker Drive, huddling around makeshift fires. During the mornings, these people could be seen ransacking Chicago's garbage dumps for food after the trucks had pulled out. In this climate, it was no wonder the affluent were hated. Is it a surprise, given the national mood, that the club owners could reduce ballplayers' salaries with no fear of public outcry?

Herbert Hoover was far from an executive activist, but when he did make a decision, it always seemed dead wrong. When the press reported his unpopularity, he took it personally, like some ancient tyrant reacting to the messenger's bad news, and he became less and less accessible to reporters. In contrast, Franklin Roosevelt would give frequent press conferences and build a further bridge to the people with his informal "fireside chats." F.D.R. combined the even-handed equity of Jeffersonian democracy with the strength of autocracy in a benevolently socialistic despotism, and, in retrospect, it's doubtful any other approach would have worked as well.

Meanwhile, Terry's Giants were about to convene in Los Angeles to prepare for *their* new season under *their* new boss. The autocratic McGraw, distinctly of the old school and as blind to change as the outgoing President, had made every decision, never consulting with his players. Terry, in contrast, held a skull session before each game, listening to every suggestion and implementing some of them. McGraw, like Hoover, had begun to walk away from the press; Terry, at least for now, opened that journalistic door again. Terry could understand the sorrow of the Depression, and so could his friends on the team, men who came from rural towns—many in the poor South, some in the Dust Bowl—towns like Meeker, Waldo, and Gause, in rural Oklahoma, Arkansas and Texas. Maybe Terry *was* wealthy, but his wealth had come exclusively from shrewd judgment and hard work. Unlike McGraw or Hoover, Terry understood how fundamentally the country had changed; like F.D.R., although he would always be the boss, Terry was also one of the boys. Hubbell remembered Terry as "a real good baseball manager, and when he took over in 1932, he was perfect for the players," adding that "of course, he had been through the McGraw bit." Joe Moore put the difference between the two more succinctly, telling me simply that "McGraw was a driver; Terry was a leader."

When the October 1933 issue of *Baseball Magazine* came out, F. C. Lane was already discussing Terry very perceptively. "Terry and McGraw are in striking contrast," he began: "Their managerial methods are at opposite poles. McGraw was the autocrat of the diamond. His was the imperial purple; his the regal scepter. Players, to him, were little beyond automata who batted and ran bases as he pulled the strings." Terry, on the other hand, seemed to Lane "cold, unemotional and rather unapproachable," although, in truth, Lane concluded, "he is none of these things." Lane also said:

> Terry is a young man who has had to work for his living. He has worked on and off the diamond. Long ago he learned the value of efficiency. He is business-like in all his methods. If he is coldly calculating at times, it is

because he is after results. He has no hallucinations. He has resolved to make good.

Terry does not sit upon the bench like an executive at a desk and push a button for a subordinate to perform a certain task. That was McGraw's method. Terry is a player. He is the leading player on the team, and he manages not by driving nor even directing, so much as he does by leading.

Lane went on to quote Terry's declaration that his way was "different from McGraw's": "The managerial policy which I have adopted is built upon defense rather than offense. The Giants do not usually need to score many runs. All that we must do is score more than the other fellow. Our system is built upon air-tight pitching. We commonly play for one run. I have said to the players many times, 'If we can hold them to the seventh inning, we can win.'"

Another new wrinkle, surprisingly, was Terry's greater concentration on fundamentals. An observer of McGraw might have thought he would drill his men until they wept, until the basics of the game became reflexive, but apparently he was less of a stickler for the fundamentals than Terry. Terry particularly concentrated on the running game, sometimes putting the whole squad through two-hour sessions in the sliding pit. He also had his infielders and pitchers do extensive work on the fielding of bunts, drills so extensive that the *Times* quoted Fred Fitzsimmons as saying "he had learned more baseball in the two weeks here than he did all the time he played under McGraw."

Things, in short, had changed for the Giants, and the most important difference by far involved the new feeling that everybody was working in partnership. Joe Moore told me that "back in our day, we were called the family team—we were very close. We lived, all of us lived in the same neighborhood in New York, up in Washington Heights. And…our families were very close; we visited, we sat in the park together and what not. But we were a pretty close ballclub." The new harmony Moore described was important. Terry wasn't simply running a team, as his predecessor had, he was part of it; stale pieties like "playing ball" and "teamwork" began to take on real meaning. In 1933, the practicality of the team's "family values" would become very plain.

Most experts picked the Giants to finish no better than sixth, but they hadn't noticed that, due to Terry's quietly persistent shuffling and trading, the 1933 team was very different. When the official roster was released, however, they *did* notice. John Drebinger wrote that the Giants had been subjected to "one of the most intensive and extensive overhaulings ever undergone by a major league club." More than half of the 1932 club was gone. A few days later, Drebinger added that Terry had "set a record for dismantling a ball club," that there had been so many trades in such a short time it looked like "a jam in a six-day bike race." In a column he called "The New Deal on the Diamond," John Kieran even directly compared Terry's boldness to Roosevelt's. Terry had acted at least as decisively as the country's new manager, Kieran said, adding that, like F.D.R., he had done "everything but throw the old cards out the window and call for a brand-new deck."

How much had the team changed? Take the situation at catcher. Of the 1932 catchers, only one, Fran Healy, remained. The three newcomers were Gus Mancuso, Harry Danning, and Paul Richards, all of whom would have lengthy major-league careers—which should give some indication of Terry's eye for talent. It's been argued that the success Terry's teams enjoyed in the mid-1930s was made possible by McGraw's players, but considering the trades Terry made in 1932 and would continue to make in the next few years, this seems preposterous. The writer who eventually became the most stentorian Terry-basher was Joe Williams of the *New York World-Telegram*. In December 1932, he wrote: "Terry wants the 1933 Giants to be his own ball club. The 1932 team was McGraw's. Bill is willing to stand on the revised roster.

If he has made mistakes, he is ready to suffer the consequences." Williams' comments were made some time before Terry's "revised roster" would show what it could do. Like McGraw, Terry was going to make some bad trades, but, from now on, the Giants were exactly what the papers started to call them, the Terrymen. After they started winning, McGraw himself insisted he'd had nothing to do with their success.

It becomes particularly hard to understand why Terry's critics persist in claiming he won because of McGraw's players when they don't explain how he did so much better with those players than McGraw had. Compare the years each man managed "McGraw's team," beginning with Ott's first season, 1926, excluding 1932, and ending with 1939, two years after Hubbell had begun to slip and three years after Terry had retired as a player: From 1926 through 1931, McGraw's Giants finished an average of 8.17 games out of first place; from 1933 through 1939, Terry's Giants finished an average of only three games back. The contrast becomes even more marked when looking at the managerial records of McGraw and Terry from 1929 through 1937, which were not only the greatest years Hubbell, Terry, and Ott ever had, but also the only seasons Hubbell won more than 13 games. (Hubbell averaged 20.2 wins annually for those nine years.) During the years McGraw managed in that period, his teams averaged ten and a half games back, while Terry's averaged two and a half games *ahead.*

In any event, most reporters felt the 1933 team was very different. When they asked Terry what he thought, he bet a hat—his usual bet—that the Giants would finish anywhere from third to first, and they were no longer disposed to take him lightly. Travis Jackson should come back strong from his bad knee, Terry said. Fred Fitzsimmons should have a good year, Hubbell will be terrific as always, and Gus Mancuso, the best catcher in the league, would be able to handle even "Tarzan" Parmelee. "The changes we've made should give us more power than any other club in the circuit next to Philadelphia," he told John Drebinger, "and we have them stopped, because we'll have the better defense." He also asked the writers not to forget "the very promising youngster, Johnny Ryan."

A couple of days later, the annual Baseball Writers' indoor picnic honored McGraw, who actually left the track in Havana and flew up to New York to attend. He walked in to boisterous and lengthy applause, a noisy reception that went on for several minutes. As usual, invitees included figures from all walks of the sporting life, dignitaries such as football's "Hunk" Anderson and wrestling's Ed "Strangler" Lewis. The writers, breaking from tradition, made no fun of their tired friend McGraw; the only number they sang that made reference to him, to the tune of "Molly Malone," was called "Oh, Where Will You Find Another Like John J. McGraw?" Frank Frisch was present, but nobody noticed the asides of which he must have been guilty during the song. Terry was also in the hall, John Drebinger reported in the *Times*, "his dark hair, free of even a few straggling touches of gray, offering a sharp contrast to the snow-white locks of the ruddy-faced McGraw," but, like Frisch, he appears to have been innocent of formal comment. Left relatively alone at the party and possibly a little miffed by the writers' musical hint that nobody could replace the old Giant manager, Terry must have been thinking that McGraw was taking a hell of a long time to ride off into the sunset.

On February 17, a week before training camp opened in Los Angeles, outfielder Len Koenecke's contract arrived on team secretary Jim Tierney's desk at the Polo Grounds. Every player was now signed. "I can't recall when it was ever done before," Tierney said in the *Times*; "I guess it should stand as a record." What Tierney meant was that nobody was holding out when the spring camp opened, and everyone was eager to play. This may have been because the players still remembered the salary gouging of 1932, but it also may have been because this was Terry's team, not McGraw's.

Meanwhile, the country was closer to actual collapse than it had been since the Civil War. Roosevelt had been in office less than a week before he responded to the financial panic by closing the banks. The Giants, fortunately, were too hard at work to worry overmuch, although, like everybody else, they had no access to cash. Terry told John Drebinger of the *Times*: "The boys may be broke, but they are eating very well at the hotel, and that is all ball players ought to do in training. Eat well, sleep well, and concentrate on what is going on in the workouts. That they can't raise any money makes it all the easier to maintain training regulations, although I will say I never saw a better behaved bunch of fellows on a ball club than we have here."

As if the Depression weren't difficult enough, there were several natural disasters of crushing magnitude during the same period. The soil erosion in the Dust Bowl, at its most severe in 1933, was the best known, but there was also very heavy flooding in the northeast, and, at 5:50 p.m. on Friday, March 10, one day before F.D.R.'s first fireside chat, southern California suffered a major earthquake. The quake killed 130 outright, injured at least 5,000 and did $45 million in damage. Severe aftershocks continued through the night, sending debris from half-ruined buildings into the streets, while residents huddled in parks and other open spaces to try to sleep.

The Giants, back at the Biltmore in Los Angeles after beating the Cubs that afternoon, at first thought the earthquake was nothing serious. "At first I was inclined to take it for a joke," Terry told John Drebinger. "I remember making some crack about guessing the shock of the Giants' finally winning a ball game being too much. But when I started getting reports how bad the thing really was, boys, I'll admit I was plenty scared."

The other Giants were plenty scared, too. Willie Schaeffer, the trainer, was still at the ballpark, taking a shower. After the earthquake hit, he panicked and ran, and when he came to his senses, he was standing on second base, naked, dripping water, and looking at a huge crack in the grandstand clock tower. "Fortunately, the stands were empty," Drebinger commented, although he didn't say whether it was Schaeffer or the fans who were fortunate.

It didn't take long for the rest of the Giants to get outside. Hughie Critz left a thick steak on the table and ran out into Pershing Square, in front of the hotel. Jim Tierney grabbed a rosary and ran down ten flights of stairs. Everybody gathered around Terry in the middle of the square, and, by this time, Schaeffer, who had shaken off his fear and put on his clothes, arrived. It was getting cold and the players, showing precious little concern for Schaeffer, sent him back into the hotel four separate times to retrieve sweaters and overcoats. It was still too cold to sleep outdoors, however, even with the warm clothing, so when Schaefer told the team that the ballpark seemed relatively safe, most of the players hailed cabs. Once they arrived there, they went into the dressing room and tried to sleep on the uniform trunks. Glenn Spencer, a pitcher, thought it would be safer back in his hotel room, but he was too nervous to stay by himself, and his roommate, Gus Mancuso, had gone with the others to the park. Terry went with him to the hotel, calmed him down, and spent the rest of the night in the bed vacated by Mancuso. The next afternoon, during the Saturday game between the Giants and the Cubs, aftershocks made the stands sway slightly four different times. Unbelievably, the seven hundred fans in the stands stayed for the whole game.

Terry was getting nervous. He said the team would have to break camp and go to Phoenix if the tremors didn't quit. He said he couldn't train his men properly if they couldn't get any sleep. Although the aftershocks grew worse the second night, the quake seemed to be over by the following day, a Sunday. The game that day went well for the Giants, and Terry was obviously able to concentrate: he went 2-for-5, hitting a three-run homer in the bottom of the ninth inning that won the game and shattered the windshield of a car parked just beyond the out-field fence.

Back at the Biltmore, Terry slept well, at least until 5:15 Monday morning, when the worst aftershock of the prolonged series actually tumbled some of the Giants out of bed. Most of the players ran for the streets, with the rosary-wielding Tierney again getting down ten flights in record time. Now Terry, angry and frustrated, reached for his phone. He was going to ask Willie Schaeffer how long it would take to pack the players' gear. He couldn't reach Schaeffer, however, and, when Terry calmed down, he had a reasonable discussion with the prayerful Jim Tierney. The two men agreed the big aftershock really *had* to be the last one, and they decided to stay. Later in the day, reporters from the *Times* asked Terry about his threatened move to Phoenix, and he laughed. "Some of the boys are frankly scared," he said, "and I'll admit those shocks are beginning to get me too. But unless matters get worse I guess we'll be able to struggle through."

Terry and Tierney were right. The earthquake was over at last, and the rest of the camp was uneventful, at least seismologically. Now everyone could look back on the general panic with relieved smiles, as did Terry, who talked of how difficult it had become at the training table, what with all those peas rolling off all those knives. While it was certainly a coincidence, equivalent to a meaningless baseball statistic, historians concede that the economic "bottom" of the Great Depression was reached at the time of the great Los Angeles quake, and the long, slow national recovery began when the shaking stopped. The Giants' 1933 season began in earnest after the earthquake, too, and it would also be characterized by dramatic recovery.

In fact, it turned out to be a good spring. Hubbell, Schumacher, and Fitzsimmons were throwing well. As March progressed, the Giants swept a two-game series from the White Sox, then took two in a row from Pittsburgh. Travis "Stonewall" Jackson, however, was still hurting. In 1931, he'd played a full season and hit .310, but in 1932, he appeared in only 52 games and his average dropped more than 50 points. In the off-season, Terry had found him a surgeon, and Jackson had come to Memphis for an operation, but it didn't seem to have done any good. In fact, for Jackson, 1933 would be disappointingly similar to 1932: he'd end up with a .246 mark in 53 games. Terry told me that once, on the road in Cincinnati, "Stonewall" even broke down: "I had him in Cincinnati, in the hotel bedroom, with a newspaper and a pillow, and he was crying...and I said, 'Look,' I says, 'you're your own worst enemy. You make yourself like that.' I said, 'Hit that ball outside. Hit it to the opposite field. Don't hit it down to left field, hit it the other way.' And the pillow was for home plate, and the paper was the bat, and I showed him how to stride."

The right-handed Jackson had a good excuse for hitting so predictably to left. When he was seventeen, playing for Little Rock, he had been very badly hurt. He and the center fielder, both running at top speed, hit heads. It was bad, indeed: the center fielder's frontal sinus bones were pushed into his right eye, which he lost, and Jackson himself didn't wake up until after they'd operated on him in the hospital, stitching up a gash so wide it connected his eyebrows. The physical scar was permanent, and so was the mental one; he always shied away from the plate a little, both turning and hitting to the left. Jackson apparently took Terry's advice, though, since he had a better year in 1934. By 1935, he was hitting over .300 again.

Injuries continued on the team, some of them freakish. Around the time Jackson was reaffirming that his legs were bad, coach Billy Southworth, feeling the itch to play, spelled Joe Moore in left and badly wrenched his knee. A week later, on the last day of March, Terry was hit square on the nose by a hard foul ball during batting practice. There was plenty of swelling (one writer suggested a resemblance to Jimmy Durante) and a vivid shiner. Southworth, an old friend and ex-roommate of

Terry's, came over with some ice to help keep the swelling down.

In the meantime, Southworth had submitted his resignation, apparently asking Terry to use his wrenched knee as his excuse for quitting. He possibly felt a little foolish, maybe a bit elderly for a young man's game. Anyway, he left for Ohio the next day, and the writers immediately got suspicious. Guessing that something had been kept from them, they grew inventive. None of them had been at that early morning batting practice to actually witness Terry getting clocked. Wasn't saying you got hit in the nose by a random foul tip a little like saying you had walked into a door? The standard explanation for a black eye was a fist fight. Southworth was known to like his whiskey, and he left for good right after the incident. The writers didn't come out and say all of this, but they implied it, despite denials from all concerned and the lack of hard evidence that there had been any rift in Terry's and Southworth's long-standing friendship.

Nonetheless, Terry remained on good terms with the reporters who covered the Giants, and also utterly involved in his own new administration. One night, he was sitting with several writers in the dining car of the team train during the spring trip north, talking about the Giants, and he never noticed when the lights in the diner were turned down. He kept talking as the car was shunted around the railroad yard, not figuring out that the diner had been disconnected from the Giant's team car until he realized it hadn't moved for some time. Terry and the writers had to run around the yard until they found the team's train, which was starting to pull away.

When the Giants played their first game at the Polo Grounds, the day was sunny, but very cold. The band from near-by Manhattan College played the national anthem, and Mayor John P. O'Brien led a march across the field, shoulder to shoulder with John McGraw, attending in his civilian capacity as vice-president of the Giants. McGraw went over to the Giants' dugout and shook Terry's hand, but the encounter was diplomatic and per-functory. O'Brien tossed out the first ball, but his throw was so high that the crowd cheered, prompting him to laugh. Mancuso was able to catch his next effort.

Then Hubbell took over. He gave up four hits and no runs, walking two and striking out thirteen. The Giants scored only one run—all they needed—on consecutive hits by George "Kiddo" Davis and Hughie Critz. Hubbell needed no help from the bullpen, pitching a complete game. This was simple baseball, unglamorous but efficient, the kind of low-scoring game that Terry had built this team to play. It was the same style of ball they would continue to win with in 1933.

The season wasn't going to be easy, though. For one thing, the injuries persisted. If a player looked as though he might be able to get back into the regular lineup, another was often dis-abled, evening things out. The Giants were behind the Braves by two runs on April 21 when Terry tried to shake things up in the eighth inning by putting the still-lame Jackson in at shortstop. He got the desired result, both from the crowd (an ovation) and from Jackson (an infield hit in the ninth), but the Giants still lost, 3-1. Jackson's legs were still bothering him, though, and he was benched again the following day. Worse, on April 24, Terry him-self was injured when he was hit by a pitch thrown by Brooklyn's Joe Shaute. The pitch broke his wrist, and he wasn't even award-ed first, since the home-plate umpire, Ernie Quigley, ruled that the pitch had first hit Terry's bat and was therefore a foul strike. *How in hell, then,* Terry presumably asked, *could it break my wrist?* He left the game fuming. He nearly passed out from pain on the bench and was ministered to by the team doctor. On the bright side, Hubbell shut out Brooklyn 4-0, grudging them four hits, only two of which reached the outfield, walking three, and strik-ing out six. The papers noted that he was working on a streak of 22.2 scoreless innings. The next day, Terry managed from the dugout, his right arm in a cast. It was the first time he had been out of the lineup since 1929, ending his streak at 468 straight games. By late May, Terry began putting himself in as a pinch-hitter, and he did pretty well for an invalid; in his first at-bat, he knocked one out of the park to beat Brooklyn. When he finally got back in the regular lineup on June 3, he hit another homer, and the Giants won handily, 11-3.

The real story, however, remained the pitching. In the games just mentioned, Terry's two shots were part of the Giants' total of seven runs. The Giants' opponents in those two games got a total of just one. When the Giants' hitters faltered, the team could still win, and often it would need only one run to do it. On May 7, for example, Hubbell beat the Reds, 1-0, in the first game of a doubleheader, and Schumacher beat them, 5-0, in the second one.

Nearly two months into the season, Terry's system had proven so efficient that the team had won more than it lost, even with *both* himself and Jackson out. It was a very tight race, though, and still early. A hard-headed businessman and ruthless taskmaster would find this the worst time to give his hard-pressed employees profitless work, but Terry arranged for his team to do something no big-league squad had ever done, or has ever done since. It was a decision that had to be called sentimental.

Hal Schumacher—the appealing kid who had been first awed by Terry, then bowled over by his suggestion that they room together, and finally terrified at the prospect of being so close to the new manager—was graduating from St. Lawrence in June. Schumacher told me he had not quit college to play baseball by choice: "Don't forget, that was during Depression days," he said. "I had to leave school, because I didn't have enough money to finish school. I tried to give baseball a crack, to earn enough money to come back in the fall—which, fortunately, I was able to do."

Terry knew Schumacher had worked hard to earn his degree and admired him for that. Schumacher was another man that matched his era—like Terry, confronted with a tough situation, he had worked hard and come out well. So Terry took the team upstate, to Canton, to watch Hal put on his cap and gown and to play an exhibition game against the St. Lawrence team. When he told me about how potentially embarrassing the trip was, Schumacher laughed.

> I had just started in the rotation, and was pitching, going along real good, and suddenly they said we were stopping at St. Lawrence University for an exhibition game, and it was going to be on commencement day, and that after the ceremony they were going to play the university a baseball game on our athletic field. I got into the chapel, and I looked around, and said my God, what am I doing here? I felt a little bit self-conscious, as you can imagine, wearing a robe! When I walked up to get my diploma, I'm sure they nudged each other. When that was over…that was the happiest moment of my life, to get through with that ceremony!

Tough ballplayers though these guys were, they all put on jackets and ties for the pre-game ceremony. In the pictures, they looked good; one might have mistaken them for a group of insurance salesmen, even deans. Like Terry, the other players were fond of and respected Schumacher, who, at bottom, was probably as happy about being given the day as he was to get through it.

Once the brief recess was over, Terry returned to work. Less than a week later, he made a major trade with the Dodgers, acquiring Lefty O'Doul. He sent them Sam Leslie, and, in addition to O'Doul, he received Watty Clark, a left-hander who had been one of only two National League pitchers to win twenty games the previous year. Some journalists suggested that this trade iced the pennant for the Giants, since the thirty-six-year-old O'Doul could still hit and Terry now had a second quality lefty on the staff. As it turned out, O'Doul did hit well, but Clark was a bust, winning only three games the rest of the season. Nonetheless, it quickly became clear Clark wasn't needed. On July 2, the Giants' pitching staff had the best day in its history—whether under McGraw or another manager, either in New York or San Francisco, where the team later moved.

It was a Sunday, and there was a doubleheader against the Cardinals scheduled at the Polo Grounds. Before the afternoon's business began, Dizzy Dean dropped in on the Giants at their pre-game meeting with the express intent of needling them. When Terry explained that they were planning strategy, specifically how to pitch to the Cardinal hitters, and politely asked Dean to leave, Diz said that it was okay, he didn't mind staying. Dean then offered to go over the weaknesses in the St. Louis lineup himself, which, apparently, is exactly what he did.

Dean's bravado was an obvious attempt to unsettle Terry's players, but, on this particular day, it didn't work. Although both games were one-run affairs, neither was won by Dean's Cards. In the second game, Roy Parmelee, who walked nobody, beat Dean, 1-0, although Johnny "Blondy" Ryan was badly spiked and had to leave the game. In the legendary first of the two contests, Hubbell beat Tex Carleton and Pop Haines, also 1-0, but it took him 18 innings to do it. On that day, the Giants shut out the Cardinals for the equivalent of three nine-inning games. Taking nothing away from a pretty good performance by Parmelee, Hubbell's outing was truly incredible. It still stands among a half-dozen or so can-didates for the greatest game ever pitched.

Although Hubbell was something of an iron man—he hit for himself in the bottom of the eighteenth inning and would have pitched the nineteenth had he needed to—he very likely threw two hundred pitches against the Cardinals, give or take an elbow-deforming screwball or two. Terry, in a pennant race, didn't want to risk using him in a new mid-season exhibition game meant to pub-licize baseball—the first All-Star Game, on July 6. McGraw, who had been nominated to manage the National League squad, had said Hubbell would start. Terry asked McGraw not to start him, and the former Giant manager acquiesced. It was their last dispute.

The fans were disappointed, of course, although Hubbell did come in to pitch the last two innings. In the game, four players had two hits apiece—Terry and Frisch for the Nationals, Jimmy Dykes and Babe Ruth for the Americans—but only one really mattered. Ruth's two-run homer in the third inning gave the American League a 4-2 victory and handed John McGraw a loss in the last game he'd ever manage. Ruth hit his shot off Hubbell's replacement as the National League starter, "Wild" Bill Hallahan, and McGraw must have wondered how Hubbell would have fared against the Babe. Fred Lieb of the *New York Post*, before he knew Hubbell had been scratched as the starting pitcher, made the following prophetic observation: "John McGraw, who will lead the National League All-Stars into action in Chicago Thursday, says he'll start Carl Hubbell. Well, Messrs. Ruth, Gehrig, Simmons, Foxx and Cronin of the American League stars should have an interesting afternoon ahead of them." In the All-Star Game the following year, Hubbell would prove Lieb's sagacity.

Following the break, the Giants' fortunes took a marked turn for the worse. At the height of their achievements, just before the All-Star Game, the Giants had lost Blondy Ryan. He had, in fact, been so badly spiked that it took thirteen stitches to patch him up, and he was sidelined for an indeterminate amount of time. When the team began a road trip after the break, it left Ryan at home in New York to recuperate. Ryan, a lousy hitter, was replaced by a much better one, the hobbled Travis Jackson, who was worse than Ryan in the field. In fact, Jackson was often intentionally walked, as he had been in the bottom of the eighteenth during Hubbell's great game, since he was certainly no threat as a runner. Although it seemed the Giants would gain at the plate what they lost in the field, it didn't work out that way.

Cincinnati manager Donie Bush had earlier told the *Times* "that boy Ryan don't hit much, but the team is winning and you can carry a shortstop for his fielding." Soon, the stiff-jointed Jackson was flubbing routine ground balls; his two errors in the ninth inning on July 3 let in two unearned runs and cost Schumacher a shutout, although he still beat the Braves, 5-2. But now, with Ryan hurt, they dropped seven games in a row and were undoubtedly ready to consult with the nearest gypsy reader. Superstitious ballplayers might have thought Ryan was a human talisman, the quality of good luck incarnate. Leveller heads would have said the Giants they were being hurt by Jackson's fielding and that a zealot like Ryan simply could invigorate a team. In any case, even the writers made frequent comments about the short-stop's absence and paid close attention to the timetable of his scheduled return.

On July 10, Terry phoned Ryan, and Blondy asked permission to come back right away, but Terry told him he shouldn't rush his recovery. Terry said he wanted him to go to St. Louis for the next series, but that he wouldn't put him back in the lineup until he was sure he was healed. Nat Gerstenzang of the *New York Post* underlined Ryan's intangible importance by saying that although "his batting average is so obscure you won't find it without a microscope," the Giants should have a brass band at Union Station in St. Louis when he arrives. The next day, the Giants lost to Dizzy Dean, 2-1; both Cardinal runs were unearned, one of them resulting from one of two more errors by Travis Jackson. Further, this was a game in which a notable insult was added to the injury of loss. Dean had visited a children's hospital earlier that day, where one kid had asked him to strike out Terry for him. Dizzy had said he would. After he left the kids' ward, Dean complained to a pal, "He *would* have to pick Terry." In fact, Dean had little luck with Terry for most of the game. In the bottom of ninth inning, he got his last chance. The Giants had already scored a run on three singles; there were two men on, one out, and the Cards were ahead by one run. The batter was Hughie Critz. If Dean could force him to ground into a double play, the game would be over; if he walked him intentionally to load the bases, he would get another shot at Terry, who was on deck.

Dean walked Critz. Then he came off the mound and walked toward the plate. Halfway there, he stopped, explained to Terry what he had to do, and why, apologized, and walked back to the rubber. Then he struck Terry out on three pitches. The next man up was a flabbergasted Mel Ott, who popped out to end the game.

For the Giants, though, the important thing was Jackson's miserable performance in the infield. A healthy shortstop would at least have sent the game into extra innings. Gerstenzang said the need for Ryan had become "obvious," and Will Wedge of the *New York Sun* voiced hope that Blondy "was rushing to the rescue." One unidentified Giant—considering how he was fielding, it might even have been Jackson—told the *Times*, "Boy, we sure need Blondie in there at short." On or about July 11, Ryan himself got into this act. Rud Rennie of the *New York Herald-Tribune* had breakfast with Terry on July 12, and Terry was cheerful. "Read this," he said to Rennie, handing him a small yellow sheet with "Western Union" printed across the top: "THEY CANNOT BEAT US STOP EN ROUTE STOP J C RYAN."

Terry, knowing it could only have a positive effect, told everybody about Ryan's wire, writer and player alike, right away. As soon as the team returned to the Polo Grounds, he posted it on the same bulletin board on which Meany had found the announcement of McGraw's retirement the previous year. It became the Giants' battle cry, and, in addition, since everybody knew what a weak hitter Ryan was, it elicited a laugh from fans all over the country.

It was what the team needed though. On July 12, the day Terry showed the wire to Rennie, they got back on track. Schumacher snapped the seven-game losing streak with a 3-0 shutout over St. Louis. There was little question that Ryan's telegram and his subsequent return to the starting lineup were important factors in the Giants' season, whether the credit belonged specifically to Ryan's infectious hustle or the primitive beliefs of some of his teammates. Wearing a football shinguard, he starting playing shortstop regularly again on July 13. After that, the Giants kept winning and were never in really serious trouble again.

The pattern of the Giants' season rarely changed in 1933; nearly every game seemed to be decided by one run, usually in Terry's team's favor. By August 21, the team was seven and a half games ahead of a second-place bunching of Pirates, Cardinals and Braves, but Terry still firmly promised he'd allow "no let-up," secure though the National League flag seemed. Practicing what he preached, Terry hit a game-winning homer in one of two wins over the Pirates on August 25. Terry and the Giants could smell blood, and, on August 27, their enthusiasm boiled over. The Cardinals, now managed by Frisch, sent Dean against Schumacher in the first of two games, but Schumacher had one of his worst days of the summer, losing, 7-1. In the second game, possibly frustrated by that very lopsided score, Terry and the Giants instigated a rhubarb that, in its severity, reminded observers of the days of McGraw. Umpire Ted McGrew called Frisch out at first, then changed the ruling to safe. It was a very bad call. It made Terry—*Terry*—"white with fury," according to Rud Rennie in the *Herald-Tribune*. He charged McGrew in a rage, and the umpire was seen to thumb Terry out of the game.

Fifteen minutes later, however, everybody in the stands was startled to see Terry still on the field. Ott and coach Tom Clarke, both of whom had appeared to keep their respective cools during the dispute, had been tossed instead. Later, Ott told the confused writers that Terry had shouted to McGrew that he couldn't eject the only first baseman the Giants had (Sam Leslie was now with the Dodgers), and that the umpire had seized on Ott and Clarke, innocent bystanders, as surrogates. Whether this is strictly true is debatable, since National League President Heydler briefly considered a suspension for Ott, who was apparently more active in the dispute than anyone had reported.

Terry was a shrewd psychologist, a man who would sleep in the bed next to a pitcher frightened by an earthquake, who understood the value of Ryan's telegram, and who certainly saw the value of maintaining (or feigning) testy relations with the Brooklyn Dodgers. Here, though, his reaction seemed spontaneous, even though it did serve to rekindle the Giants' fires at a crucial point in the season. John Kieran of the *Times* felt Terry's explosion was both important and genuine, saying that heretofore he had been "just a fellow who picked the pitchers since McGraw moved out," but that now "he had demonstrated to the fans that he was something more than a fellow out there putting in an afternoon." Kieran went on to say that "the fans stood up and roared approval of Memphis Bill's explosion. They never knew that he cared. He won his spurs. The old Guard among the Giant rooters has fallen in behind him."

On the September 19, it all paid off—the wholesale trades of the previous winter, the great year the pitchers were having, the energy, the hustle, the hard work, and even the occasional detonation of placid sorts like Terry and Ott. At exactly 3:15 p.m., one of the writers in the press box at Sportsman's Park waved down to Terry and shouted that the second-place Pirates had lost the second game of their doubleheader with the Phils. It no longer mattered what happened in the game the Giants were playing with the Cards. They had won the pennant. Players in the dugout stood up, and, when the scoreboard verified the report, several tossed their caps and waved their arms. Terry said this was his biggest thrill in baseball, and he told reporters, twice, that the team had done it because of its remarkable "spirit" and "fight." He said he was going to ask Judge Landis for permission to add infielder Charley Dressen to his post-season roster, since Travis Jackson remained half helpless in the field, but he added that first he had to ask his players what they thought—a strategy *most* unlike his predecessor's.

As a player, at least for one of his caliber, Terry's year had been unexceptional. His broken wrist had sidelined him for several weeks, so he recorded career lows in hits, doubles, triples, home runs, and slugging average. His .322 batting average was his second worst, but, even so—it was a dead-ball year—he led the other Giants. Nonetheless, this Terry was a far cry from the hitter who'd had nearly seven hundred total hits in the three-year period from 1929 to 1931 and who had hit well over .350 in each of those seasons. On the positive side, though, these Giants (five games in front) were an even farther cry from what they had been under McGraw, when Terry was recording such impressive statistics.

By 1933, Terry the manager had become more important to the Giants than Terry the player, and his employees, reacting to the new regime, had become cheerful and optimistic. On the train back to New York, Tom Clarke was talking to some writers when Blondy Ryan walked along the aisle of the Pullman, looked down and grinned. "They can't beat us," the *Times* reporter heard him say. "It's an old bromide now. But the Series won't go over six games. They can't stop a derring-do team like this, with Terry at the head," Ryan said. He then made a reference to the bad hop that had cost the Giants the Series in 1924—"unless they sprinkle some pebbles at third base."

On September 20, at 6 p.m., Terry and his men arrived in Grand Central Station and were greeted by two bands (one from George Washington High, the other composed of Pullman porters), a couple of official city greeters, fifty policemen and ten thousand citizens. Some were catching commuter trains, but most were fans. Even the commuters stayed to cheer the team. The crowd broke through the police line, mobbing and backslapping until the players finally got outside the terminal and into a fleet of waiting cabs. From there, they were driven to their homes, mostly in Washington Heights. As Joe Moore indicated, Washington Heights was well-known as the Giants' enclave in the city; even Damon Runyon's fictional "Baseball Hattie" lived there with her husband, who, in his story, pitched for McGraw.

The next morning, there was a gathering at the Polo Grounds for a motorcade to City Hall. The first to arrive was a fan known only as "Goldy." He arrived at eight in the morning, adorned with numerous cowbells. Hubbell got there next and signed autographs while he waited for the others. Terry, exercising the head man's privilege to be late, didn't show up until a bit after eleven, when the parade started downtown. There were ten cars with a motorcycle escort; traffic waiting for them to pass at cross streets honked. At the corner of Spring and Lafayette, the men of Engine Company Number 20 stood at attention in front of their firehouse, and, as the Giants went by, they turned on their siren. The same thing happened in front of Company Number 31 on Lafayette and White.

At City Hall, another big crowd had waited two hours in the rain to get a look. The people yelled at Ryan—"Oh, you, Blondy!"—and shouted for Hubbell to stand up. They called for Ott, who was standing shyly behind the much larger Roy Parmelee. They sat through the obligatory mayoral address, during which Mayor John P. O'Brien made both the usual lame jokes (the Giants had passed on the California earthquake to the rest of the league) and a predictable effort to associate himself with glory (he, too, had once managed a baseball team, at Georgetown). O'Brien also suggested that the Giants' perserverance could be taken as a model for the entire country: "Your performance might well be taken as a shining example for men and women of today, particularly business men and working men, who are striving in these times of stress to go forward in the face of great economic odds. We might all well take pattern after you and when the days seem darkest fight the hardest and keep fighting until success is achieved." The crowd listened patiently in the rain. Then Terry got up, and asked, "Would you like to meet some of the boys?" The crowd went nuts.

After every player was introduced, one by one, and after Terry said again that this had been a team effort, the Giants headed back to the Polo Grounds. The rain persisted, however, and the game against the Dodgers was postponed. Terry went to his office, left the door open as usual, and started going through his mail. There was a lot of it, and one writer said he resembled a man looking for checks. A number of the letters made him chuckle, since they began with the words, "As one of the few who picked you to win…"

The American League champions were the Washington Senators, a fine offensive aggregate that had led the majors in hitting and finished a comfortable seven games ahead of Ruth, Gehrig, and the Yankees. Their best hitter was left-fielder Heinie Manush, who'd had a better year at the plate than any Giant except Terry, and they still had Goose Goslin in right. They also had Joe Cronin, a player-manager like Terry, at short. All three players would later make the Hall of Fame. Grantland Rice expected great things from the conflict, and, as he often did, he expressed himself in regular verse. "There's Cronin marching to the plate," he wrote in the *Sun*, "As Hubbell's 'screw ball' flies; / There's Terry, in his clash with fate, / Beneath World Series skies."

The Giants had plenty of time to take it easy before the Series, and they even scheduled a charity exhibition with the inmates at Sing Sing prison. (Terry said the park had the highest outfield fence he'd ever seen.) A dozen Giants, including McGraw, were photographed in stylish fedoras for a national hat company's advertisement. The ad's copy was addressed to Terry, the bettor of hats, and it read, "Tell us frankly, was it 'Blondie' Ryan or ADAM HATS that brought you the good luck to win the pennant?" Jack Doyle, euphemistically called "the veteran betting commisioner" by the *Times*, said this Series had prompted the heaviest gambling action in years, probably another indication that the national mood was improving. Doyle's odds, however, were 6-to-5 against the Giants.

The Giants would not have known how to be favorites. They made no comments about the unfavorable odds and indulged in no braggadocio, and, when it was time, they simply went to the ballpark. The umpires were already there, hanging out glumly around first base. Westbrook Pegler of the *Post* said they looked like "sheriff's deputies preparing to solemnize a hanging." Walter Johnson, the former Senator who had been the hero of the 1924 Series, was now only a spectator; he edged his big frame down to a row just in front of the press section. A little red plane appeared in the oval of sky over the Polo Grounds; it was chased off by a big black official-looking one with the letters "P. D." on its side. Al Schacht, an ex-Senator pitcher who still worked at ballparks as "The Clown Prince of Baseball," put on a visor and used a pillowcase for an apron to impersonate the aristocratic tennis star Helen Wills Moody. A second-rate band, half-hidden in the fold of the lower stands in left, played the anthem, and somebody with a big voice yelled, "Play ball!"

Terry's strategy was simple. He pitched Hubbell, who allowed five hits and struck out ten, and let Ott, who went 4-for-4 with a homer, swing away. The Giants won the first game, 4-2, and, as John Drebinger wrote, they won it with "two quiet unassuming young men, epitomizing the spirit of the New York Giants." After Terry made the last out of the game at first, he flipped the ball to Hubbell and ran back to the clubhouse with his arm around the pitcher's shoulder. Once inside, the players cracked open beers and discussed the game. Terry took a long swig from his bottle. "What a game," he said, looking around and waiting for questions from the press. Did he relax after Hubbell fanned the first three Senators? No, not with eight more innings to go, not even with Hubbell. Which Senator was most dangerous? Terry said Hubbell should answer that one, and Carl thought for a while. Finally, he said, "Cronin," with no further comment.

The diehard Giant fans were at the Polo Grounds again the next day. "Goldy" was there with cowbells on, and there was a second eccentric, a man wearing a tall hat plastered with pictures of all the Giant players. He extracted an autograph from a resigned John McGraw, who had seen worse.

The Senators scored first in game two, when Goslin hit a homer in the third inning, but New York came back with six runs, batting around in the sixth. O'Doul, pinch-hitting for Kiddo Davis, got the big hit that inning, a two-run single to center. Years later, O'Doul admitted he'd been so eager he actually stepped over the plate to get a swing at the ball, and that he should have been called out, but plate umpire George Moriarty either didn't see the infraction or was a partial observer. The inning was also notable for Joe Moore, who hit two singles, both on first pitches. Moore was such a notorious first-ball hitter that some opposing managers fined pitchers who started him out with a strike.

That was all the scoring in the game, which the Giants won, 6-1, and after Terry again made the last out at first, he flipped the ball back to his pitcher, threw his arm around a player's shoulder— Schumacher's this time—trotted out to center field, and into the clubhouse. The Giants, who were supposed to be a low-scoring team with great pitching and a fine defense, had outscored the hard-hitting Senators in the first two games by a 10-3 total.

The following day, October 5, the Series moved to Griffith Stadium in Washington, where President Roosevelt came across the playing field. The dour Hoover had made a similar appearance three years earlier on the first opening day after the stock market crash, only to be poorly received by the Washington fans. F.D.R., of course, couldn't walk, so he was driven to his box. Although he sported a gray felt hat reminiscent of Hoover's, he was by no means dour, flashing his famous smile. Far from being booed, he was mightily cheered.

The President threw out the first ball that day with what John Drebinger called "a quick, decisive wind-up," and, just then, the clouds that had threatened all morning gave way to the sun. The Senators, capitalizing on the omen, got to Fitzsimmons and won, 4-0. It looked to Cronin as though the momentum might have shifted to his club. It looked to Terry as though he'd pitch Hubbell the next day.

One of the features of game four was a piece of baseball legend that turns out to be fine as legend, but less satisfactory as truth. It will be remembered that Terry had asked Commissioner Landis for permission to add Charley Dressen to his staff, in case Jackson was unable to play. Shortly before the Series, Landis had agreed, and Dressen had been brought up from the Southern Association. Game four was tied 1-1, until the Giants scored once in the top of the eleventh inning. In the bottom of that inning, Hubbell got into deep trouble, loading the bases with one out to bring up Cliff Bolton—the same Cliff Bolton who had also just been brought up from the Southern Association. Here, says legend, Dressen called time out, ran to the mound, and told Hubbell exactly how to pitch to Bolton, who then grounded into the game-ending double play.

Dressen actually had nothing to do with the double play. Terry told me that Ryan and Hughie Critz talked him into letting them play deep in the infield, to set up the double play, and he added that he was happy they had done so. The result was all that mattered, anyway. They made the double play, as promised; the Giants won the game, 2-1; and they were one victory away from the World Series title, with Schumacher scheduled to pitch next. Giant fans were pleased, especially the great dancer Bill Robinson. A *Times* reporter saw him charge through a police cordon to shake Ryan's hand. "It was the first time in my life that I ever was nervous even a bit," Robinson told Ryan. "I was worried until you picked up that ball, Blondy. And that ball meant fifteen hundred and forty bucks to me." Not only was the famous "Bojangles" Robinson a better dancer than Jack Doyle, he was apparently a better handicapper, too.

Few expected the Senators to put up much of a fight in game five, but it went into extra innings. Schumacher was knocked out of the game in a three-run Washington sixth, and the great Cuban pitcher Dolf Luque came in for the Giants. Neither team scored again until the top of the tenth, when Ott hit a controversial homer into the temporary bleachers in left center. It could have been called either a ground-rule double or a homer. After some discussion, however, the umpires ruled it a homer, and Ott jogged the rest of the way home from second base. Luque provided some entertainment in the bottom of the inning. By then, Richards Vidmer, now writing for the *Herald-Tribune,* had decided to leave the arena; he was in the clubhouse with Hal Schumacher, who was sitting on a bench and listening to the radio.

"Two out," said the announcer. Vidmer was watching Schumacher, who sat quietly on the bench, head down.

"Cronin singled," the announcer said. Vidmer saw Schumacher close his eyes. His shoulders drooped a little.

"Schulte walked."

Now Joe Kuhel was up. Kuhel had hit .322 and batted in 107 runs in 1933. Schumacher couldn't stand the inactivity. He turned around, reached for his socks, and put them on methodically. For quite a while, there was no sound from the radio, then Vidmer and Schumacher heard a noisy stamping of feet in the grandstand overhead. The announcer came back on.

"Kuhel fanned."

In fact, he had fanned on three pitches, thereby giving Luque his only Series decision in a twenty-year big league career, and delivering the Giants the championship.

Schumacher jumped up, but he still couldn't believe it. "Is it over?" he asked a clubhouse man. The man nodded. So he jumped over the bench he'd been sitting on and positioned himself by the door. Vidmer watched the whole scene from further back in the room; pretty soon he could hear the thundering and yelling as the team came down the passageway. When the door was thrown open, the first man through was Terry, and Schumacher grabbed him and shook his hand.

And so the celebrations began. The Giants picked up their paychecks, dispersed, and returned home to be received like so many conquerors back from the war. Dolf Luque returned to

Cuba. Batista had just deposed the legitimate government, and the United States didn't like it. When Dolf landed in Havana and was mobbed at the airport, he found papers that ran his picture with the caption, "The only Cuban the United States recognizes." Hughie Critz received a big parade in Greenwood, Mississippi, led by the Greenwood Drum and Bugle Corps; after that, he was fed at a dinner hosted by his parents. The upstaters turned out to cheer on Hal Schumacher for the second time in a season, but they seemed a little tired after the first party, and the *Times* noted there were only "hundreds of village folk," not a thousand, to hear the mayor and a state senator take political advantage of the young pitcher in the Dolgeville town park. However, the larger community of Lynn, Massachusetts, planned a real party for Blondy Ryan. Although he was tiring of the limelight and managed to sneak into town unnoticed, his father, a Lynn policeman, made a couple of calls. When Blondy drove into Central Square later that day, a crowd was waiting for him. The fans made him park, get up on a soapbox, and make a speech. While he was talking, the Lynn policemen pretended to give him a ticket, and when somebody told him, Ryan, sensing no mischief, blew up. He had yanked the ticket off his windshield and crumpled it before an embarrassed constable could ask him to read it to the crowd. The "ticket" was a square of cardboard that read, "Blondy Ryan Has Put Lynn on the Map."

Meeker, Oklahoma, may have been a small town, but, because it had the biggest hero, Carl Hubbell, it went all out, setting up a full day's celebration, with bands, parades, a baseball game, and a dinner. Meeker had a population of only seven hundred and fifty, but the crowd topped ten thousand. Hubbell was introduced to the crowd by Ned Pettigrew, the Cushing, Oklahoma, manager who had given him his first pitching job. The people asked for a speech, but Hubbell balked as long as he could. When he finally obliged them, the *Times* reported that "they got a brief one." Across the country in San Francisco, O'Doul, who was travelling with Joe Cronin, found a large crowd waiting at the Ferry Building. Their parade was city-sized—"several thousand school children marched to the tunes of many bands"—and when they arrived at City Hall, the *Times* said Mayor Rossi gave them the keys to the city. Cronin said he still thought the Senators were the better team, apparently not realizing what that suggested about his managerial skills, and he received polite applause. O'Doul agreed that Washington would indeed have been a cinch "if they'd had Carl Hubbell pitching," drawing a big laugh.

Terry took a long way home, since he wanted to take Elvena and his younger son, Kenn, to see Niagara Falls first. When he got back to Memphis, however, he got the biggest reception of all. His parade went south on Main to Beale Street, then cut back north on Second until it got to the Courthouse, covering most of downtown and passing the Peabody Hotel twice. There were plenty of bands in attendance, as well as clumps of Shriners, Boy Scouts, soldiers, and Elks. There were also two hundred of Terry's co-workers from Standard Oil. When he arrived at the courthouse, he got a surprise: instead of the anticipated key to the city, Mayor Overton announced that the state government in Nashville had made Terry an honorary Tennessee Colonel, and he was presented with a Governor's proclamation attesting to that fact. During the presentation Emma Hardin, who was the South's answer to Amelia Earhart, flew overhead and dipped her wings in salute. Even the normally controlled Terry was moved by the enthusiasm of all of these neighbors, and he said so. The *Commercial-Appeal* quoted him as saying it was "the greatest thrill I ever experienced off the playing field" and that the Memphis welcome was "bigger and better" than the New York celebration, particularly because "here…well, it's closer to the heart." When Terry reminded the crowd that the victory had been a team effort, that "no manager wins a World Series…it's his ballplayers," he was given a big hand. The *Commercial-Appeal* added that the mayor beamed "as he had not beamed since his last election."

Then there was the obligatory banquet, hosted by Terry's old friend, Frank Gailor, at the DeVoy Hotel. Gailor had officiated at Memphis' first party for Terry, a lunch held the previous October in honor of his elevation to manager. Many of his former Polarine teammates been at that event, including fellow pitchers Forest Bradley and Joe Bradshaw, and Gailor had reminded everybody that in 1931, when he was "King" of the Cotton Carnival, Terry had been his ceremonial bodyguard. At the lunch, Terry had been presented with a hand-painted scroll, an honor he took seriously; half a century later, the certificate hung on a wall in his Jacksonville home, and he pointed it out with satisfaction. It might have been at the World Series banquet, that Mrs. Hunter Wilson rose to premiere "The Last Line-Up," a five-verse musical description of Terry's winning year.

Things were working out well in other venues, too. Terry had taken a winter job as vice-president of the Knox-Ant Corporation, an exterminating company with offices in the Peabody, and, since he was undoubtedly paid more for his name than his labor, he had time to pursue his other business interests. On October 20, a Standard news release announced it had signed him to another contract and that he would "continue with the sales force this winter as he has in the past." Why would a relatively wealthy man take a job as a salesman when he could already call himself a manager and a vice-president? Well, Terry was a very different kind of salesman. When Guy Lombardo, already a household name, made his annual tour of the country, his shows were sponsored by Standard Oil; in the winters, Terry frequently went along to act as a public relations man and road boss. In fact, what he had learned by organizing Lombardo's tours over the years certainly must have helped him later, when he planned the Giants' barnstorming tours with the Indians. The musicians would travel in a Greyhound bus, and Terry would follow in his car, often with his family, since the trips amounted to paid vacations for his kids. Terry was obviously on one of these junkets when the Greyhound forced him off the road in 1930. At every place he stopped, he would contact the local government and, as he told me, "make a sales pitch" for Standard Oil. "I travelled through all the states, from Boston to New Orleans, two shows a night," he said. "My job was to get the mayor, the governor, and make arrangements for dinner, and get them tickets to the show. We had a beautiful show; people stood outside on the curbstone, waiting to get in. We had a blues singer, a trio—oh, we had a regular set-up. That was really a beautiful deal. They gave me eight thousand dollars for that."

Plus expenses.

And there was even better economic news for Terry. A few days after the Series was won, Charles Stoneham gave him a five-year contract at forty thousand dollars per year. In 1932, he had inherited McGraw's job; now he inherited the best salary McGraw had ever made. Terry had just completed one of the most dramatically successful seasons ever for a rookie manager, and for his team, like the country itself, it looked as though good times might be coming back.

11

ARE THE DODGERS STILL IN THE LEAGUE?:
1934–1935

That sure made us a lot of money.
—Bill Terry

After the 1933 Series, the writers were converts to the Giants. In December, the Associated Press rated the Giants' victory the year's "greatest team feat," and it voted Hubbell 1933's best athlete in any sport. It also picked the Giants to repeat. So did Johnny Ryan, who worked the team's chances out mathematically. The addition of outfielder George Watkins had improved the team by twelve percent, he reasoned. Jackson was now healthy, and that meant the club would be ten percent better. The ball was livelier, which could only help the hitting of Terry and Ott, giving the Giants a six-percent edge, while Schumacher and Parmelee were at least two percent more effective due to the experience they had gained. Ergo, the 1934 Giants, would be a full thirty percent better than the 1933 team that had surprised the league, then startled Washington in October.

Whether or not he took Ryan seriously, it's understandable Terry made few changes in his squad in the fall and winter of 1933; he had to give up Kiddo Davis to get Watkins, but that was about his only shuffling. Early in 1934, the new optimism still prevailed, as symbolized by the broad presidential smile, and Terry himself even suggested a connection between his team's projected prosperity and that of the nation. "I expect baseball to take a new lease on life next season," he told the Associated Press in January. "Additional money has been put into circulation. Thousands have gone back to work and have money to spend on pleasure. The NRA codes will provide them with time off for baseball games."

The NRA, or National Recovery Administration, was one of several new bureaus created to fight the Depression. For some reason, these agencies were always given three letters. The TVA (Tennessee Valley Authority) and the WPA (Works Progress Administration) would also become well known, but the NRA caught the public imagination first. It was the new administration's most visible innovation, as much a psychological rallying point as a practical agency. Its "codes" included guidelines for higher wages and fewer hours of work. If a business displayed the NRA symbol, a blue eagle glowering aggressively over the words "We Do Our Part," it became a player on Roosevelt's team and was required to observe NRA rules, although participation was entirely voluntary. The country, however, took the NRA enthusiastically to heart—it represented the substitution of hope for F.D.R.'s nemesis, fear—and it was bad business not to play for the NRA team.

But by the time Terry made his January comments about the NRA and its beneficial effects, the country had begun to stumble again. There had been warnings: stocks had taken another scary nosedive on July 21, and, by November, a steady economic decline had set in. Terry's comments, coming two months after the decline began, indicate how much everyone wanted the NRA to work. By the summer of 1934, America was more resigned, if not disillusioned. In 1933, NRA Director Hugh Johnson could speak of the Blue Eagle as an icon, the Holy Spirit of recovery: "May God have mercy on the man or group of men who attempt to trifle with this bird," he had said, and people had taken his words seriously. Now, in 1934, when a dusty blue pigeon interrupted a Giants game until it was shooed off the infield, several of the writers felt no qualms about suggesting that the bird was actually the NRA eagle, reduced, like the agency itself, to a sorry state.

Although Terry's hope that the New Deal could improve the team's attendance was unfounded, he was nothing if not fiscally enterprising. His Giants had been one of just two teams in the majors to finish in the black in 1933, and, with a profit of $59,416, they were the only club that was more than marginally successful. (The other team that made money, the Phils, cleared only $3,184.) Even the Yankees lost at the gate, and, in 1934, Ruth took another pay cut, to $35,000; he was now taking home less than half of what he'd made only three years earlier. Now, a little more than a week after he voiced his confidence in the NRA, Terry made a casual remark that he quickly realized could become lucrative.

On January 24, Terry sat with the press in New York just prior to heading down to Miami for spring training. He was asked to comment on the Giants' chances, particularly with reference to their competition. He was in an expansive mood and tried to give the writers his estimate of each team's ability. All of the papers printed what he had to say about the teams that seemed most dangerous, the Cubs, for example, and the Cardinals. Most papers, including the *Brooklyn Eagle*, ignored what he said about the Dodgers.

What Bill Terry said about the Dodgers that morning was offered amicably, as a joke, he said, and Hal Schumacher, who was in the room, agreed. Cardinal shortstop Leo Durocher disavowed Terry's seriousness with a great deal of energy, saying the comment was obviously just a "throwaway" and that Terry had a very deadpan sense of humor. Only two of the writers considered the joke funny enough to bear repeating. Rud Rennie of the *New York Herald-Tribune* was one:

"Do you fear the Dodgers?" he was asked.

"I was just wondering," said Terry, "whether they were still in the league."

Terry thinks that the Cubs have been strengthened...

And Marshall Hunt of the New York *Daily News* reported the comment this way:

> The Dodgers? Will they give trouble? Mr. Terry grinned. He said he hadn't heard much about that outfit in a long while and he wondered whether they're still in the league. He's had letters from Travis Jackson and William Watson Clarke. Both have put on plenty of weight...

Hunt suggested the remark was humorously meant, and both he and Rennie made so little of it that they immediately turned to other matters. Bob Quinn, the grandfather of Cincinnati's recent general manager, was the new Brooklyn business manager, and, after reading Hunt's account, he went to his phone and made two calls. The first was to Terry; the second was to Hunt, who reported what Quinn had told him in his column the following day:

> Why, dammit, in your paper this morning you quoted Bill Terry as wondering whether the Dodgers are still in the league.
>
> I've found out that you didn't misquote Terry. I called him up this afternoon and he verified everything.
>
> If Terry persists in ridiculing the Brooklyn club the element of competition will vanish. No one will come either to Ebbets Field or to the Polo Grounds if they think the games are a breeze.

At this point, some reference should probably be made to floodgates. A chance, facetious remark had been reported in an offhand manner by only two of nine metropolitan dailies, but it suddenly became one of the major sports stories of the year. It seems certain that nothing would have come of it had Bob Quinn not leapt like a cougar attacking a mouse. At any rate, the writers kept the story alive for the rest of the week, although they usually commented on the salutary effect it would have on attendance, and their tone was aways amused.

None of the writers was entirely convinced that Quinn's rage was genuine, and there were frequent references to a probable improvement at the gate. Conjecture here is truly hard to resist. Terry never referred to his famous remark and its aftermath without laughing. "That sure made us a lot of money," he told me. Schumacher also remembered the incident: "It was a joke, yeah," he told me. "It was a joke. I was there when it was said, I think I was negotiating with Bill, and Bill *kiddingly* said to 'em, 'Are they still in the league?' And it *was* kidding. But as *he* mentioned, it was the greatest thing that ever happened to the gate."

What a shame that no one wiretapped the conversation between Terry and Quinn in January of 1934. Did they cook the whole scheme up between them? Quinn was a business manager, while Terry was an acknowledged business wizard on his way to becoming a multimillionaire. Terry's remark was obviously jocular. If Quinn didn't understand that before talking to Terry, Terry would have made it clear to him; Terry was always known for speaking his mind. And however he said it, what Terry said about the Dodgers had been said before. In fact, the *Post's* Nat Gerstenzang had written a column about the Dodgers on the day Terry made his comment, and it's conceivable that Terry had read it before going to his news conference that afternoon:

> Some one smuggled a telephone directory into The Dugout, and thus we were able to check the fact that there is a Brooklyn baseball club.
>
> Ever hear of it? Many years ago there was such an

organization. Reference to dusty files indicates that the Dodgers clinched sixth place last summer and promptly went to sleep. They haven't been awakened yet. Compared with them, Rip Van Winkle was an insomniac.

If it's not impossible that Terry read Gerstenzang's piece on January 24, it's equally tempting to imagine that Quinn also saw it, prompting his extreme reaction to Hunt's column the next day. There is no doubt Terry knew that angering Brooklyn fans would make him money. The only question is whether there is sufficient circumstantial evidence to convict him and Bob Quinn of engaging in a merry conspiracy.

A month later, the baseball world was given a jolt. Although John McGraw had not really been his legendary self for a full decade, he still symbolized baseball. In January, he went to Joe Leone's birthday party at Leone's famous restaurant, a party in which George M. Cohan performed "Give My Regards to Broadway" for the last time. McGraw, at play among his oldest friends, seemed to enjoy himself thoroughly. A couple of weeks later, however, he left a party celebrating the Giants' victory after staying only an hour. On February 16, he was taken to New Rochelle Hospital in New York, running a high fever. One of his visitors there was a friend in the priesthood, and another was Francis X. McQuade, the former Giant co-owner who had been forced out by Charles Stoneham, a man who also didn't have much time to live. These two visits must have made McGraw see that his time was getting short. On February 25, he hemorrhaged and died. There had been a heavy snowfall, so the town of Pelham Manor, just north of New York City, paid its workers overtime to plow the street in front of the McGraw home, where the body was going to be laid out. His widow Blanche was inside, in a state of nervous collapse.

The rest of baseball was similarly devastated; immortals may lose their divinity, but they are not supposed to die. Even Terry was shocked. Despite their differences, despite Terry's contempt for McGraw in his later years and for his stiffened methods, the two went back a long way. He released a statement to the press in which he admitted candidly that he'd learned most of what he knew about baseball from McGraw. He also said he considered McGraw the greatest manager of all time. Since Terry would not have said that if he didn't mean it, he was very likely referring to McGraw's knowledge of the game, not to the way he actually handled his teams from the time he first began making questionable moves in the 1924 Series until his ouster in 1932. Terry left Florida at 10 a.m. the day after getting the news and headed north for the funeral. At St. Patrick's Cathedral, the priest who had visited McGraw in the hospital celebrated a high requiem mass. The *Times* said there were more than three thousand people in the church, a social spectrum extending from state supreme court justices to "men in tattered coats and soggy shoes"—a reminder that McGraw had always been a soft touch for the jobless. After the service, the casket was put on the 12:30 p.m. train to Baltimore, where McGraw was interred that afternoon. The only members of the organization who took that train along with Blanche McGraw were Charles Stoneham and Terry.

McGraw's death was 1934's earthquake, the big upheaval for the team in the spring. Once the ordeal was over, little else happened to interfere with what seemed their smooth progress toward a second consecutive flag. The Giants came out strong: if anything, Terry's method was working even more effectively. The country itself blundered on, lurching between hope and fear. On the positive side, Hollywood's spunky movies reflected the national determination to beat the Depression. William Powell and Myrna Loy, full of optimism and martinis, starred in *The Thin Man*, a movie in which the good guys survive a hostile world without ever losing either their humor or balance. Martinis—themselves a form of quick and decisive action—were the drink of choice in the post-Prohibition 1930s; even Roosevelt had a martini or two most nights, although he's said to have made a lousy one.

On the negative side, however, no courageous fiction could disguise the reality of what was happening in agricultural middle America, an area that was first called the Dust Bowl in 1934. Winds, which picked up dry topsoil and blew it thousands of miles, even far out into the ocean, had begun in 1930; now they were at their most severe. After the winds took the soil, grasshoppers descended in Biblical quantities to finish off whatever grain and yellowing grass was left. Everybody on the Giants was aware of these "black blizzards," whose clouds could be seen as far east as Schumacher's Dolgeville, but men like Travis Jackson, Joe Moore, and Hubbell (himself an "Okie") must have felt the impact more severely, since their families lived in the southern tier, the center of the storms.

In the Dickensian paradox of these times, simultaneously hopeful and dismal, the Giants kept playing hard. In the face of the whirlwind and the plague of locusts, while working out of a city with at least an optimistic facade, they did their part. In such an atmosphere, where it was possible that persistent effort would go unrewarded, it was certain that to make no effort at all was socially immoral. Hugh Johnson had said the chief value of the NRA was teamwork, that it had replaced "wolfish individualism" with "concerted action," that his Blue Eagle was a "symbol of solidarity," that there was now a "willingness of the American people to act together as one person." He could just as easily have been talking about Terry's Giants, who were one of baseball's all-time great *teams*. No single player on these Giants could be called, in today's sense of the term, a "franchise," not Ott, not even Hubbell. The weakest links, like Ryan, were as vital to the team's success as the strongest. Terry, partly through trades but largely through the personal style of his leadership, had made a team so suited to the Depression that it might also have been given one of those three-letter labels—NRA, TVA, WPA, or NYG.

The team opened on April 17 at the Polo Grounds; Hubbell

pitched a complete game and allowed the Phils only one run to the Giants' six. The next day Fred Fitzsimmons beat the Phils again, 6-2. The day after that, Roy Parmelee shut them out, 2-0. Only Parmelee failed to go the distance; Dolph Luque came in for him halfway through the eighth inning. The Giant rotation had an ERA of 1.00, and Hal Schumacher hadn't even pitched yet. Schumacher would end up with twenty-three wins in 1934, more even than Hubbell, for the second-highest total in the league. The only problem was that the only fellow who would win more games—seven more, in fact—played for St. Louis. He was a tall and skinny kid who went by several names—sometimes Jerome Herman, which was his preference; sometimes Jay Hanna, which had been given to him by his parents, the Deans, at his christening; sometimes just plain Dizzy.

The Giants led for most of the spring, and they were still comfortably in front on July 10, when Terry took over for McGraw again, this time as manager of the National League team in the second All-Star Game. This was the first All-Star Game in which the managers were the men who had won the two pennants the year before, a practice that, of course, still continues. The fans voted for the players, and Terry was the top vote-getter. Second was Babe Ruth.

In 1933, Hubbell had pitched his marathon, eighteen-inning shutout just before the All-Star Game in Chicago's Comiskey park, and Terry had asked McGraw not to start him. This year they played at the Polo Grounds, and Hubbell was rested and ready. Terry started him, but Hubbell immediately got into trouble when Charlie Gehringer singled and went to second on Wally Berger's error in right. Then Heinie Manush walked. There were no outs, and coming up was the man who had won the first All-Star Game with a two-run homer, a fellow named Ruth.

Hubbell threw four pitches to Ruth. One was a ball. The Babe swung at the second one and missed it. The next two were called strikes.

Hubbell had, as they say, settled down. The next batter,

Gehrig, swung and missed with the count at 3-and-2; since the hit-and-run play was on, Manush and Gehringer advanced to second and third. Nevertheless, there were two outs now. Next on the menu was Foxx, whom Hubbell struck out on five pitches to end the inning. Paul Gallico had to leave the park, and his column in the New York *Daily News* breaks off here, reporting that, after Foxx struck out, "the crowd lifted the Polo Grounds six feet off the ground with a roar and then set it down again."

When the Americans came up again in the second, Al Simmons took a ball, then swung and missed on three straight pitches. Cronin swung and missed twice, took a ball, then struck out swinging. In one of baseball history's most legendary performances, Hubbell had struck out five of the game's greatest hitters in a row, and only Foxx, who fouled one pitch off, had made contact. The spoiler was Yankee catcher Bill Dickey. Hubbell later said Dickey didn't try to smash the ball; he just waited for it, sending the pitch into left "with a shove of his powerful wrists." "He hit as good a ball as ever I pitched to any batter," Hubbell continued. "Bill's a very smart hitter." Dickey simply told me: "Well, I was lucky, I got a little hit over shortstop. It was a line drive. But he struck out five pretty good men."

The last man up in the inning, Lefty Gomez, was a notoriously weak hitter, even for a pitcher. When he swung and missed Hubbell's first pitch, he heaved his bat clear across the diamond to second base. Maybe he was trying to get Hubbell out of the box in the only way he figured he could. Frisch, playing second, yelled to Gomez that he might want to leave it there and complete his at-bat without it, since the bat seemed of no use to him anyway. Gomez was above response. He retrieved his bat and struck out swinging on Hubbell's next two pitches. Thereafter, Gomez liked to remind people that he was one of the great hitters Carl struck out that day.

Hubbell, of course, had many great days on the mound, and it seems a shame that only his flashy All-Star performance in 1934 is well remembered. He's still the last New York Giant to pitch a no-hitter, still the man who threw eighteen innings of shutout ball, still a standard of control. (In 1934, he walked thirty-seven men, less than half of Dean's total, although Dean led the majors in wins with a 30-7 record.) Hal Schumacher searched for the proper description of Hubbell, finally deciding the simplest way of saying it was the best: "I think he, I think…nobody ever lived that was any better than Hubbell."

By mid-September, it didn't seem that there was much to worry about; the Giants were five and a half games up, and, during one rain-out, Dizzy Dean interrupted his card game long enough to say this to a *Times* reporter: "The Giants are in. There's no use kidding ourselves. Paul and I will beat them tomorrow, but after that it don't matter." Then he started talking about next year. Terry announced that Schumacher was looking so good he'd start him in the first game of the World Series.

However, on September 16, the teams played the double-header Dizzy had been talking about, and if there was an identifiable point where the Giants started their 1934 slide, this was it. They dropped the doubleheader, and, as Dizzy had promised, the Dean brothers won both contests. Dizzy beat the combination of Roy Parmelee and Hal Schumacher in game one, and, in game two, which went eleven innings, Paul beat Hubbell. Although the Giants clearly never gave up, these two games gave the Cards the impetus they needed. They got red hot, and from here on in the real question was whether they could keep it up.

The flamboyant Dizzy Dean sometimes convinced the fans (and possibly even the writers) that "me 'n' Paul" were the sole reasons for the team's success, but a word should be inserted here about the other twenty-three men on the "Gas House Gang." Rip Collins played first, and, in 1934, he would tie Ott for the league home run title. Frankie Frisch might have slowed down a little, but he was still effective at second, ending the season with a .305 batting average; further, though relatively new at it, he was already a fine manager. With Pepper Martin at third and Leo Durocher at shortstop, the Cards had one of baseball's greatest infields, one talented enough to keep Burgess Whitehead on the bench. (Whitehead was the man whose fielding, according to Terry, was instrumental to the Giant successes of 1936 and 1937.) There were even a couple of good pitchers whose names weren't Dean: Tex Carleton won sixteen games for St. Louis in 1934, and ex-Giant Bill Walker, who won twelve, had a 3.12 earned run average that was .31 better than Paul's 3.43 mark. This was definitely a team with more than two stars, and only the volume and persistence of Dizzy's declamations made the papers and their readers ignore its depth.

In any case, by the end of September, only two weeks after they dropped that doubleheader to Dizzy and Paul, New York had blown its five-and-a-half-game lead. John Kieran saw a Cardinal pennant as inevitable:

> By this time Bill Terry may have some vague idea that the hand of fate is clutching at his epiglottis. He spoke some words in jest early last Spring and now they are about to be flung back in his teeth in wrath. The Brooklyn cry is, 'Revenge, doubled in spades!' Now the delightful Dodgers are about to open fire on them with malice propense, compounded quarterly since last February when Bill Terry attempted to rub out Brooklyn with a devastating phrase.

Still, it's very debatable whether Terry's crack was, as Frank Graham's chapter title in his *The New York Giants* would have it, "The Gibe That Cost a Pennant." The real reason for the Giant collapse in 1934 had nothing to do with fate and little to do with Terry's irony. After all, the Giants *had* taken fourteen of the twenty games they had already played against the Dodgers. The Giants, who had played an unusual number of extra-inning games, were simply tired, and, as a result, they were playing bad baseball. Here's Kieran's account in the *Times* of one game in late September:

> The outfielders were falling over their own feet. The infielders were playing pat-a-cake with the ball. A stranger could have rolled a barrel through the infield and no Giant would have laid a hand on him or the barrel.

By September 27, the Giants were still one game ahead of the Cardinals, but the teams were even in the loss column; St. Louis had four more games against the Reds, while New York had a couple of days rest prior to its season-ending, two-game series against Brooklyn. As Terry's team helplessly cooled its heels, St. Louis took its first two games from Cincinnati. Now, on September 29, the teams were even, and the Giants had to get serious against the team Terry had kidded in March.

DODGERS SET TO KICK
GIANTS OUT OF RACE AT
POLO GROUNDS TODAY
—*Brooklyn Eagle* (front page)

The games were played at the Polo Grounds, but it almost seemed like Brooklyn. Despite a wet field and weather so ominous that most people stayed away, assuming the game would be called, three thousand Dodger fans turned up. Most of them sat in the lower stands on the third base side, behind the visitors' dugout. All of them came with a purpose. Roscoe McGowen of the *Times* said that when the Giants came onto the field, they directed "a tremendous roar of derision" at the team and manager, "with, of course, several references to Memphis Bill's Winter wisecrack." In the Dodger dugout, a Western Union messenger handed Brooklyn's rookie manager, Casey Stengel, a wire signed by fifty fans. It said, "You'll win the undying gratitude of Brooklyn if you knock Bill Terry and his Giants flat on their backs." Casey read the telegram aloud to his players and yelled "This calls for a special meeting!" He then ejected the press. Although Stengel was hardly an inspirational leader, he must have found the right words to say on this occasion because his team beat a nervous Roy Parmelee and New York handily, 5-1. In the seventh inning, after the Giants' inept fielding had let in one run, one Dodger tossed a small rubber ball on the field, implying that New York might do better work by using the tools of children.

BROOKLYN DODGERS 5; NEW YORK GIANTS 1
ST. LOUIS CARDINALS 6; CINCINNATI 1
YES, INDEED, MR. TERRY, THE DODGERS
STILL ARE IN THE LEAGUE
—*Brooklyn Times-Union* (front page)

Meanwhile, Paul Dean had won his nineteenth game. As recently as September 7, the Giants had led by seven games. Now they were in second place, one game back, with one contest left in the season. The best they could hope for was a tie, and, to accomplish that, the Cardinals had to help them by losing at home.

The next day, the Dodger fans were back, like sharks at a feeding frenzy. The weather had cleared, bringing more of them to the park. Even so, the Giants rose to the occasion. They got to Ray Benge for four runs in the first inning, forcing Stengel to replace him with Dutch Leonard, a kid who would spend twenty years in the majors and eventually win more games than Dizzy Dean. New York led, 5-3, in the eighth inning. The scoreboard, however, reported that the Cardinals were leading the Reds, 2-0, in their third inning, with Dizzy Dean going after his thirtieth victory. But the Giants weren't out of the race yet, and Terry made a serious effort to win. When the Dodgers got two hits and another run off Fred Fitzsimmons in the eighth inning, Terry immediately pulled him for Hal Schumacher and sent Hubbell running out to the bullpen. While Hubbell was throwing a couple of warm-up pitches, a cloud darkened the field for a minute and, just then, the crowd roared. Terry, who was standing on the mound with Schumacher, looked up at the scoreboard, then turned and walked slowly back to first. The score was now 5-0, Cardinals, after four innings. As the Giants game continued, there was one out, and Schumacher quickly got another. Then he let in the tying run on a wild pitch. The scoreboard showed that the Cardinals had added another run in the bottom of the fifth inning, and, by this time, the sun was completely hidden at the Polo Grounds.

Terry's game went into extra innings, but if he didn't yet know the Cards had won the pennant, he certainly knew he had very little hope. Still, he refused to give up. When the Dodgers got two hits off Schumacher in the tenth, he brought in Hubbell. Hubbell struck out the next batter, and the following man was intentionally walked to load the bases. Then an error by Ryan let in a run, Glenn Chapman hit a long sacrifice fly that scored another, and Buzz Boyle singled home a third. Hubbell struck out Lonny Frey to end the inning, but now it made no difference. The scoreboard showed the Cardinal final: Dean had won, 9-0. The Giants could be forgiven for going down one-two-three—Critz, Terry, and Ott—in the bottom of the tenth. The high-flying Giants had fallen, completing what John Drebinger called "one of the most astounding descents in the history of major league baseball."

The writers persisted in saying the Dodgers had beaten the Giants in retaliation for Terry's crack, and they supported this by pointing out that throngs of Brooklyn fans had come to watch the two games, adding that these throngs had booed Terry with energy whenever he came to bat. In fact, the Giants, unlike the Cardinals, were a bunch of tired, slumping athletes. As far as the Brooklyn fans booing him, Terry could only enjoy it, since they had to pay him for the privilege. But there would have been more money still had the Giants won—in those days, a lot more—and, in any case, Terry hated to lose. When he had an encounter with the frisky Brooklyn manager right after the game, he was in no mood to offer congratulations. After all, the games had been relatively meaningless to Stengel, who had benefited as much as anybody from the attendance boom at Dodger-Giant games. Still, Terry tried. "If your ballclub had played all season the way you did the last two days," he said, "you wouldn't have finished sixth." This grudging compliment, however, was misinterpreted, and Stengel responded sharply:

"No," Casey replied, "and if your fellas had played all season long the way you did the last two, you wouldn't have finished second."

Terry, angry, moved toward Stengel, thought better of it and walked away.

By the time Terry met the reporters a little later, he'd had time to cool off. The *Times* said he told them that he'd been held responsible for the great win in 1933, and so, he said, he'd take the blame now. You couldn't criticize the players, he said, since they had just done "what I told them to." Terry didn't want to become to kind of boss who tried to pass the buck. One of the reporters, talking to Frank Graham, reacted this way: "I don't like him as well as you do. In fact, I don't like him at all. But I'll say this for the guy. He has plenty of class and when he gets licked he talks like a man." Terry was also a man who tried very hard *not* to get licked, and, in this tight season, he may have felt the need for an extra effort at the plate. Whether or not that was the case, he *did* bounce back from his disappointing performance of the year before, hitting .354 (his third-highest season's average) and scoring 109 runs.

Following the 1934 season, Terry rested for about a month, then began reorganizing. On October 29, he announced that only Ott and Hubbell were non-negotiable, although he probably should have included Joe Moore, who ended up third in the Most Valuable Player balloting after Dizzy Dean and Paul Waner. He said he was having what amounted to a garage sale and "almost anything anybody wants is for sale or trade." He laughed at the report that he'd give the Cardinals Hubbell and fifty thousand dollars for Dean; after all, even though he had faltered late in the year and Dizzy had won 30 games, Hubbell had led the league in earned run average for the second straight year. "I wouldn't trade them even," Terry said to the *Times* reporters. Two days later, one day after he turned 36, Terry made a major trade, one which he later said was largely responsible for the team's strong showing in 1936. He sent Johnny Vergez, Ryan, a couple of little-known players, and a lot of money to the Phillies for "Rowdy" Dick Bartell. Charles Stoneham had resisted at first, reminding Terry about the Depression and saying the price was way too high, but Terry had insisted. He told Stoneham the trade would bring the Giants a pennant in two years, and the owner gave in.

Terry made one more trip to New York to attend a three-day owners' meeting, but he wasn't able to make any other trades, and he intimated he would play with the hand he'd drawn for 1935. But before he left, he invited the writers to lunch at the New Yorker, issuing what Roscoe McGowen of *The New York Times* considered "a declaration of war on the Dodgers." Why not? It seemed to have worked last year.

His new player, Bartell, was the topic. When Bartell was a Phillie, he had badly spiked a popular Dodger rookie, Lonnie Frey, and he was particularly disliked in Brooklyn. Terry called the reporters together to tell them that Bartell would be "protected" whenever the Giants moved into Ebbets Field. "We're not going to stand for his being spiked by somebody," Terry said, "and if he is—why, somebody else may suffer for it." In what was undoubtedly mock surprise, McGowen told Terry "his statement about Bartell was certain to bring repercussions in Brooklyn, as well as undue emphasis in headlines."

As if he didn't know.

Even though it was the season of his most bitter loss, in some ways Terry had been at the peak of his career in 1934. His family was healthy and secure; his son was in prep school; and the man who once had to hock his wife's wedding ring had moved everybody into a new home, a big stone house in English manor style that stood directly across the street from their church. His team had drawn three-quarters of a million fans to the Polo Grounds in the middle of the Depression; not only was that the highest attendance figure in the league, it was just about twice the business the world-champion Cardinals had done in Sportsman's Park. Terry had also become a valuable commercial commodity, and his picture appeared in advertisements countrywide. Many were for Rockefeller's gasoline: "I want fast starting, instant response to my signals, and plenty of wallop," he said in one ad. In another, he said, "Next to baseball, I know motor fuel best. And let me tell you, folks, it takes a leader to deliver the goods—in baseball or in motor fuel." There were also the old ads for hats and some new ones for cigarettes that read, "WILLIAM (Bill) TERRY says: TWENTY GRANDS tallies the smartest double play in the cigarette game: quality to thrift!"

In the 1930s, Terry's fame was not limited geographically, and he even helped give a Hollywood star her stage name. Actress Ruth Terry replied to my query, saying "Walter Winchell didn't think my real name was an appropriate stage name for me, so he supposedly took the last names of Babe Ruth and Bill Terry. That's the way I was billed from then on, and that's the way it appeared in the press—Ed Sullivan's column, etc." Ruth Terry admitted she never met Bill Terry or even saw him play, adding, "I don't believe he knew I took his name."

Terry, or at least his club, was even celebrated in Tokyo. When the Japanese created their first professional baseball team on December 26, 1934, they called it the Yomiuri *Giants*.

Back home, Terry was unquestionably the best-known private citizen in Memphis, and he probably embodied its particular spirit even more than its mayor, "Boss" Ed Crump. Memphis is a city unique in its combinations of flavors from the north, south, east, and west. It sits on a bluff on the eastern side of the Mississippi, facing the old frontier, and it's possible to get to an old eastern town such as Cincinnati in about the same day's trip it would take to reach a new western one like Fort Worth. Memphis is the first city of the Mississippi Delta, but it's much closer to Missouri than to Louisiana. It draws from all of the American worlds, and non-Memphians notice this quality of the city, as Westbrook Pegler did when he covered the Cotton Carnival for the New York Post in 1934. "Memphis is New York in lower case," he wrote, "with a whiff of Natchez and Vicksburg and even Des Moines." He was particularly impressed with the way Memphians could combine work and play. Sure, the Carnival was a rite of spring, a "three-days' hullabaloo," but it was getting a lot of good publicity for cotton and producing a lot of good will for the manufacturers who staged the event. Beyond that, as Pegler recognized, it brought tourist business into town, helping out the cotton magnates' brothers in commerce. It was a kind of Mardi Gras, of course, but, as Pegler said, "a Mardi Gras with practical implications."

However, Memphis' success, and Terry's, were pretty much theirs alone. Although baseball didn't lose as much money in 1934 as it had in 1933, the times were still bad. Even the solvent Giants were not as profitable and had to be cautious. When Schumacher insisted on a raise after his twenty-three-win season, Terry told him not to hold his breath. Schumacher wanted a salary of $10,000, but Stoneham told him he wouldn't go any higher than $9500. Schumacher was adamant, saying he'd hold out; but Stoneham was just as stubborn. Terry could find only one way to resolve the impasse. "He said, I'll tell you what I'll do," Schumacher told me.

He said, "You go ahead and you have a good year," and he said "I'll pick up the five hundred dollars, and I will pay the additional five hundred dollars to you." And I sort of looked at him with a question in my eyes,

and he said, "Well," he said, "yes, I promise you that."
And he's told the story till the day that he died, that he
picked up the additional five hundred dollars out of his
own salary. Now, that refutes the other end of it, about
Bill Terry being cheap. I thought, "Oh, well, he'll get it
out of the old man, or someplace or another like that."
But he swore that to the day he died.

Now the Giants again began to rebuild. Terry obviously had
great hopes for Dick Bartell, both as the keystone of the new team
he envisioned and as an incitement to Brooklyn riot.
Unfortunately, Bartell had one of his weakest years in his first year
with the club. Some say that Terry tried to get the fiery shortstop
to control his temper, and that both Bartell and his average wilt-
ed under the restraint. All Bartell said was that "Stoneham just
was furious, because he gave five players and sixty thousand dollars," but that Terry told Stoneham to have patience and faith,
both of which were rewarded in 1936. Whatever the reasons,
Bartell dropped from .310 in 1934 to a career-low .262 in 1935.

The Giants trained in Florida in 1935, and, when everybody
arrived there, the team won approval from no less a figure than
the grandest old manager of baseball himself. When their two
teams played each other to open the exhibition season, according
to the *Times*, Connie Mack of the Philadelphia A's said to Terry,
"Bill, you have a wonderful team this year and I don't know who
can possibly beat you." Then he proceeded to beat him, getting to
Hubbell for three runs in the first inning. The rest of the week was
equally mediocre, involving Giants losses to Rogers Hornsby's St.
Louis Browns and Joe Cronin's Red Sox. Then, on St. Patrick's
Day, the Giants played the Cardinals, who started Dizzy Dean.

Dizzy liked to call himself "the Master," and, when he said
it, he didn't always smile. John Drebinger said Dean "swept majes-
tically" through the first inning. In the second, "the Dean strode
with imperial gait to the mound to continue his matchless display," but then he ran into a little trouble. The Giants scored

seven runs, to which injury was added the insult of "some fearful jockeying from the bench, with the pitched voice of Dick Bartell leading the chorus."

Dean had a standard response to his own poor performance, and if it smacks of poor sportsmanship, such an attitude was fairly common then: if you hit him, he'd hit you. You didn't have to hot dog it, running the bases in a taunting manner after a home run; he'd deck you no matter how you behaved. Against the Giants, he absorbed four runs with relative equanimity, but then Hank Leiber came up with the bases loaded to double in three more, and Dean's temper took over. He threw four straight fastballs at Phil Weintraub's head, then four more at Terry's.

While there was little reason to scare the life out of Weintraub, Terry, on the other hand, was a line-drive hitter who could make a pitcher's job hazardous, too. Dean even insisted that Terry once hit a ball through his legs, which was caught on the fly at the wall by the center fielder. In Terry's first at-bat in one game, he socked the ball into Dizzy's shin, and he almost took his glove off with another rope the second time he came up. The third time Terry walked into the batter's box, Pepper Martin called time out and ambled over to the mound. He asked Dean if he would accept some advice. Dean said, sure. Pepper said, "I don't think you're playing deep enough," then he hurried back to third. Besides, whether Dean's "dusters" to Weintraub and Terry had been thrown out of emotion or as strategy, they worked. Even though the walks loaded the bases, the next two men up wanted no part of Dean, and he got out of the inning on Jackson's strikeout and Davis' fly.

Still, with a pitcher like Dean—"Oh, he was *fast!*" Terry said to me—such "strategy" was truly dangerous. Terry apparently did a very slow burn after the brush-back pitches, because it took him four full days to respond. When he did, after another pre-season game with St. Louis, he sounded a bit catty. It was Dean's habit to kibitz in the Giant clubhouse whenever the two teams played, as he had done on the morning of Hubbell's great eighteen-inning shutout. Now Terry declared, rather icily, that the next time Dean called, he would not find the Giants at home. Drebinger said that "it seems the Giants are not at all accepting the idea that some of those high balls the elder Dean blazed at their heads last Sunday were accidental." Or perhaps it was the game itself that made Terry edgy, since the Cards, on their way to an easy win, scored seven runs of their own in the first inning.

When the Giants finally opened the regular season in Boston, there was a jovial hullaballoo, but it had little to do with Terry's men, who were public-relations bridesmaids again. It was Babe Ruth's first game for the Braves. In the spring, Terry had said it was bad business for the American League to let the greatest gate attraction in the game's history go over to the National League, and, for now at least, he was right. Every politician in New England was there, from Massachusetts Governor Curley on down. There were bands and marching soldiers; planes flew over Braves Field; even cannons were shot off. Ruth obliged, hitting an enormous homer off Hubbell, followed by a hard line drive that the *Times* said "almost cut the legs from under Manager Bill Terry" for a single to right. Terry, who was always entirely willing to give credit when due, said the ball was hit so hard he didn't even see it, adding that "it's uncanny the way Ruth delivers when he is under pressure." Ruth also made a dazzling fielding play that would have been a highlight on today's evening news, running all the way in from the outfield to rob Hubbell of a Texas Leaguer. Ruth drove in a total of three runs, which were all his new team would need to win a 4-2 game. Even when the Giants opened at home against the Braves a week later, the record crowd wasn't there to see either Terry or Ott, although Ott won the tight game with a clutch hit in the eleventh inning. The fans were there to see the Babe. Ruth, however, went 0-for-4, and, pretty soon, the fans' fascination with him would become merely sentimental, after which it would, like the Babe's skills, swiftly evaporate.

Terry batted in the National League's only run in the 1935 All-Star Game, which the Nationals lost, 4-1. His team had been comfortably in first place at the mid-season break, but, as the second half began, their luck started to run out. Freddie Fitzsimmons chipped a bone in his elbow, Terry broke Clydell "Slick" Castleman's finger with a line drive in practice, and both pitchers were lost to the starting rotation. Hal Schumacher had already won thirteen games, eleven of them in a row, but now the Reds shelled him, continuing the attack on Hubbell, who was entirely unsuccessful in relief. The final was 13-6, and the loss cut the Giants' lead to five games. There were nearly three months left in the season, but Schumacher would win only six more games. In an ominous echo of 1934, it became apparent that the Giant pitchers, the ones who weren't injured, were wearing down, while the Cardinal staff was still strong. Not only were Hubbell, Parmelee, and Schumacher pitching too often for the good of their arms, the Giants also had the misfortune of playing many extra-inning games in 1935. The Giant lead was only a game and a half on July 25 for a doubleheader in St. Louis, and Schumacher and Parmelee took both ends, but the heat in Sportsman's Park was equatorial—the paper said it was ninety-four degrees, but it must have been much worse on the field. After working six innings in game one, Schumacher went back to the dugout and collapsed. Doc Hyland, the Cardinal corpsman, later diagnosed it as heat prostration and said Hal would be fine. As Schumacher explained it to me, it was a lot more serious than that:

> Oh, yeah, oh yeah—I'll never forget that. As I walked back—it was at *least* one hundred ten degrees out on the mound—I walked back, I remember going in the dugout. That's the last thing I remember, until I came to in the clubhouse, and I was packed in ice. And it happened they had these old-fashioned ice-coolers where they had to throw ice cubes around the coils, instead of the refrigerated stuff; and the firemen were there, and they packed me, shoulders, *everything*, my entire uniform. When I got back into the clubhouse, Dr. Hyland—the St. Louis doctor, club

doctor—came over, and he said, 'I want to tell you something. You're a pretty lucky young man.' I said, 'What do you mean, Doc?' He said, 'When I first got to the bench, you didn't have any heartbeat.' That's how close I was.

Harry Danning caught both games in the dangerous Missouri heat, and Schumacher explained to me how Danning was getting desperate for the erratic Parmelee to finish the second one: "That's the ballgame where, where Danning caught the doubleheader, and how he ever did that...He was a real, real iron man, and Roy was wild, and all that Danning kept saying during the ball game—I didn't hear it, but that's what they told me afterwards—'*get* the ball over, Roy! *Please* get the ball over!'"

The Giants had shoved the Cards back into third place, and they were three games up on the second-place Cubs. Hyland was right about Schumacher, who wasn't adversely affected; he won his next start, 8-2, driving in three of those runs himself.

The problem was that it was only July, not September, and the Giants' lead wasn't all that big. Now they began to slip again. Through July, they had gone 60-33; in August and September, they were 31-29.

On August 25, the Giants, who had led the league all year, finally fell out of first place for good. When Hubbell beat Dean midway through September, the club moved back to within a game and a half, and there was some revival of hope, but not for long. The Giants quickly lost four straight to the streaking Cubs, and that, for all practical purposes, was that. The Cubs proved to be the story in 1935. They had a great defense—three regulars led the league in fielding average—and two of these, catcher Gabby Hartnett and second baseman Billy Herman, also batted .344 and .341, respectively. It was Herman's best season as a hitter, Hartnett's second best, and both men are now in the Hall of Fame. Add to this a pitching staff with two twenty-game winners and four more men in double figures, and the result is a formidable outfit. The Cubs had a string of twenty-one consecutive wins in September, when it mattered most. Their overall record for that month was 23-3. Even the Cards, who closed nearly as well as they had the year before, couldn't catch them. As far as the Giants were concerned, it was beginning to be whispered that they had an unpleasant habit of folding in the clutch.

That kind of shot is always cheap and usually undeserved. Terry knew this, so he tried to turn to more constructive concerns. On September 20, he said that while he was not yet finished, he had to reasonably expect defeat, and he started talking about a "drastic shake-up" before the next season. On September 22, the day the Giants were officially eliminated, he said he wanted to find himself a replacement at first so he could manage from the bench. Although he'd had a typically fine year (his season's average was .341, which would match his lifetime average), he was, at thirty-seven, beginning to feel pain in his legs. Fortunately for the 1936 Giants, however, he wouldn't follow through on this impulse to stop playing.

Then, on December 8, he made what was probably his most important move in 1935, trading for Burgess Whitehead, the fine Cardinal second baseman who would combine with Bartell and Terry in providing the Giants with one of the tightest infields in baseball. This infield would play a large part in the Giants' success over for the next two years. Even Dizzy Dean, who always pretended to be a lot dumber than he was, told the *Times* he was impressed that Terry had picked up "the best second baseman in the business, or the next best, anyhow, outside of Billy Herman."

While it's true Dean's praise was that of a loyal teammate and pal, Whitehead *was* one of the best-fielding second basemen in the league, possibly even better than Hall-of-Famer Billy Herman. In any case, Terry felt the pennants he won with the Giants were principally the result of trades like this one. He believed Mancuso brought him the 1933 championship, and that Bartell and Whitehead were the keys to what came next.

12

HARD WORK PAYS OFF: 1936

The idol of my early days was definitely my dad. He was the bravest man I ever knew. He never complained, and he never acted scared even when he was dying of Hodgkin's disease in 1951 and 1952. No boy ever loved his dad more than I did. I'd do anything to make that man happy. All it took from him was a sharp look, and I knew what was right and what was wrong.

His real name was Elvin, but they called him Mutt. He was a damned good ballplayer, but he had to work in the mines all his life to support our family during the Depression in one of the poorest parts of the country—in dust bowl country out in Oklahoma. I know that's why he felt so strongly about my making good in baseball.

—Mickey Mantle

That the ravages of the Depression were by no means restricted to the Oklahoma lives of the Mantles and the Hubbells may be seen in the example of Burgess "Whitey" Whitehead, who grew up in North Carolina. His father had lost everything in 1930, including the banked savings of a lifetime, and, soon after that, his health began to fail. Whitehead dropped out of the University of North Carolina, where he'd been a Phi Beta Kappa, gave up his plans for law school, and began to play professional ball in order to support his parents. His decision is reminiscent of both Hal Schumacher's and Hughey Critz's. Schumacher had played ball in order to earn enough to pay his college tuition, while Critz had turned to baseball after the family cotton business had gone bust. While baseball certainly didn't thrive during these years, it was generally a healthier business than most. In talking about Whitehead, *Baseball Magazine* made the point: "Into what other profession could he have jumped in those dark days and made sufficient honest money when it was sorely needed?"

People reacted to the agony of the Depression in a number
of ways. At first, the most common response was simple despair.
In 1932, less than a week after Terry replaced McGraw as manager, a kid from George Washington High hanged himself in the
makeshift basement flat where he was living with his mother and
unemployed father. George Washington was the same Manhattan
high school whose band would greet the Giants after the team
won the pennant in 1933. The boy left no note, but his father said
their poverty had made him despondent. Terry's own need to be
absolutely sure his family would survive becomes more understandable in the light of stories like this, which were not uncom-
mon. In any event, Terry was able to keep the wolf from his door,
and then some. In early January 1936, he even made his eighteen-
year-old son, Bill, Jr., the business manager of the Greenwood,
Mississippi, club in the Cotton States League, a team Terry had
just bought.

Still, not everybody was despondent. After F.D.R. took over,
there was exhilaration, the sense of new possibility. The scholar
and critic Edmund Wilson wrote about the "barbarism" of the
era of big business, and how the collapse of what he called that
"stupid, gigantic fraud" gave him "a new sense of freedom." But,
as it became apparent that social revival would not come soon,
people began to look at life with an irony that sometimes
approached the desperate. If the country didn't actually get hys-
terical, it often got zany. John Kieran made a tongue-in-cheek
suggestion in the *Times* that baseball issue long-term bonds to
pay players' salaries. Kenneth Burke came up with an idea for a
WPA-style boondoggle, when he proposed to put the unemployed to work paving the Sahara "with a mixture of wheat,
steel, cement, corn, and automobile parts." Michigan Senator
Arthur Vandenberg thought a project to move the Rocky
Mountains might do the trick, economist Stuart Chase suggested an army of workers to bail out Long Island Sound, and
Edward L. Dyer, a retired army officer, seriously proposed mercy

killings, "where the persons are of no use to themselves or anyone else [but *only* then]."

In baseball, with all respect to Casey Stengel's Dodgers, the
most representative eccentric was Dizzy Dean, whose outrageous
stunts provided the fans with the escapist fun the decade used as
therapy. Among his other talents in this regard, Dean was a mas-
terful teller of all-American tall tales. Take his account of how
Terry ended up as manager of the Giants: Diz, having bunted for
a base hit, went to second on Terry's bobble, got to third because
of Terry's bad throw to second, and scored after kicking the ball
out of the third baseman's glove—all of which so upset John
McGraw that McGraw quit that very night. Actually, Dean did
score in just that fashion in a game against the Giants in
McGraw"s last year, but the contest was played in early May;
McGraw left in June.

If the flamboyant Cards pretended to treat the Depression
with contempt, facing it down with a wisecrack and a challenge,
Terry's Giants simply worked—and worked hard. They always
knew they had a tough job at hand, so they accepted the fact and
rolled up their collective sleeves. They weren't particularly interested in headlines, unless the headlines were the kind that
brought customers to the park; they weren't particularly chatty,
either. Terry's team, like Terry himself, thought words less elo-
quent than actions. The Giants were simply very good and very
consistent, at a very high level. Ott, the team's slugger, would win
the home-run title in 1936, with thirty-three. He'd win it again in
1937 and in 1938, producing an average of 33.3 homers per season over that three-year span.

Before the spring season started, however, the Giants moved
a little further away from their past. After McGraw's death,
Charles Stoneham was the sole owner and the last of the three co-
founders to be associated with the team. Now, in the dead of winter, Stoneham fell ill. He had never liked publicity—he seldom
even watched games from his box in the Polo Grounds, preferring

instead to stay by his window in the distant clubhouse—and he may have felt shamed by a debilitating disease that he probably knew was terminal. (Ironically, it was Bright's disease, which affects the kidneys, the same illness that killed Giants star Ross Youngs in the late 1920s.) Stoneham was the man responsible for giving Terry McGraw's job, and Stoneham respected Terry; he knew he was the most reliable and discreet man in the organization, so Stoneham called him to ask for help.

Terry came to New York from Memphis at Stoneham's behest and found a weak and dying man. He asked Terry to take him personally to Hot Springs, Arkansas, where at least he'd be more comfortable. He didn't want any reporters to know about the trip. He wanted to take along his black servant, whom Terry remembered only as "Alfred" when he told me the story, and he asked Terry to square that with the segregated hotel at which they were planning to stay. He also requested that Terry get his doctor down there.

"When do you want to go?" Terry asked.

"As fast as we can get the tickets," Stoneham said.

Terry made the necessary calls, then he, Stoneham, and Alfred boarded a south-bound train. When they arrived there, a week before Christmas, they were shown into a large suite with a separate room for Alfred, so that he wouldn't be seen in the halls. Stoneham's doctor was already there. Terry remembered seeing the poor man drained of enormous amounts of fluid, nearly filling two two-gallon buckets. Then Stoneham asked for a drink, and, while they were sending out for one, he said again, "I've got to have a drink."

Terry called Stoneham's son, Horace, and told him that if he wanted to see his father alive, he'd better get down to Arkansas quickly. Horace came, and Terry went back home to Memphis.

Charles Stoneham lived only a short time longer. He died on January 6; the press was told of his illness only after his death. He was embalmed in Little Rock, then put on a train for Newark, New Jersey. Terry joined the train at St. Louis. As had been the case when McGraw died, Terry was the only Giant player in the funeral party. When the train arrived at Jersey City, Charles Stoneham's birthplace, a requiem mass was held in All Saints' Church, where he had served as an altar boy. He was buried in nearby Holy Name Cemetery.

And so the transition became complete. McQuade had been forced out, then McGraw. Both had subsequently died, and now the principal owner, Stoneham, had passed away. The old guard was gone. It was now completely the Terry era. Horace Stoneham was 32, something of a rich kid, and he neither interfered with Terry's decisions nor enjoyed his respect. Terry ran his own show.

Terry illustrated his business acumen from the start, when he tried to sign Buddy Hassett. After the 1935 season, Terry had been frank about his aches and pains—how his legs were giving out, how he played with pain all the time now—and he knew he needed a good first baseman, either as a frequent substitute or a full-time player. Hassett was a standout for the Yanks' great double-A team at Newark. The problem was that the Yanks were less than eager to trade Hassett to a team they guessed they'd have to play in the post-season, so they decided to keep him at Newark until they could deal him elsewhere. When it became plain he couldn't get Hassett, Terry bought Sam Leslie back from the Dodgers. Sure enough, on that same day, the Yankees let Brooklyn have Hassett to replace Leslie. Stengel and the Dodger front office thought very highly of Hassett, too; they sent Newark thirty-five thousand dollars and two players for him.

Toward the end of February, the Giants caught the train for camp, which was now in Pensacola. On February 24, Terry held the first practice, witnessed by a hundred and fifty students from his latest business venture, a baseball school for young men with hope and tuition; John Drebinger called it the "Bill Terry School for Higher Baseball." It was a typical Terry project, meant to be both high-minded and practical. The school provided professional training for most kids, since it was, as Drebinger said, "within reach of the pocketbook of the average American boy," and it also served as another sort of farm system; later, in March, the *Times* announced that "eleven young graduates" had been "shipped to Greenwood," which was, of course, Terry's own team. The school, which cost each student twenty-five dollars a month, was essentially non-profit, but the advantage to Terry was that he could scout young players at their own cost. It turned out to be a more expensive venture than he'd thought, however, partly because he hadn't calculated the cost of first aid supplies—the kids were forever banging themselves up—and, after a couple of years, he abandoned the project.

Terry was even being friendly with the writers. He had chartered and skippered what one *Times* reporter called a "handsomely cabined motor launch," holding his press conferences on it. He even occasionally invited them to share a social cruise.

The writers loved it, of course. Years later, one of them, Sam Andre, wrote another, Ken Smith, reminiscing about that spring. Smith, who was by then working at the Hall of Fame in Cooperstown, New York, sent Andre a group picture, and Andre thanked him. It reminded Andre of their youth, of the party at which it was taken, and, finally, of a time they went out on Terry's boat. Andre and Smith had decided to turn down Terry's invitation because an Associated Press photographer had threatened to stay onshore with the players, thus gaining an unfair advantage over those who sailed. As Andre wrote Smith:

Terry passed us in the hotel lobby but stopped long enough to ask if we were all set for the fishing trip. We explained the situation. Only words he uttered were, "Be on that boat tomorrow." That was good enough for us. He ordered the camp gates locked and the players were not to pose for photos under any circumstances, though we didn't find out about it until we returned from the trip. Big Bad Bill...indeed.

Those who are convinced that Terry was terrible may find this incident hard to believe—all those writers getting along so well with him, and the man at the helm having no apparent intention of going three miles out so that he could throw a few of them overboard.

It was a good, comfortable, relaxed camp, but, only a week or two into it, things become more serious, when Terry wrenched his left knee. He had said he might quit after the 1935 season, when John Drebinger reported in the *Times* that Terry "had been trying desperately for more than a year to find an understudy who will help take the pressure off his own aging legs." Now he had been given an opportunity to bow out gracefully. He had already signed Sam Leslie, an eight-year veteran who had hit .308 for Brooklyn the previous year, so first base could be professionally covered. Quitting now would be sensible. It might even be good business.

Instead, Terry left immediately for Memphis to put himself in the care of Dr. Spencer Speed. Speed was the man who had restored Travis Jackson in 1933, and Terry didn't waste time; as soon as he was hurt, he caught the train.

Happily, Dr. Speed said an operation wouldn't be necessary. He drained fluid from the knee, said that a couple of weeks of rest would suffice, and agreed to go back to the camp with Terry. Terry now had an in-house "Knee Man" in attendance. He put on a bandage, started working out right away, and seemed no worse for wear. He said that during the exhibition season, he'd play the first few innings of each game, then let Leslie take over.

Still, if the ailing knee wasn't enough to hint that his playing days were running out, what happened next should surely have given Terry a clue. Pensacola gave him a "Day," announcing through an official proclamation that it would take place on May 13th—a Friday. The superstitious McGraw would never have consented to a celebration of any kind on such a date; however, the more pragmatic Terry saw it as a potential boost for attendance, so the party was held.

When the Giants and the Indians left on their annual barn-storming tour back north (the tradition had begun in 1934 and would continue for more than two decades), Terry was healthy, though fragile, and the team was intact. Joe Moore, the notorious first-ball hitter and superb left fielder, led off, Whitehead batted second or third, and Ott hit cleanup. Terry, in what seemed a pre-mature concession to a decline that never seriously affected his hitting, sometimes put himself as far down as eighth in the order. The trip north was a typical one, balancing occasionally great baseball against the travails of constant train travel through rural America. Barnstorming in this era was colorful, to say the least—more so than spring training, more so even than playing in the minors. When great (or even good) teams arrived in baseball-starved, pre-TV communities, it was no small event. There was generally a brass band, officials with keys to the city, maybe a local vaudevillian or two. The players slept on the train, in Pullmans with cramped upper berths, getting off to play games in the afternoons. There were usually dogs on the field, sometimes even sheep.

The Giants were far from a sure bet to win the pennant in 1936. Terry's knee problem wouldn't go away, although he could play. Travis Jackson's knees were probably even worse, and he was playing third, a more physical position than first. Whitehead, a small guy who had never completed even a half-season for the Cards, hadn't proved he had the stamina to play regularly at sec-ond. Dick Bartell, at short, was the only really dependable man in the infield, with the possible exception of Sam Leslie, Terry's understudy at first who, as John Kieran had said in *The New York Times*, was a "stout feller—but he's no Bill Terry." If Terry's bad legs hampered his fielding, they also hurt his ability to run. In fact, the entire team was slow. Their stolen-base figures are espe-cially revealing. Of the ten Giants who played most regularly, four (including Jackson and Terry) stole no bases at all. Their fastest man was Whitehead, and he had fourteen steals, which was a respectable number for that era. Still, nobody else stole more than six bases, and the team total for the regulars in 1936 was thirty.

Here a few words should be said about the fielding of the first baseman the Giants were soon to lose to injury and age. It wasn't Sam Leslie alone who was "no Bill Terry." Terry was very likely one of the three greatest fielding first basemen in history, the other two being Hal Chase and George Sisler. In fact, Terry may have been the best ever. Fred Lieb, who saw all three play, thought so, although he admitted that those who favored Chase or Sisler had an argument. William Curran, the contemporary authority on the art of baseball defense, saw only Terry play, but he thinks Lieb is probably right:

> If I close my eyes I can still see "Memphis Bill" with his slouching, negligent air stretch at the last instant and gather in a throw, wide and in the dirt, with a casual flick of the wrist. He always appeared to be the only person in the park not worried on an errant toss, and I am sure that the fielding averages of a generation of Giant infielders are points above what they deserve to be.

Nor should it be forgotten that, in addition to being a great hitter and a fine fielder, Terry also had exceptional speed and a superior arm. Travis Jackson, who was with the team from the early 1920s, remembered one spring in Tampa, Florida, when a couple of Washington players bet him he couldn't find anybody on the New York squad faster than Goose Goslin. He surprised them by nominating the young Terry. The race was from home to first, and Jackson probably knew Terry had once beaten Jim Thorpe's Giant record for that distance. At any rate, Goslin was beaten so badly that, halfway down the line, he just gave up. "When Terry went past him, he quit," Jackson said in the *Times.* Then he gave his assessment of his old manager's overall skills:

> Terry was one of the best all-around players I ever saw. He could field, he could run, there's no doubt about

his hitting and he had such a strong arm he could have stayed up there as a pitcher. He was a case like Babe Ruth, someone who could both hit and pitch in major league style.

Although it's certainly debatable whether Terry's strong arm meant he could "stay up there" as a pitcher—as Hubbell might have said, control has something to do with it, too—Terry was certainly the multi-talented athlete Jackson described, a fact often overshadowed by his reputation as a hitter.

The Giants opened at the Polo Grounds on April 14, with Hal Schumacher going against the Dodgers. If an opportunity to re-stoke the fires of inter-borough distaste had been lost earlier in the spring, now it presented itself again and was apparently duly acted upon. Terry refused to pose for a picture with Stengel because, he said, he remembered how the fans at Ebbets Field had razzed him in 1935. Stengel was equally huffy. However, the possibility they were feigning this animosity, like boxers at a weigh-in, must have eluded the press. Dan Parker of the *Daily Mirror* said "they should both be fined for acting so silly," apparently forgetting there could have been a direct correlation between this kind of silliness and the more serious matter of the size of the gate.

The Giants made several harmful early errors, with Bartell, supposedly the only reliable infielder, accounting for two. Then they settled down and won 8-5 on a couple of late-inning homers, with Bartell accounting for one.

The next day, Terry's starter was not Hubbell, but Harry Gumbert; Terry knew Hubbell often had bad luck against Brooklyn. The first inning was placid enough, but, in the second, there was some trouble. Dick Bartell said one thing or another to Van Lingle Mungo, the large Dodger pitcher who was his particular enemy. Then he hit an easy grounder to first baseman Buddy Hassett who was playing in his first major-league game. Hassett ran across the bag for the out, which should have ended the play, but then he felt the earth move, and, looking up, he saw the oversized Mungo bearing down on Bartell, who was slowing down. Hassett moved out of the way, but Bartell wasn't so lucky. Mungo checked him like a hockey player, and Bartell was sent sprawling. He rolled twice, got up spitting profanities, and attacked the Dodger pitcher. Trying to be helpful, the rookie Hassett pinned the veteran Bartell to the ground. "Then I look up," Hassett told me. "We're playin' in the Polo Grounds, and I can't find a gray uniform. I'm looking at all white uniforms. All Giants, and if they wanted to Sunday me, they coulda killed me. All of my fellows are over there, taking care of Mungo. And I got up, and I said, 'Hey, fellas, here he is, he's all right. Let me outta here!' And that was my initiation."

Eventually, "Beans" Reardon, the ump, threw Mungo and Bartell out of the game, running all the way from third base to do it. Gumbert took all this in stride and pitched a decent game; the Giants won again, 5-3, this time on a two-run shot by Mancuso.

They won the following day, too, making it a sweep, though they probably shouldn't have. The play that gave the Giants the game was Brooklyn-bizarre. The Dodgers were leading by one run in the bottom of the ninth, with two out and men on first and third. Hank Leiber hit a high fly to short left. The game looked over, but the left fielder, ex-Giant Freddie Lindstrom himself, didn't see shortstop Jimmy Jordan running out for the ball as he was coming in. They banged heads, the ball fell, and both Giant runners scored, ending the game. Lindstrom, who lasted only a month more before he quit baseball for good, claimed that sort of mishap had never happened to him before he joined the Dodgers and said he just couldn't take it anymore.

Before the Giants' first game at Ebbets Field, Terry, claiming he was worried about what angry Mungo supporters might do to Bartell, announced he was requesting police protection for the shortstop, even though Bartell had a severe sinus condition and was too sick to play. The New York writer Lee Allen asked mildly whether Terry "was motivated by publicity considerations," but it's clear Allen didn't have to ask the question. The only problem with Terry's "Flatbush Plan" was that when the Dodgers got riled up, they usually got riled up enough to win. It had happened in September of 1934, and repeated itself now; Brooklyn swept the Giants in the two-game series. That was the situation with rivalries then. Beating the Giants was serious business in Brooklyn and St. Louis, not to mention Chicago.

By late June, Terry was beginning to be seriously affected by his various ailments. John Kieran had written several ominous columns in the *Times* in April regarding the inevitable and possibly imminent departure of "Memphis Bill" from the active ranks, pointing out that his knees were still bad and cruelly adding that "grayish streaks are beginning to appear in the once jet-black locks of Bill Terry." Terry didn't play himself often in the early part of the season, and even though the team was chugging along nicely, Kieran was concerned. "If Bill Terry sits out many games the team will lose a big part of its punch," he said. "Without his fancy fielding and his big bat, the Giants wouldn't be the same team."

Kieran was right; the Giants wouldn't be the same. It now seemed likely that Terry wouldn't be able to help, even in a limited capacity. In addition to the chronic knee problem (Dr. Speed said it was a torn semi-lunar cartilege in the left leg), he had broken the little finger in his glove hand. It was nearly halfway through the season, and he'd only appeared in 26 games; every time he tried to play on a regular basis, he'd do something to the knee again. His longest string of consecutive games had been seven. On July 9, in St. Louis, he made the expected announcement:

TERRY'S PLAYING CAREER BELIEVED
AT END WITH OPERATION NECESSARY
Giant Manager Will Postpone
Treatment of Knee Till Fall

But Is Likely to Remain Out
of Line-up—Star Since 1923

That day, they lost to the Cards—to Roy Parmelee—and the following day's game went thirteen innings. Terry really tried to win this one, making so many substitutions he finally had to put himself in on defense. James P. Dawson said in the *Times* that, in defiance of his own edict of the previous day, Terry "hobbled to first base with his bad left leg and broken little finger on the right hand." It didn't make any difference, though, since he neither made a play in the field nor had a chance to bat, and St. Louis won, 5-4.

In the third and last game of this series, Dizzy Dean was knocked cold by Burgess Whitehead's line drive, but the Cardinals won anyway, 9-3, showing the Giants that even attempted murder wasn't likely to get them back on track. The next day, they were in Wrigley Field, where at least they split two games with the Cubs, but the Cubs beat them, 6-1, the following afternoon. The day after that, Hubbell threw a two-hitter, and the only run the Cubs scored was unearned, but Chicago still won, 1-0, to take *that* series. Then the Giants were given a day to brood.

Next, they went to Pittsburgh for a doubleheader on July 15. They took a 4-0 lead into the sixth inning, when the Pirates tied the game. In the bottom of the tenth, Freddie Fitzsimmons loaded the bases with two out, then threw two straight balls to Woody Jensen. Terry became desperate and brought in his master of control, Hubbell, who threw Jensen balls three and four to walk in the run and give Pittsburgh a 5-4 win.

At this point in their road trip from hell, the Giants' record stood at 41-42, and they were eleven games behind the Cubs, who were at 50-29. But then Hollywood took over—in the middle of that Wednesday afternoon at Forbes Field, at the absolute nadir of the Giants' fortunes in 1936. In a moment reminiscent of Walter Johnson's walk to the mound in the last game of the 1924 World Series, Bill Terry, nearly crippled, started himself in the second game.

National League President Ford Frick, sitting in a box in the front row, tried to talk him out of it. So did the home plate ump, Ernie Quigley—the same man who had shown little sympathy when Terry had broken his wrist, but who was now alarmed when he saw how badly Terry was limping as he handed over the line-up card. Many of the writers also thought Terry was making a dumb move.

The New York Times writer James P. Dawson, however, understood the romance of the scenario. He wrote that "Bill Terry virtually pulled himself from a hospital cot today at Forbes Field to save the Giants," that "he forgot the pain in his left knee and the danger to the broken little finger of his glove hand," and that when he came up to bat for the sixth time in the ninth inning, "he heard the deafening cheers of a crowd of 15,000 on hostile territory that must have been music to his ears." The fans had reason to cheer. Terry had already won the game by driving in three runs with a single, a double, and a triple; all he had needed to complete the cycle was a home run—the only hit that wouldn't have required him to run the bases. Arthur Patterson's account of the Giants' 14-4 win in the *Times* was properly awed. Patterson suggested that Terry "loses half his inspiration for the Giants when he is on the bench," and he pointed out that the old player's fielding on this day was just as startling—note his use of the word "actually"—as his hitting:

> He had his first chance for heroics in the opening inning, when he came up with the bases loaded. He drove a sharp grounder to second, however, and it went for a double play despite Terry's spurt of stiff-legged speed which missed safety by inches. In the fourth Terry doubled to left. In the fifth he struck the decisive blow, a single which rolled through Woody Jensen in left field and went to the scoreboard to score three runners. Six runs were tallied before the Giants could be quelled in that session. Again, in the five-run seventh, it was Terry

who supplied the big blow, a 400-foot triple over Paul
Waner's head in right field.

Not only was Terry a leader on the attack, but his play
afield actually sparkled. He started a first-to-second-to-
first double play in the first inning to keep [Al] Smith
out of early harm and his famous "spread" was vital in
two other twin-killings.

With their manager active again, the Giants were new
Giants, or, rather, the Giants of old. Ott hit his sixteenth
home run, the first for the club on this trip; Joe Moore
snapped out of a long slump with two doubles and a single; Mancuso made three hits and every Giant except
[Eddie] Mayo scored at least once. And Mayo was
thrown out at the plate on a squeeze play which missed
success by a whisker.

Terry's gamble worked. The Giants took the next two games
from the Pirates, the first on a homer by Ott and the second on a
shutout by Hubbell. Then they split two games with the Reds.
Against the Cards on July 20, Hall-of-Famer Hubbell beat Hall-of-
Famer Dean in ten innings, 2-1; both pitchers went the distance.
Hubbell wouldn't lose another regular-season game for nearly
eleven months. Years later, Burgess Whitehead still believed the
Giants' resurgence in 1936 was due to Terry's self-reactivation; "He
sparked us," Whitehead told me, "and we got our confidence back."

Terry, who was not about to let his team relax after it had
been jolted from its June hibernation, kept trying out new things.
After the Giants started winning, he set up what the Times called
"a complicated system of money prizes for hitters who drive in
runs." Both the incentive and Terry were paying off. Here's how it
worked: The basic unit of currency was the two-dollar bill. A
player was fined two dollars for hurting the cause, rewarded by
the same amount for helping it. If he missed a sign, didn't cover a
base when he was supposed to, or failed to drive a man in from

third when there were fewer than two out, it cost him. Conversely, he earned a bonus for each run batted in. Pitchers were docked for losses and paid when they won. Frank Gabler was a Californian, and once, after he collected for winning a game in relief, he went out and blew his earnings at the movies. *San Francisco* was playing, and he wanted to see how Hollywood handled earthquakes, since he said he was quite familiar with the real thing. Whenever there were more bonuses than fines, which was most of the time, Terry paid out the difference himself. Remember what Hal Schumacher said about the value of the dollar in the 1930s: it was possible to buy nearly two dinners with a couple of dollars.

For the rest of the season, Terry's revived Giants looked nearly as good as the high-scoring Yankees across the Harlem River. On July 30, in what the *Times* called "another one of Carl Hubbell's matchless exhibitions of his pitching craft," they beat the front-running Cubs, 3-1. While the Yanks' pitching wasn't quite that good, their hitting made up for it; they beat Mickey Cochrane's Tigers, 13-3, on that same day. And so it went, on through the dog days: The Giants persistently climbing in the standings, the Yankees easily maintaining and extending the big lead they'd had all year long. The Giants sometimes won with a power offense, but what they really counted on was their superior pitching; since they had a disproportionate number of the old and wounded on their roster, they weren't too swift on the bases, and they were downright mediocre in the field. The Yankees, on the other hand, had it all—first-rate pitching (with the possible exception of Bump Hadley), good fielding, enough youth to have some speed on the bases, and hitting, of course, hitting. The 1936 Yankees were the first team in history with five players who batted in more than a hundred runs, and they did this when there was still a week left in the season.

Meanwhile, the Giants kept winning, and it was becoming very hard for them not to think in terms of getting into the Series, particularly since it was now the turn of a weary St. Louis team to fade in the stretch. On August 24, the Giants had a day off, but the Cards played and lost. This meant that as they travelled to Cincinnati to open a series against the Reds, the Giants were tied with the Cardinals for first. When they won the first game of the series the next day (their thirteenth straight victory), the Giants were alone on top of the league. What happened to their chief rival was more significant. The Cardinals collapsed. They lost the first game of their doubleheader with Boston (now temporarily called the Bees), 20-3, and even Dizzy Dean couldn't pull out the second one, although, at 5-4, it was somewhat closer. The Giants were, very suddenly, out in front by a game and a half, and it was Hubbell's turn to pitch.

Hubbell won, of course, while the Cards, vanishing like a pleasant dream on a cold morning, lost big again, 10-4. In what may have been a desperate statement of faith, Cardinal owner Sam Breadon renewed manager Frankie Frisch's contract for another year, but the fact remained that the Giants now had a lead of two and a half games. The Hollywood scenario was being noticed by everybody now, and even though the Giants' winning streak was about to end, the persistent invincibility of Hubbell went on and on.

Terry, however, was a mere mortal, and the stretch drive was getting to him. He had been hitting well, so he'd been playing himself fairly regularly, but he was drained. In the clubhouse after a doubleheader with the Reds, the Giants' second in as many days, he sat exhausted on a bench for a half-hour before he could even muster the energy to take off his uniform. The writers marvelled at his intensity. As Dawson said in the *Times,* this was a man "who a few years ago frankly confessed his interest in the game was more or less monetary and who could easily turn to investments that would give him a life of comfort." Terry's self-sacrificing passion to help his team seemed at odds with the picture of him as an unemotional businessman.

The Giants now looked with interest across the league barrier to the powerful Yankees. August 28 might have been the best day for a comparison of the two teams. On that day, the Giants, still following their implausible script, won their fifteenth straight game. They had taken twenty-two of their last twenty-three, and, since that seminal win on July 15, they had lost only five. Only *five*, in a month and a half; their winning percentage for that span was .875. Still, they took neither chances nor breathers. When they beat the Pirates in Pittsburgh on July 28, with Fitzsimmons outlasting Waite Hoyt, they did it on a pinch-hit single with the bases full in the top of the fourteenth inning. The pinch-hitter, of course—remember the Hollywood script—was Terry. Louis Effrat described it for *The New York Times*:

> Colonel Bill Terry came off the coaching line at first base today in a dramatic fourteen-inning struggle with the Pirates at Forbes Field and by the power of his bat raised the Giant victory string to fifteen straight. The man who has piloted his club through one of the most amazing victory marches in the history of baseball slashed a scorching line drive past the reach of Floyd Young to center field, chased in two runs that broke a 1-1 deadlock and charted the Giants on the victory course.

A second half such as the one the Giants enjoyed should have troubled any potential opponent, but the Yankees were apparently too busy scoring runs to worry. On August 28, they were in their ballpark, across the river from the Polo Grounds, playing a doubleheader against the Tigers. They took the first game, 14-5, and the second one, 19-4. The second game was called after seven innings, on account of darkness; the excessive amount of time the Yankees had taken in piling up runs had prevented them from scoring still more. Had they played one more inning, they might well have gone over the twenty-run mark; as it is, scoring thirty-three runs in fifteen innings indicates a relatively healthy offense.

While the Yanks' powerful offense was a factor in virtually all their games, it seemed that the Giants either hit very well or not at all, as was the case in three successive games against the Boston Bees, from August 3-6. The first was a Hubbell game, a low-scoring affair that the Giants won by a single run. The second was a pitcher's game, too—Fitzsimmons allowed only one run—but there were also two homers by Ott, plus one by Jimmy Ripple. In the third contest, Ott hit two more homers, as the Giants scored eight times, but the less reliable Frank Gabler was pitching, and Boston got four runs. In the first of these three games, then, pitching won for the Giants; in the second one, it was a combination of pitching and hitting; in the last, hitting alone. This team could win in a variety of ways. In fact, they'd now won four straight, but, as usual, the papers took no particular notice; this time it was because Jesse Owens had just won his third gold medal at the Berlin Olympics.

Meanwhile, on September 11, Hubbell won again, his twenty-third victory of the year and thirteenth straight, as the Cubs scored just one run off him. Over in St. Louis, Dizzy Dean must have felt bitter frustration. He was nearly as good as ever, often having flashy days when he was better than anybody, but Hubbell, like some persistent Oklahoma lawman, just kept coming. Dizzy, whose health was a little more fragile than it had been in 1934 and 1935, was this season's limping hare, while Hubbell was giving the tortoise a new aura of glamor.

By September 21, the Giants were six games up, and, although their "magic number" to clinch the pennant was two, Terry still had the cart and the horse in their appropriate positions: win the pennant first, then think about what comes after. Still, he told the *Times*' John Drebinger that he was "already planning a definite course of prep work for the World Series clash with the Yankees." He made a point to announce that he would rest a number of his veterans, especially himself, although the list also included Joe Moore, Mel Ott and the infielder Drebinger now called "the venerable Travis Jackson." He also announced his probable post-season starters: Hubbell in game one, of course, and Feddie Fitzsimmons in game two.

As Walter Johnson had shown in 1924, though, a good plot will milk the suspense. Winning the pennant took a few more days. The team lost a doubleheader to the Phils in Baker Bowl, even though Terry played and had a couple of hits. The next day, Hubbell pitched and won, but the Cards had been stubbornly winning, too, and the Giants still needed to earn one more victory. They got it on September 24, at Boston, when Hal Schumacher not only went the distance, but also singled home Jackson, who scored the winning run on a close play in the tenth. Al Lopez was catching for the Bees and argued the call, but it stood. So the feat was accomplished—one of the three or four greatest comebacks in baseball history, and certainly the least remembered. Now even skeptical writers felt the comeback had been due in large part to Terry's courage.

After winning the pennant, some ebullience might have been expected from the players, but this was a serious team in a solemn era. The clubhouse celebration was so muted it surprised the *Times'* Drebinger, who was puzzled by the self-control of "this singularly reserved team," and wondered if it was the rhubarb after the game-ending play that "threw something akin to a chill on the Giants themselves as they reached their dressing room— it was, at any rate, not the sort of reception any one likes to hear after having achieved something remarkable indeed." Drebinger may have been frustrated that everybody was taking the victory in stride. In any event, he saw the hyperbolic vacuum and he tried to fill it. He wrote that the Giants' stretch drive "was perhaps as spectacular as anything the game had ever seen since the miraculous Braves of 1914 lifted themselves from the cellar into a pennant and world championship," and he went on to comment about Terry again:

Utterly disregarding the advice of physicians, who warned him that playing on his crippled left knee might

maim him for life, and tearing off the splints protecting
a broken finger, the indomitable man from Memphis
jumped into the line-up and by the sheer brilliance of
his individual peformance had a most astonishing inspirational effect upon the others.

Terry's statistics for his last year as a player were relatively
modest on paper—he batted .310 in seventy-nine games, knocking in only thirty-nine runs—but there has seldom been a better
example of how meaningless numbers can become in the evalua-
tion of performance. In this case, the performance was, in the
admiring words of Drebinger, "brilliant," "astonishing" and
"inspirational."

It was the view of many sober thinkers that the Giants'
1936 fate depended on two lone and heroic individuals: Terry
had brought them the pennant, now it was up to Hubbell to win
them the Series. Even bookies' odds dramatically reflected this
belief. Jack Doyle announced that the Yankees were favored to
win the Series by 20-to-11, or nearly 2-to-1, but he also said that
Hubbell was the pick to take the first game, by 5-to-3. Doyle
added that those odds would surely change by game time, and
that Hubbell would also go off as a 2-to-1 favorite. If that was
the feeling, then, shouldn't the Giants have figured to take at
least the three games Hubbell was scheduled to pitch? After all,
he hadn't lost since July 13, and though nobody knew it at the
time, he was going to extend his regular-season streak in the
spring of 1937 until it reached twenty-four straight. Drebinger
even ran a subhead in his column that read, "IT'S A HUBBELL
SERIES."

But the New York Yankees had won twelve straight World
Series games going into game one with the Giants in 1936. They
had swept the Pirates in 1927, the Cards in 1928, and the Cubs in
1932. What's more, the 1936 Yankee team wasn't weakened in any
really appreciable way. True, the Yankees didn't have Ruth, but

they had Gehrig, who batted .354 on the year and led the league with forty-nine homers. Gehrig batted in 152 runs, while the other four Yanks to top one hundred in that category were Tony Lazzeri (109), George Selkirk (107), Bill Dickey (107), and a graceful young rookie named Joe DiMaggio (125). The total number of runs batted in by these five players came to exactly six hundred. Even if this was no longer "Murderer's Row," the team was still capable of aggravated assault.

Still, the Giants were starting one of the greatest pitchers in the history of the game, and Jack Doyle was not the only one to give them a chance. Earlier in the year, Dizzy Dean had explained that he was paid more than Hubbell because he could really bring fans into the park, adding that the comparatively colorless Giant star was only a pitcher. On the day before the Series opened, however, Dizzy was asked what he really thought, and he told a reporter for the Associated Press this: "Carl Hubbell? Hubbell's the best pitcher in the game—including Dean."

The Giants did win game one, with Hubbell picking up the victory, but there was more to the contest than great pitching. There's an old *Movietone News* segment about the game during which announcer Ed Thorgersen gushes all over Hubbell, but the film and commentary are much more telling when the subject is Terry. There was a steady, light rain that day, and, as the game wore on, the grounds became treacherously wet. In the newsreel, Thorgersen refers to Frank Crosetti "wading" to second on a double in the top of the eighth. It was wetter still in the bottom of that inning, when Terry "walloped the soggy ball to center for a single and hobbled to first, apparently bothered by his ailing knee." Terry was hurting noticeably, but, even so, he called for a sacrifice bunt, which would force him to run. Hubbell was ahead by a run, in form, and had only three more Yankee batters to face, so Terry need not have risked further injury. When John Kieran questioned Terry's decision later on in the *Times*, he made the point that "a one-run lead for Hubbell was as safe as money in the bank." Still, Terry preferred to take chances with his leg rather than the game, so he had Ott bunt. Terry ran as best as he could, and he made it to second, drawing a throw that allowed Ott to reach first safely.

The next man up was Jimmy Ripple, a solid .305 hitter. Terry knew the Yankees could see how poorly he was running, and he figured they would never expect a second straight bunt, particularly with a powerful hitter at the plate. He was right. Ripple sacrificed, advancing the two runners. Terry can be seen on the film running very gingerly, taking almost mincing steps, and Thorgersen's voice-over has him "limping and pulling up at third." Then McCarthy ordered Gus Mancuso intentionally walked.

With the bases full, Yankee pitcher Red Ruffing had too much to think about, and walked Whitehead, forcing in the first run of the inning. The Giants scored three more, making it 6-1, on Jackson's sacrifice fly, a hit by Hubbell himself and a throwing error by Frank Crosetti, which gave Hubbell a much bigger lead than he needed. It's arguable that there would have been no scoring at all had Terry not ordered those two bunts.

And so the Giants beat the Yankees, and they beat them convincingly. How could it have happened? Pat "Blubber" Malone, the veteran Yankee pitcher who had once played on the Mud Hens with Terry, later explained: "Oh, we expected Hubbell to beat us, anyhow."

The Giant fans were probably less complacent. My God, they must have asked, is it possible? Even DiMaggio had been defused, grounding out on the first pitch in his first at-bat, lining into a Whitehead-to-Terry double play a little later on, and ending up with one single in four tries. Terry, on the other hand, had the first Giant hit, which was also the first hit of the Series, then hit that second single in the eighth. So far, he was batting .400. Maybe the team with the waning old hero could beat the club with the rising young star after all. There'd be no doubt of it, said Kieran, if the Giants could just manage one thing: pitch Hubbell in every game.

The first game encapsulated everything the 1936 Giants did best. It had a great pitching performance, certainly. Frank Graham went so far as to say it was Hubbell's greatest, surpassing even his no-hitter in 1929, his World Series wins in 1933, and his five straight strikeouts in the 1934 All-Star Game. Additionally, any team that could get six runs off Red Ruffing (nobody ever relieved him) was hitting pretty well, and the Giants were nearly impeccable in the field. Whitehead made one great play that probably saved a couple of runs in the top of the eighth, after Crosetti doubled and Hubbell bobbled Rolfe's bunt. With men on first and third and nobody out, DiMaggio hit a line drive that seemed a sure hit, but Whitehead got to it, picking it off the ground ankle-high. Whitehead later told me:

> We could've gotten a triple play on that had Bill thrown the ball to third base. Crosetti was on third. It was drizzling rain, not a heavy rain, but, you know, a fine drizzling rain. See, I caught the line drive DiMaggio hit and relayed it to Bill and he caught the guy off of first. Bill said the reason he didn't throw across to third was the ball was kind of slick and he was afraid he'd throw it away."

The game also had a couple of other hallmarks, lest anybody forget how the team got to the Series in the first place: it had the courage and the managerial savvy of Terry, which was particularly evident in the four-run Giant eighth inning.

The weather that day encouraged those hoping for another Hubbell start, when the drizzle became a deluge after the game that continued well into the evening, dousing the field so thoroughly that Judge Landis announced the next morning that game two would have to be postponed. When it was finally played the following day, on October 2, the weather was superb, and the patrons had a right to expect another pitching masterpiece, this time from the Yanks' Vernon "Lefty" Gomez. Even though he was having a mediocre year, he was far from finished (he would lead the American League in wins and earned run average in 1937), and John Drebinger said he was the only Yankee pitcher "with the chance of spinning a game which might match a Hubbell performance." He was going against Hal Schumacher, who had struggled all year with a sore arm. Although Schumacher was still capable of a great performance, on this day, the odds favored Gomez.

Gomez won the second game, and although he wasn't very sharp, allowing four runs, he didn't have to be, since the Giant pitchers allowed eighteen. It was the worst pounding the New York Giants had ever taken in a World Series game, the worst they would ever take, but it was not a particularly unusual score for the powerful Yankees, and it suggested that the dream might be over. Even Gomez got a hit.

After the game, Terry said DiMaggio was "the kid for my money," Gomez admitted it was "a great feeling to be in there in the ninth inning with a fourteen-run lead," and Frank "Gabbo" Gabler tried to cheer up the Giants by asking them to consider the positive fact that nobody got killed. Kieran wondered if the strategy had been to tire the Yankees out by making them run all those bases, and he ended his report with this: "The Giants haven't lost hope. They still have Carl Hubbell on their side."

There was never any disagreement about the importance of "King Carl" to the Giant effort. Drebinger even went so far as to say that, should Fitzsimmons lose his start the following day, "only the lone, lean figure of Hubbell looms between the crushing McCarthy machine and the world title"—and this comment came with the Series even, 1-1. Fitzsimmons *might* win, in other words, but Hubbell certainly would. Everybody still considered him invincible.

Game three, across the river at Yankee Stadium on another fine day, was the pivotal one in the Series. The grandstands were decorated with flags, and the new concrete bleachers, being used for the first time, were completely filled with the colorfully shirted. The old pro Fitzsimmons was going against the spotty Bump Hadley. Fitzsimmons gave up a solo homer to Gehrig in the second inning, but then he settled down. After Jimmy Ripple homered in the fifth, reaching virtually the same spot in the bleachers as Gehrig and tying the score at 1-1, the Stadium crowd became increasingly pro-Giant. It was possibly because Fitzsimmons was pitching such a splendid game; through seven innings, he'd allowed only two hits, the other being DiMaggio's double in the fourth. Or maybe it was because the Giants were the underdogs, especially after giving up eighteen runs the day before; Drebinger went so far as to make a Biblical parallel, calling the Series a contest between "the pygmy" and "the big guy." Whatever the reason, the customers in the American League park were rooting for the visitors, and it looked very much as though the David from Manhattan might surprise the Bronx Goliath a second time. A win would put the Giants a game up, and, with Hubbell scheduled for the next day, that would mean, or so oddsmaker Jack Doyle might have argued, a two-game Giant lead was a sure thing.

In the top of the eighth, the Giants threatened again. Bartell singled. Terry bunted, but the ball went right back to Hadley, resulting in a fielder's choice, and Bartell, not Terry, was out. This meant that, instead of having a healthy runner on second base, they had a near-invalid on first. Ott, next up, singled to center, moving Terry to second; had Bartell been on base, he would at least have gone to third, maybe even scored. Then Ripple grounded to second. There was no chance to double up either Ott or Terry, both of whom advanced a base; had Bartell been on third, again he might have scored. Gus Mancuso was up next. He hit the ball well to left, but Jake Powell caught it for the third out. And so, as is so often the case, great outcomes hinge on things as small as one poorly executed bunt.

In the bottom of the eighth, the Giants lost their luck, their confidence, and probably the World Series. The Yanks were beginning to trouble Fitzsimmons, who gave up a single to Selkirk and walked Jake Powell, after which Joe McCarthy tried a couple of sacrifice bunts. The first one worked, but Fitzsimmons fielded the second bunt, throwing Selkirk out at home. Now there were two out, men on first and third, and Frankie Crosetti was up.

As it happens, some thoughtful soul, mindful of posterity, recorded the entire radio broadcast of game three of the 1936 Series. The announcer called what happened next:

> He's in pitching position, there's the stretch... Johnson, going down on the pitch, Crosetti bangs one off...Fitzsimmons' glove...for a hit! And of course Powell came home...I'm sure that will be scored a hit; it was a bad bounder, right to the left of Hadley, or of, uh, Fitzsimmons, who managed to knock the ball down, but right behind him about fifteen or twenty feet and before Whitehead could come in and recover, Crosetti, a fast man, had crossed the bag. From where we're broadcasting today, we cannot see the official scorer. But we are going to score that as a hit.

One infield hit and one frustrating 2-1 loss may not sound like much, but it was the beginning of the end of the Giants' impossible dream, the last-minute shredding of a script that was getting too bizarre even by Hollywood standards. The papers knew it, and they started talking about destiny again, almost as if the bad bounces that beat the team in the 1924 Series and that Blondy Ryan had feared would reappear in the 1933 Series had indeed returned, a dozen years later. Although the writers, absolutely Attic in their devotion to the concept of fate, would not be satisfied with a simpler analysis, there is a much less tragic possibility, one that hinges on how hard the ball was hit and how far over toward second Whitehead was playing. Crosseti told me that "I hit the ball hard, I really did," and that after it hit Fitzsimmons' glove, it "bounded toward second base." Terry said the ball "bounced over his [Fitzsimmons'] head." The accounts of the game support the belief that the ball was hit to the first-base side of the mound, and Crosetti said that after Fitzsimmons deflected it, "I beat it out pretty easily, I think." Right after the game, Fitzsimmons himself said Whitehead was moving to cover second when the ball was hit. With a pinch-runner on first, Terry would have been guarding the bag, meaning there would have been an enormous hole between first and second. If Crosetti hit the ball as hard as he remembered, to the first-base side, and had Fitzsimmons never touched it, the ball might well have shot through that hole for a single, anyway. Fitzsimmons is supposed to have lost the whole Series single-mittedly on this play, but it's not out of the question that, had he let the ball go, the outcome would have been precisely the same.

Besides, how could you say the Giants were a defeated team? They *had* played the better game, and fate or luck had certainly been a large part of its ending. And they were only one game behind; with Hubbell due to pitch next, their luck could certainly change. After game three, the writers found Terry in the clubhouse, to which he repaired after every game to avail himself of the hot towels Willie Schaefer had ready for his knee. Terry made it plain that he didn't think there was an inevitable outcome in store to which he had to resign himself. He knew the writers were going to ask him him how in the world he thought he could stop these Yankees, who could win either by flood or by fluke, so before they had a chance to say anything, he answered their question: "Hub tomorrow," he said, and he started to dress for the street.

The next day, in front of the largest crowd ever to see a Series game, Hubbell gave up four runs in the first three innings and went on to lose, 5-2. This sad game (the *Times* called it the "dethroning" of "King Carl") ended with thousands of exuberant Yankee fans throwing at least as much paper on the field as would be used for a ticker-tape parade up Broadway. The fans, like everybody else, knew that once you beat Hubbell, you'd beaten the Giants. Their manager silently agreed. When one reporter told him this would be the most profitable series in history and said the winners would divide more than $178,000, Terry asked him wryly, "How much do the losers get?" Still, he had to play out his string and, like any other hero, he wanted to do so. There was at least one more day. He'd start Hal Schumacher.

"In the '36 World Series I pitched the best ballgame I ever pitched in my life," Hal Schumacher told me, and Gus Mancuso and Harry Danning, his catchers, agreed with him. In a great career, this game, particularly its third inning, was Schumacher's finest hour. The bases were loaded with nobody out in the third, when Schumacher struck out both DiMaggio and Gehrig and then got Dickey to fly to Ott. He walked off the mound to a tremendous roar. The Stadium fans were cheering the Giants again.

After that, Schumacher settled down pretty well; in the next four innings, he gave up only a double and a walk to DiMaggio, plus a single to the pitcher, Pat Malone, and another one to Dickey. In the ninth, he had to face Gehrig with two on and two out and the game tied at four, but he got Gehrig to ground to Whitehead, who forced out DiMaggio at second base. The Giants took the lead in the top of the tenth, when Joe Moore doubled, Dick Bartell sacrificed him to third, and Terry hit a sacrifice fly to score him. Terry should have struck out on a 2-2 curve from his old buddy, Pat Malone, but umpire Cy Pfirman missed the call; Pfirman seemed to realize his mistake, but despite lengthy objection by Malone and Dickey, the ruling stood. Terry had another chance, this time with a full count. Now he hit the long fly to left that brought Moore home. Even though the ball he hit was properly Jake Powell's, it was taken by DiMaggio, who had the better arm, but even he couldn't throw out the hard-running Moore at home. The last play of this game lingers in memory: a great older player, working his next-to-last game, hits a long fly to a great young player, just finishing his first season; the old player, who knows the young one has a strong arm, hits the ball *just* far enough to make that arm ineffective. "I'd have given Joe a hundred bucks if he'd thrown Moore out on that one," Terry told the press after the game.

Schumacher had an easy time of it in the bottom of the inning, which ended when pinch-runner Bob Seeds was caught trying to steal second with two out. "I was in jam after jam starting that ball game," Schumacher told me.

> And I'd get into situations like this: you got the bases loaded, nobody out; DiMaggio, Gehrig and Dickey were up. So you can appreciate just exactly how I felt out there. Well, I struck out DiMaggio, I struck out Gehrig, and Dickey popped up. I had ten strikeouts—wasn't a strikeout pitcher—finally beat 'em 5-to-4 in ten innings. This may sound like bragging, but to me it was the best that I ever did.

If it was the best he ever did, it was also the Giants' last gasp. Possibly sensing this, they spent a lot of time celebrating afterwards. Moore and Schumacher posed for a bunch of pictures. He said he'd given Gehrig curveballs in the bottom of the ninth, that in fact he'd thrown mainly curves all day, adding that he hadn't had time to get nervous. Terry, who seemed to have forgotten the pain in his knee, said Fitzsimmons would start the next game, followed by Hubbell—but, he caught himself, qualifying that comment with, "If there *is* a next day; you know, you've always got to say that, because one game can end it." But however manic the Giants and their sponsors were for the moment—and a little innocent self-delusion never hurt anybody—the reality was stated quietly by Joe McCarthy: "They've got to win two and we need only one."

In game six, the Giants got two runs off Gomez in the first inning, but the Yanks came back with two in the second, one in the third, and two in the fourth. Then the Giants scored another run in the fifth. Going into the seventh, it was 5-3, Yankees, and, in the bottom of that inning, with Bartell on second, Terry got his last professional base hit. He singled to center, after which DiMaggio fumbled the ball for an error that allowed Bartell to score. Had Terry not had the bad knee, he would have made it to third base easily, but, in his hobbled state, he had to stop at second. As a result, he had the next man up, the slugging Leiber, sacrifice him to third. By now, the Yankees knew Terry was willing to take chances with his leg, so they weren't surprised by the sacrifice, but the bad knee meant Leiber never got to swing away at a time when a long fly would have tied the game. Still, with the Giants behind only 5-4, the game was far from out of reach. In the eighth, each team scored again once, making it 6-5, Yanks.

In the top of the ninth, though, the 1936 Yankees—the Yankees of game two—returned. They batted around. DiMaggio got two hits in the inning and the team scored seven times, even though nobody hit anything more than a single. In the bottom of the ninth, the Giants did the only respectable thing: they went quietly, three men up and three men down, and the Yankees won the last game, 13-5, and the Series, 4-2.

DiMaggio and Terry crossed each other's paths more than once in the 1936 Series. Not only did DiMaggio catch Terry's long run-scoring drive in the tenth inning of game five and make his only post-season error on Terry's single in the seventh during game six, on one occasion, he also out-faked "Memphis Bill." This also happened during game six, in the Yankee ninth, before any of the runs had scored. DiMaggio had opened with a single, Gehrig had singled him to third. Then Dickey hit a slow grounder to Terry at first. At this point, DiMaggio stopped between third and home. "I stopped," DiMaggio remembered, "waiting to see what move Terry would make. I figured he would come right at me and force me to make the break. I thought I was gone."

DiMaggio had evidently forgotten how bad Terry's legs were.

Instead of running toward the trapped DiMaggio and forcing him to choose which way to go, the hobbled Terry made the decision for him; he cocked his arm toward third, and, as soon as DiMaggio saw that, he broke for the plate and scored. DiMaggio later said that getting Terry to throw behind him was his biggest thrill of the Series. So if Terry deserved some credit for stimulating the Giants' four-run eighth in game one, DiMaggio was worthy of a similar nod for starting the seven-run Yankee explosion in the last inning of the final game.

After the Series, DiMaggio said little, although his apparent nervousness in fielding Terry's hit and his evident delight in getting Terry to make a strategic error in the field both bespoke respect. Terry did make a comment, offered with his usual terse conviction: "I've always heard that one player could make the difference between a losing team and a winner and I never believed it. Now I know it's true."

And so everybody went home. DiMaggio went back to the West coast, where, unbelievably he had agreed to do an old-fashioned baseball vaudeville turn. Terry returned to Memphis, where he and Elvena were met at the train station by their two youngest kids, eight-year-old Kenn and Ray, who was three. Terry admitted he was going to have an operation on his knee, but he wouldn't comment on the rumor that he might buy the Memphis Chicks. By any objective standard, he had enjoyed a truly great year, a season probably greater than the one of his first pennant in 1933. He had never had a finer hour as a player, and few experts doubted he was a superior strategist to the comparatively unimaginative Joe McCarthy, who was often dismissed as just a "push-button manager." Just before the Series started, John Kieran wrote an article for the *Times* discussing the relative merits of McCarthy and Terry, and, while he conceded that McCarthy had maintained a good team by bringing up younger players, that the Yankee manager was a good "builder," he said Terry was simply "the foremost leader of his time, surpassing, perhaps, even his illustrious predecessor." Even McCarthy had confessed he'd been impressed, that he'd had no idea the Giants were so good. When the Giants went their separate ways in October 1936, they dispersed cheerfully, contemplating "next year" with more hope than resignation.

13

THE LAST GREAT YEAR: 1937

*I just saw Carl Hubbell's son the other day, over in Cooperstown, and he
was telling me about how his Dad told him about when I pitched against
him over in Shawnee, Oklahoma, in a dust storm—Carl was from
Meeker, a town near there, but they didn't have any facilities. It wound
up it was so dusty that the ball went up in the air with men on base, we
were in the field, our infielders lost the ball, it dropped, they scored the
winning run and the game was over. The dust blowing—they had a big
water tower behind the center field fence, and whenever you could see
the water tower, it was a little better than when you couldn't see it.*
—Bob Feller

That dust storm in Shawnee was fortunately little more than
a reminder, a last wheeze, since the soil in the southern tier had
begun to slowly reestablish itself after the summer of 1935.
Baseball, too, was coming back. When Cincinnati General
Manager Larry MacPhail introduced night baseball to the majors
in 1935, he'd done so to attract people who couldn't afford to skip
a day's work. The economic success of his experiment had been
viewed with great interest by the owners; but now that times were
somewhat better, they felt they didn't need lights to make a profit. Crosley Field in Cincinnati remained the only major-league
park to offer night games, and it would stay that way until 1938.
The winter meeting was in Montreal, and, on his way there in
December 1936, Terry stopped at the Giant offices on West 42nd
Street, where the writers caught up with him. He was in no hurry
to get to Canada, he said. "We won the pennant and we've still got
the team intact that did that, so why can't we wait and see what
the other fellows have to offer?"he told the *Times*. Somebody told

him he was going to be a day late for the conclave, and he was genuinely surprised, although not much concerned. He said he hadn't known that, but if he had, he would have taken his time, anyway, because he had arranged to stop for a visit with Bill, Jr., who was attending the University of Virginia. Since Terry made no mention of his son and his association with the Cotton States League, it may have been that running the Greenwood club was just a summer job for a college student.

The winter was otherwise uneventful, although Terry did discover he couldn't conditionally retire as a player with the option to return again should he so choose. As a result, Stoneham drew up a new contract that somehow got around the legal technicalities; Terry would officially quit for good, but Horace Stoneham would maintain the freedom to hire him again as a player if necessary. Terry signed the new paper and went home, where he made the last adjustments to the spring training schedule.

It had been under McGraw that this schedule became comparatively glamorous. McGraw was always sure to pick a camp he liked (maybe one like Sarasota, which came with a millionaire host), and, as already noted, he made sure to use classy hotels on the subsequent trip north. Terry built on what McGraw had wrought, and, by 1937, the annual southern swing had become downright rococo. In 1937, the Giants started out in Havana, where they spent three and a half weeks. Then they played several games in Florida, hooked up with the Indians in Gulfport, and finally meandered on up the map toward the Polo Grounds.

Terry's motives for training in Havana were not the same as McGraw's. McGraw had loved the city for its swank racetrack and numerous bodegas, of which Sloppy Joe's was only the most famous. Terry's reasons for taking the team there were eminently sensible. For one thing, there was much less danger of losing a number of training days to bad weather, as had been the case in San Antonio, Augusta, and even Sarasota. For another, Cuba was cheaper, and the times, if better, were still lean. There may even have been the psychological element of a brief escape from reality—if flying down to Rio cheered up Fred and Ginger, maybe a month in Havana would invigorate Hubbell and Ott.

When they got to Cuba, though, they soon found out the camp wouldn't be all rum and sunshine. The Cuban teams were less sparring partners than very legitimate opponents, and the Giants didn't win a game against them for weeks. This was partly because the Giants were rusty, while the Cubans had been playing league games all winter. But it was also because many of the Cuban stars were black—skilled players who couldn't work in the majors. Not only were they a pool of entirely untapped talent, they had plenty of motivation to show up the league champion Giants. One of these men was a pitcher, Ramon Bragana, who nearly shut out Terry's club the first time he faced them that spring. Terry was impressed. "This Ramon Bragana who beat us yesterday, with only six hits, is just about as great a pitcher as I ever saw," he told a *Times* reporter after the game. "He had speed, a wonderful assortment of curves and perfect control. He didn't pass a man, and eighteen of the outs were pop flies or fouls." Even today, Bragana is occasionally remembered. In a recent baseball newsletter, an old Cuban pitcher named Rodolfo Fernandez reminisced about that spring in 1937, a year he played on the Trujillo team with Satchel Paige, Josh Gibson, and James "Cool Papa" Bell. Asked to list the best pitchers in that Cuban league, he named Bragana first.

The great Cuban teams were only part of the problem in the spring of 1937, however; there were also plenty of indications that the old Giants were exactly that—*old*—even though Jackson had finally quit playing, and Ott was still only twenty-eight. Hubbell, for instance, said he wouldn't learn any new pitches, because that was tough for "a fellow my age," and he added that he was now throwing the curve more often than the demanding screwball. Terry, however, was tougher to figure. Witness this headline in the *Times:* "TERRY, WORKING HARDER THAN

EVER, PERPLEXES THE BASEBALL EXPERTS." Terry had been adamant about wanting to retire as a player, and, yet, in one intra-squad game, he'd chosen to pitch for both sides. He insisted that somebody else was going to play first this year, but he worked out harder than any player, even to the extent of wearing a rubber shirt to lose weight. His limp was far less noticeable than it had been in the Series, and the writers concluded that he was keeping himself in condition "in case." What they didn't say, and what will stay a matter of conjecture, is whether he hoped the "case" might arise. There was always in Terry that conflict between his mature common sense and his love of a game for the game's sake. If it turned out to be an inescapably sound business decision—if all his other candidates for first were hurt, for example—Terry probably would have *leapt* back into the lineup, bad leg and all.

By late March, when the Giants began their barnstorming tour with the Indians, the biggest story in baseball was the ingenuous kid with the great fastball who was pitching for Cleveland. Bob Feller had been packing ballparks throughout the south, and Terry decided he could make a good situation even better by starting Hubbell against him. He was possibly even thinking back to the last year's Series, in which he himself had been the great old hitter in gallant decline—the perfect foil to DiMaggio, the great rookie—and he may have recognized that there would be the additional draw of matching a superb control pitcher against a hard thrower. Whatever the case, he calculated he'd get more people to buy tickets if he pitched *his* old master against the sensational kid. He was right. On the day Feller and Hubbell squared off for the first time, thirteen thousand fans showed up at the Pelicans' park in New Orleans, beginning a pattern that would continue over many of the years the two teams travelled together in the spring. As Feller told me, "About every three days, the batteries would be Hubbell and Mancuso and Feller and Pytlak. I'd be pitched three innings, every three days. I guess that was part of the sell—no, it was the sideshow."

So far, so good. The Giants had begun to have a good spring, and now they also had the enormous luck to be playing a team that had a pitcher who was the biggest draw in baseball. Unfortunately, that pitcher was still young, and still wild. In that first encounter between Feller and Hubbell, there was a near tragedy—Hank Leiber was seriously beaned. Harry Danning was watching from the bench. "I saw Hank Leiber get hit," he said to me, "and he didn't even move." At the time, decades before batters used helmets, the blow didn't seem very bad; he was hit on the back of the head, but not only did he remain conscious, he never even fell down. He simply bent over in pain, rubbed his head for a while, and walked off the field without any help.

Leiber wasn't unaffected, though. The next day, he confessed that his head was still "buzzing," and, although the doctors couldn't find any major injury, he was, for all practical purposes, out for the season.

The next day, the Indians beat the Giants in Tyler, Texas, and the following game was the dusty one in Shawnee. Although Hubbell pitched, Feller's memory is inaccurate: while he presumably saw everything from the bench, he never got into the game. Most of the Indian pitching that day was done by Denny Galehouse. Another Indian pitcher, Nebraskan Mel Harder, was impressed by the Oklahoma weather, which he described for me: "I remember that game well," he said. "I can't understand why they played. You were practically eating dust that day. I know when we got back to that hotel, even the hotel rooms had dust in 'em."

Eventually, the team started on what John Drebinger called "its wierd journey 'Northward'," putting the word in quotes because the itinerary veered so randomly across the map. Players and writers lived on and worked out of the trains, which explains why they knew each other so much better in this pre-jet era. They all have memories of those long trips. Denny Galehouse recalled that there was only one dining car, so the Indians and the Giants broke bread together, but he also said the two teams generally

picked tables on opposite sides of the aisle; Mel Harder remembered that there were never enough seats, so the team that arrived
first *ate* first. Bob Feller told me the writers were usually pretty
outrageous:

> There was a club car where all the New York and
> Cleveland writers sat around and got drunk. They had
> their own band—they'd get out and start playing instru-
> ments when we pulled along the siding to let another
> train go by. A couple of nights the police came and
> threw 'em back *on* the train. Crazy things.

Giants catcher Harry Danning was a non-drinker, so he
chose not to blow off steam that way, but he never turned down a
good game of chance. On the train, Harry told me, "we'd talk
baseball, play cards a little; if you got up after seven in the morning, you haven't got a seat in the poker game. I used to play hearts
with Luque, [Giants' coach Pancho] Snyder and Dick Bartell, for
a quarter for a hundred points, screw the low man, and all that
stuff. We had a lot of laughs." But Harder said two weeks was a
long time on a train, and eventually you grew tired of looking at
everybody. Besides, he added, "we always started out pretty
friendly and everything else, but by the time the thing was over,
why, we were playing pretty hard against each other." Even
though the teams played in different leagues and these were
meaningless games, the players still hated to lose.

When they finally returned to Manhattan, which must have
looked like green-towered Oz after the long trip, the Giants and
the Indians played their last exhibition game of the 1937 season
on April 18 at the Polo Grounds. The game was truly something.
Hubbell and Feller went head-to-head for eight innings, and
Feller "very clearly and decisively outpitched mighty King Carl,"
according to John Drebinger. A photo on the *Times* sports page
showed Feller striking out one of the nine men he retired that
way. The picture was significant in that the pitch was on the *out-*

side corner, and the batter was the still-shaky Leiber; it looked as though the kid whom Drebinger called "our youthful tormentor" had no interest in committing death by baseball. In the ninth inning, though, Feller was replaced by Paul Andrews, and the Giants came back to win by one run, 5-4, on a hit by Joe Moore. The attendance was an astonishing 31,486, easily a record for a meaningless spring game. It was also reported that New York's training season had been the most financially successful ever by a team. Counting the games in Havana and Florida before hooking up with Cleveland, the Giants drew a total of approximately 175,000 paying customers.

The Giants opened the season against Brooklyn at Ebbets Field. The game began with the now-traditional booing of Terry, and it continued with a play in which the Dodgers' Cookie Lavagetto ran from first base to second while the Dodgers' Babe Phelps passed him, returning from second to first. (Phelps was correct, by the way, and Lavagetto, who hadn't seen Joe Moore make one of his great catches, was out.) The game concluded with Hal Schumacher earning his own 4-3 win with a sacrifice fly in the top of the ninth. The real highlight, however, came on the second pitch of the game, a called strike that Dick Bartell disputed. Bartell was, after Terry, the *persona* most *non grata* in Brooklyn, and, as he turned to question the integrity of "Beans" Reardon, the home-plate ump, he was hit in the chest with a ripe tomato. "One thing about Brooklyn," Harry Danning later told me, "I never brought lunch over to Brooklyn—they used to throw it at you." Harry always looked at the Dodger-Giant rivalry as a friendly battle of wits, or a tough game of hearts. He laughingly remembered the time Ott, Leiber, and Moore got lost in Brooklyn and asked a policeman for directions. The cop, recognizing the three of them, steered them wrong to keep them out of the game.

In the early months of the 1937 season, Hubbell was the big story—not only for the Giants, but for baseball. On May 4, he pitched a strange game, striking out ten while allowing six runs, but he still won his nineteenth straight regular season contest. In doing so, he tied Rube Marquard's 1912 record. For the first time the *Times* printed a box listing each win. On May 9, Hubbell earned his twentieth victory, beating the Cubs, 4-1, and James P. Dawson of the *Times* gave him the accolade the writers reserved as their ultimate: "Hubbell was Hubbell yesterday." Now he was tied with Marquard for most consecutive wins over a two-year period and, on May 13, the record became Hubbell's alone, as he beat the Pirates, 5-2, despite Arky Vaughan's two homers.

Hubbell's twenty-second win was notable for a couple of related reasons. First, his opponent was Jerome Hanna Dean; second, if Hubbell was Hubbell again that day, Dean was also Dean. After Dizzy was called for a balk in the sixth inning, which resulted in a 3-1 Giant lead, Dean started knocking Giant batters down, one after another. Terry told me he threw at everybody in the lineup with the exception of Hubbell and Whitehead, because they were his friends. The seventh batter to be dusted was Jimmy Ripple, who bunted toward first to force Dean to cover the base, precipitating a spectacular rhubarb in which the Cards' Don Gutteridge was knocked cold. Gutteridge was a particular favorite of Cardinal outfielder Pepper Martin, who was infuriated. He challenged all the Giants who were still on the bench to come out on the field and discuss the matter, but he was so obviously out of control that nobody took him up on it. Even after all this, Dean stayed in the game. When the action resumed, the first thing he did was throw at Giant first baseman Johnny McCarthy, knocking his cap off. However, it didn't do Dizzy much good. He still lost, 4-1.

Hubbell won two more games, but when he tried for his twenty-fifth straight, the string ran out. In the first game of a Memorial Day doubleheader at the Polo Grounds, in front of a sixty-thousand-plus crowd that was the second biggest in that park's history, Hubbell lost to the Dodgers. Brooklyn's Babe Phelps later admitted the team was gunning for him. "Why, we loaded up with every left-hander we could into the lineup," Phelps said.

"The trick was to get up ahead of the plate and hit Hubbell's screwball before it broke." Despite Phelps' claim, it wasn't strategy that deposed Hubbell. He gave up five runs before he was pulled with one out in the fourth inning, and he allowed them in very uncharacteristic fashion, striking out only one, giving up seven hits, and, even more unusually, throwing wild. He walked three, made a wild pitch and hit one batter, Buddy Hassett, who laughed when he told me about it: "We broke his streak, and he broke my wrist." It was 5-2, Dodgers, when Hubbell left, and Brooklyn eventually won, 10-3.

Historians have long known that the mechanical division of periods into centuries and millenia is artificial; maybe the same wisdom should be applied in baseball. Could the 1936 Giants actually have been the team that played from July 15, 1936, to May 31, 1937? In a final scene from the great 1936 script, Hubbell came back out onto the field right after his loss. He had begun his great streak on July 17, in his first start after Terry's heroic performance two days earlier; now, moments after it had ended, he was presented with the award as the National League's Most Valuable Player for the 1936 season. The presenter was "a round and very portly gentleman in a snappy tan suit," Babe Ruth.

At this stage in the 1937 season, the Giants were in second place, only two games behind Pittsburgh, but there was sufficient reason to worry, if only because it had been shown that Hubbell was not divine. While Terry's luck did not completely run out with Hubbell's streak, from now on there would seem to be less of it. On June 11, he made a startling trade, sending Fred Fitzsimmons to the Dodgers for a right-handed pitcher named Tom Baker. Baker was supposed to be a sure thing (Terry thought so, and Dodger manager Burleigh Grimes at least pretended that was the case), and he was only twenty-two, while Fitzsimmons, at thirty-five, had to be nearing the end of his career. Still, Fitzsimmons had pitched more games for the Giants than anybody except Christy Mathewson, and he was particularly effective against these same Dodgers. True, after pitching a 9-0 shutout in his first start, he had stumbled, and, after two months, his record was only 2-2 (both wins, incidentally, came against Brooklyn), but he was shocked when Terry told him the news. The same could undoubtedly be said of the Giants fans.

There *was* a reason for this trade, Terry's worst ever, and it was a sensible one. Nobody knew Baker would turn out to be the bust that he was—he would win only one game for the Giants in two seasons—and Terry had inside information about Fitzsimmons' health. He had been told by Fitzsimmons' doctor that his arm was going bad—that, in effect, the pitcher was through. Terry thought he was putting one over on Grimes, engineering Fitzsimmons' last defeat of the Dodgers. He was wrong, of course. Fitzsimmons took his arm into the shop, had it worked on, and pitched successfully in Brooklyn for seven more years, once even leading the league in winning percentage with .889. He didn't quit until 1943, two years after Terry had left as the Giants' manager.

Terry went into the second All-Star Game he'd manage with an attitude that was greatly changed. In 1934, he'd thought of the game as an exhibition, the kind of "sideshow," in Feller's phrase, whose only purpose was pecuniary. That year, the fans had picked the players, and Terry had felt this made a professional effort impossible. If he couldn't choose his own players, how could he make effective tactical decisions? As a result, in 1934, he tried to showcase everybody the fans had chosen so as to provide them with what he called "a parade of performers," and he didn't worry about winning. In 1937, however, each manager picked his team, changing Terry's outlook. Terry and McCarthy could play a game of chess, as they had in the Series, and as they had in the American Association at the end of 1923. Although Terry hadn't won a game against McCarthy when he managed Toledo, he had come uncommonly close to victory over "Marse Joe" in October, and now he had another chance.

Except for pitchers, who were now limited to three innings

apiece, he said he'd be likely to leave all his starters in at least until the Nationals took the lead. "We will play this game strictly to win," he told the Times, and so his two first choices for the mound, Dean and Hubbell, weren't surprising. The only other Giant picked to start was Dick Bartell, at short; Slick Castleman was the seventh name on a list of seven pitchers, and even Ott made the team only as a reserve, since Paul Waner was doing so well with the Pirates. Terry decided to start Dean rather than Hubbell, figuring the Cardinal pitcher was having a better year. There was going to be no old-school favoritism in this game. There was one problem with Dean, though; he'd threatened not to show up for the event. Since he had boycotted an exhibition once before, people took him seriously, but it turned out that Dean was only stalling until it became too late to take a train and somebody had to offer to fly him down to Griffith Stadium in a real plane. Dean got his plane ride, but he may have wished he hadn't. Earl Averill's single hit him on the toe in the second inning, and, although little was made of it then, this was the minor injury that would mark the beginning of Dean's slide as a great pitcher.

Despite the best efforts of Terry and his players, the Americans won the 1937 All-Star Game, 8-3. Both Dean and Hubbell were sub-par; Dean, pitching with his hurt toe, let in two runs in the third inning, and a hale Hubbell allowed three more in the fourth. Not surprisingly, most of the damage was done by Yankee players. After the game, Red Sox catcher Moe Berg suggested that Terry would have been justified in demanding that McCarthy use no more than one Yankee player at a time. Otherwise, he said, the whole matter should be referred to the Crime Prevention Society. Bucky Harris said playing the Yanks was like jumping into a pit full of rattlesnakes. Joe Cronin added that DiMaggio alone would make any team a contender.

In late July, the Giants travelled to Baker Bowl to play the Phils. It was hot—St. Louis hot—and it must have seemed even hotter in the confines of the small stadium with the notorious short (and metal) right-field wall. The customers received their money's worth, though, at least twice. First, they saw a triple play, after Ott made a great catch in right and threw to Whitehead, who relayed the ball to Lou Chiozza; second, they saw Bill Terry get thrown out of a baseball game for the only time in his career. In the ninth inning, with the Giants behind, 6-3, and Ott up, home-plate ump Bill Klem called a borderline pitch a strike and immediately heard a remark from the Giant bench. Whatever the remark was, Klem didn't like it, and he asked who had said it. Terry said, "I did." Klem asked him to repeat it. Terry repeated it. In an extremely unusual example of umpirical tolerance, Klem, who must not have believed his ears, asked Terry to repeat the remark again, and Terry did, and Terry was gone.

The cynical might note that it was a very hot afternoon and that a common metaphor for ejection from a game is "being sent to the showers." Terry's motives were probably a little nobler and a little craftier, though. His team had just blown the game by giving up six runs in the seventh inning, partly because they'd played very sloppy baseball. Did he manipulate this situation in order to light a fire under his players? It's certainly arguable. He was thrown out of the game in the ninth, when there was very little managing left to do. Whatever his intent, he had made an impression.

One element beyond the control of even the canniest manager is injury, however, and, around this time, a bunch of Giants got hurt. The day after Terry got himself ejected, Gus Mancuso was hit on the right index finger by a foul tip, and Harry Danning had to replace him. A post-game examination revealed that Mancuso had broken his finger, essentially ending his career as the Giants' first-string catcher. He was getting baseball-old, anyway, and Danning was more than adequate as his replacement. When Mancuso became healthy enough to play again in early September, Danning had established himself sufficiently so that the two were pla-tooned, and, by 1938, Danning was starting more than twice as many games as Mancuso. Then, less than a week after Mancuso broke his finger, Dick Bartell pulled a muscle so severely that he had to be carried off the field. A couple of days after that, Slick Castleman hurt his back and was sent to the hospital.

At this point in this season, Terry made one of his most unusual moves in an attempt to pump up the team: he brought back Blondy Ryan. Ryan, the little emotional catalyst of 1933, had not played a full major-league season since 1934, his last year with the Giants. He'd been out of the majors entirely since 1935; now he was playing for Milwaukee in the American Association. In re-signing him, Terry was hoping for two results: that Ryan would respond to this call, and that the Giants would once again respond to Ryan.

Ryan was sufficiently fired up to have some good days, but, over the long haul he wasn't much help, so Terry made another unusual move: he placed his great right fielder, Mel Ott, at third base. As far back as the spring, he'd said he might do this, but, remembering his sloth-footed 1936 team, he'd gone all season with the speedy Lou Chiozza at third base. Now, in early August, Ott went to third, Sam Leslie replaced the weak-hitting Johnny McCarthy at first, and Jimmy Ripple moved to right. This gave the team a lot more power at the plate and gave Ott enough solid company in the lineup to make it tough for enemy pitchers to pitch around him. The team, in general, and Ott, in particular, started hitting again. Before Terry's move, Ott had been hitting around .250, but he finished the season at .294.

The turning point for the Giants in 1937 came a lot later than it had in 1936. On August 25, the Giants, five games back and in second place, were playing a doubleheader against the league-leading Cubs at the Polo Grounds. Terry started Hubbell, but again he was off the mark, and the Giants went to the bottom of the ninth inning losing, 7-2. Danning opened what everybody thought would be the last frame of the day with a single off Bill Lee, his third hit of the game. Then Lee got Whitehead to ground out. Terry sent up Wally Berger to hit for Hal Schumacher, who had replaced Hubbell in the seventh. Berger grounded to Billy Herman at second. Herman, however, threw wide to first, allowing Berger to reach base safely, and there were men on first and third with one out.

Joe Moore was up next, and he rolled a grounder to Billy Jurges, one of the greatest fielding shortstops of all time, but, as the *Times'* Louis Effrat said, Jurges "kicked the ball all over the infield," and Danning scored. Now it was 7-3, with one out and men on first and second. Bartell followed with a single to center, scoring Berger. The Giants were still three runs down, although the tying run was at the plate in Jimmy Ripple.

It wasn't the worst time in the world to steal a page from last year's Hollywood script, and that's exactly what happened. Ripple looked at the first pitch, liked it, and sent a homer into the stands. There were more than fifty thousand people in those stands, not many of them very fond of the Cubs, and Effrat wrote that "Ripple's homer precipitated one of the greatest outbursts ever heard under Coogan's Bluff. Five minutes after that telling blow the fans were still tossing hats, score cards, papers and whatever else they were able to pick up."

The game went into extra innings, but Chicago was licked; in the eleventh, Danning's fourth single of the game drove in Ripple with the winning run. Giants right-hander Harry Gumbert won the anticlimactic second game, 4-2, and the Terrymen, who could have been five or even seven games back, now had only three games to make up. Effrat didn't need time to reflect on the significance of the day's work: "If the Giants capture the pennant, they will have to look back to yesterday's double victory as the turning point." Terry decided Hubbell might return to his old form if he were given more rest, and it turned out that he was right; in August, Hub got back into the rhythm of winning methodically. Soon, the Giants were in first place by one game. Two days later, after Hubbell shut out the Dodgers for his eighteenth win, they were up by two.

On September 7, Terry was signed to yet another revised contract, his third deal of the year. Now Terry was not only manager, he was also general manager, and his particular charge was the development of the Giants' nine-club farm system. This promotion was really more of a recognition of an accomplished fact, since Terry had been helping to develop Giant farm clubs for years; it will be remembered that he had installed his son for a while as general manager of the one he owned in Greenwood. He had even been calling himself a general manager since July, when Warren Giles of the Reds received a letter from him signed with that title. In addition, one issue of the fan journal *Giant Jottings* said he'd been acting general manager since "early 1937," suggesting the real promotion had come in January, the month Terry signed his first revised contract.

On September 30, the Giants clinched the pennant, beating the Phils, 2-1, behind a Hubbell five-hitter in the first of two games. The picture of the clubhouse celebration shows a bunch of men who seem to feel they are supposed to demonstrate elation. It looks like everybody has been told to face the camera. True, Bartell is grinning, but he was never as much a Giant as the others. Mancuso looks embarassed. The photographer has evidently asked Melton and Hubbell to wave their caps, and they are obliging, though they look stiff and neither can manage an authentic smile.

On the morning of the first game of the World Series, Leo Bondy, the Giants' lawyer and the man who had replaced Francis McQuade in 1929, was on his way to work when he was accosted by a destitute person who looked poor enough to convince Bondy he should part with two bucks. After saying thank you, the man asked Bondy if he knew how much a bleacher seat at Yankee Stadium cost, and, when Bondy told him it was one dollar and ten cents, the man turned and started walking briskly toward the uptown subway. Even in the Depression, men of integrity kept their priorities straight.

On that morning, too, Jack Doyle announced that the Yanks would be favored to win the Series, at 2-to-1 again. This time, however, he also picked them to win game one, and at the better odds of 5-to-2, even though he knew Terry was starting Hubbell. It was a bad sign when the bookies started losing faith.

As a matter of fact, it was hard to find anybody sentimental enough to pick Terry's team; about the only one to do it was Jack White, a Broadway entertainer and, by his own confession, a Giants fan since age five. "It was a tradition in my family," he told the *Times;* "Tammany Hall and the Giants. That's the way I was dragged up, and that is the way I'll always be." With the zealotry of a fan baptized and confirmed in the faith, he said the club would win in five games. Most professional handicappers were less enthusiastic, however. Detroit manager Mickey Cochrane was over at the Belmont Plaza, nibbling scotch in the rooms of Hollywood actor and baseball nut Bill Frawley. Frawley passed Cochrane a glass and asked if there was anything else he wanted. Cochrane said he'd already received his most fervent wish: for the next week, he wasn't going to be in Bill Terry's spot.

The first game was played at the Stadium on a misty afternoon. Terry himself was the final pitcher in batting practice. An unnamed Yankee, a man too young to know his history, surmised that Terry had "always wanted to be a pitcher." However, after he nearly beaned Sam Leslie, he called it quits and summoned everybody into the dugout.

Hubbell and his opposing southpaw, Gomez, both wearing number eleven, each started well. Hubbell gave up a single to DiMaggio in the first inning, but then he retired fourteen straight batters. His performance in the fourth inning was representative: he forced DiMaggio to ground to second, Dickey to ground to first, and he embarrassed Gehrig, who missed strike three, the *Times* said, "by a wide margin." Gomez weakened first, allowing a run in the fifth, while, in the bottom of the inning, Hubbell got Hoag and Selkirk on flies and Lazzeri on a strikeout. It looked as if the opening game might be a replica of the one Hubbell had won the previous year.

In the sixth inning, though, Hubbell walked the first man he faced, the weak-hitting Gomez. Then shortstop Frankie Crosetti singled, as did third baseman Red Rolfe and DiMaggio, scoring two runs. Gehrig was walked to load the bases, Terry brought the infield in, and catcher Bill Dickey, a hitter Hubbell always respected, came up. Dickey singled in a run; the bases were still filled, and Terry kept the infield in. Finally, the Giants forced DiMaggio at the plate on Hoag's grounder to Ott at third base, but then Selkirk singled to right, scoring Gehrig and Dickey. No longer able to kid himself, Terry called for Dick Coffman to take over for Hubbell.

Gus Mancuso was always embarassed about what happened next, although the Giants were behind 5-1, and the game was probably lost, anyway. Mancuso, who handled the pitchers for the boss, made a verbal slip, telling chief ump Red Ormsby that Harry Gumbert was coming in. Coffman was already on the mound when the announcement for Gumbert was made, and everybody in the Giant dugout was flabbergasted, including Gumbert, who was lounging on the bench, and particularly Terry, who was never happy with mental goofs. But since Gumbert had been officially announced, he was in the game, even though he hadn't thrown a warm-up ball. He had to come out and pitch to at least one batter, who, in this case, was Tony Lazzeri. Once he got to the mound, Gumbert was allowed a maximum of eight preliminary pitches, which he took before following the fast-thinking Terry's instructions to make *very* sure that George Selkirk stayed close to first. Gumbert undoubtedly would have thrown over there until his arm felt warm, but the Yanks wised up, and, after two throws, first-base coach Art Fletcher had Selkirk stand flat-footed on top of the bag. Although Gumbert might have gotten away with one or two more throws to first before the umps accused him of delaying the game, he now faced the plate, forcing Lazzeri to hit one on the ground to Whitehead. Unfortunately, the Giant second baseman muffed it, and another run scored. Now Coffman *could* come in, but when he did he walked Gomez on five pitches. Gomez prudently left his bat on his shoulder the entire time. It was almost certainly the only time Gomez ever walked twice in the same inning, and, unfortunately for his friends, it would provide him with another story about how much he was feared as a hitter. After getting Crosetti on a fly to left, Coffman gave the Yanks another run by walking Rolfe; then he retired DiMaggio on a long fly to Hank Leiber, ending the seven-run inning. A lot of the writers second-guessed Terry for having his fielders play the powerful Yankees so shallow. Hugh Bradley of the New York *Post* overheard this exchange between a couple of spectators, both National League managers:

"That Terry sure plays 'em close to the vest," one said. "Practically every time I looked out there on the field yesterday the infield was in."

"Yeah," agreed the other pilot sadly. "And so was another Yankee run."

The Giants had led with their best, as they had the previous year, but, this time, Hubbell had fallen down badly; Grantland Rice said it was the sad old story, "one of the oldest yarns in sport, the story of time and the years that pile up." Joe Williams simply used this subhead: "HUBBELL NO LONGER HUBBELL." The five hundred citizens of Meeker, who had closed down their shops to listen to the game on the radio and had expected, by this time, to be involved in noisy celebration, were quiet. Meeker, with all the doors shut and the radios off now, was like a ghost town. Hubbell's father made a couple of comments. "I guess we're kind of like the little boy who ran over the calf," he told the *Times*. "We haven't much to say." Then he added, "I hope that he has better luck next time." Gomez continued his strong pace throughout that afternoon, and the final was 8-1. The outcome even prompted Red Ruffing to strut in a very un-Yankee-like fashion; he said he might pitch a no-hitter in game two.

Ruffing's boast wasn't far off. The Giants started their twenty-game winner, Cliff Melton, a rookie who, as the headline resignedly put it, not only went "the way of Hubbell," but arrived there one inning earlier, in the fifth, when the Yankees tailed four consecutive hits and two runs. They went on to win the game 8-1, and the following day they beat the Giants again, 5-1, at the Polo Grounds.

After game three, Terry looked understandably tired to the writers, and he said a number of things off the record about changes he intended to make over the winter, which led the reporters to think he didn't have much hope left for the present. He also showed them two wires he'd been sent. The first one said, simply, "CHANGE SIGNALS STOP KNOWN TO YANKS STOP." Terry was exasperated by this, he said, because Yankee pitching had offered him hardly any opportunities to *give* signals. The second telegram amused him. Sent from "the son of a former baseball official," it read, "ARE THE GIANTS STILL IN THE WORLD SERIES QUESTION."

What Terry did in game four should by now be obvious. Even a skeptic could never doubt that Bill Terry would start Carl Hubbell, if Hubbell was rested and ready. The *Times* headline was blunt—"TERRY COUNTS ON HUBBELL"—and everybody hoped he would come to pitch.

He did, and it was his last great post-season moment. Not only did he have to face a great team with an overwhelming advantage, he also had to put up with the dissatisfaction of Giant fans, who booed everybody, including him. Even the writers seemed to feel a four-game sweep was certain, and Granny Rice began one of his verses with this: "A rooter of the Giants stood weeping bitter tears, / His brow was full of furrows and his system full of beers."

When the game got under way, the Giants, still wobbly after so much ill-treatment, made three errors, but they also started to hit. In the second inning, they scored six runs off Bump Hadley (a sweet revenge, if belated), and that was all they needed. Although Hubbell gave up a homer to Gehrig to lead off the top of the ninth, then he got DiMaggio to foul out and Dickey to fly out. The last man up was George Selkirk, who hit a whopping drive to deep center; Leiber caught it, turned around, ran into the clubhouse, and the Giants had won one at last, 7-3. The *Times* said the Giants were "jubilant," but the Yanks were "chagrined." Terry, indulging in some Sunday-morning quarterbacking, angered McCarthy by saying he would have started Gomez if he'd had the three-game advantage. "When you've got a team down," he told the *Times*, "cut its head off."

The next day, McCarthy obliged. Cliff Melton started the fifth game for the Giants, and he pitched respectably. In fact, the game was tied, 2-2, going into the fifth inning, when, with Lazzeri on third, Melton gave up a single to Gomez, who later scored. As a result, he could be viewed as both the winning pitcher and the offensive catalyst on that day. The final was 4-2, Yankees.

This was also the famous game in which the unpredictable Gomez did something that combined the showboating of Dean and the nonchalance of Hubbell. In the seventh inning, with one Giant on base and the tying run at the plate, he stopped pitching for quite some time to gawk at a plane that was circling overhead. Was it bravado or unflinching composure? Only Gomez knew for sure, but he was pitching so well that, as Arthur Patterson said in the *Herald-Tribune*, it would have taken an air armada to get to him. He even made the final putout in the ninth. John Kieran suggested that if he'd been asked to umpire, he probably would have done that, too.

After the game and the Series had been won, a reporter described how Yankee coach Art Fletcher began to exult. He started to rub it in, but then he caught himself, making a significant concession to the respect he evidently felt for this particular opposing team: "Hey!" shrieked the jubilant Art Fletcher. "You go back and tell Terry—well, what the heck," he interrupted himself. "He's all right. Just tell him that I hope he gets over his cold and I hope we meet him and his gang again next year."

The Giants of 1937, like the 1936 version, deserved respect. Between 1927 and 1939, the Yankees got into seven World Series winning them all. In all of those Series, they lost only three games—two in 1936, to Terry's Giants, and one in 1937, to Terry's Giants. In each of the other five years they were in a Series, the Yankees swept, four games to none. In other words, against the Giants, the great Yankees of this period were 8-3; against the other teams in the National League, they were 20-0. Not the Pirates, the Cards, the Cubs, the Cubs again, nor the Reds could take even one game from this juggernaut in a period extending more than a decade, but Terry and his Giants took three. Even those of the Dodger persuasion are invited to look it up.

14

BREAK UP THE GIANTS: 1938–1939

The Tennessee Colonel
Flushed with success
Was tossing his pearls
To the swine of the press
—New York Baseball Writers

After the 1937 Series, Terry made some season-ending comments for the press. He complained about the umpiring—not so much that it was bad, or that the umps had favored one team, but that it was lax, that the umps hadn't worked hard enough. He added enthusiastic praise for the Yankees, both as he ran down the names on their roster and when he spoke of them as a team. He went so far as to say to the *Times* that they were "the best I've ever seen—I can't recall any club in my heyday that would have beaten them."

Those were gracious words, but little attention is paid to the loser, however well he's taken the loss. Terry was close to being alone in the Giants' clubhouse by the time he was dressed and ready to leave—he hadn't even received the traditional condolences from the winning manager, who was still mighty angry over being criticized for withholding Gomez in game four (although, it must be noted, Terry didn't go over to see McCarthy either, and his praise for the Yanks always seemed to exclude mention of their leader).

Now, instead of resting in Memphis, Terry took his family on vacation to Mexico City. When he returned home, he went to his country club to play a little tennis, another game he liked, telling reporters he was "just trying to see if my legs will hold up." He also filled them in on the Giants' farm system, pointing out that the flagship club Travis Jackson was managing in Jersey City had drawn a quarter of a million fans in 1937, "and that's more than the Phillies drew." And he began, as he did every year, to look around for property to buy and then re-sell. This time, he found something that interested him so much he wanted it for himself.

Clarence Saunders was one of Memphis' most famous sons, and one of its most flamboyant. He was the founder of one of the country's first supermarket chains, Piggly-Wiggly, and he later started up Kedoozle convenience stores. It's still possible to buy a T-shirt in downtown Memphis that lists the Kedoozle venture as one of the points of civic pride, along with Beale Steet and Graceland. Saunders was not the most practical of business geniuses, however; he had already lost two mansions to foreclosure—the first was turned into the University Club, and the second, the Pink Palace, is still a prominent Memphis museum. The third, which Saunders named Annswood, was a palatial estate nearly on the Hearst scale. Terry heard that Saunders was behind on his payments again, and that he might have to give up this house, too. He bought up the outstanding debt on the place by selling a large farm he had in nearby Colliersville, and he waited for the court to start foreclosure proceedings.

Built entirely of cedar wood, Annswood had a two-story entrance hall and stood on five hundred acres of property in Germantown, just outside the Memphis city line. There was a tennis court, a swimming pool, a large lake, and a private golf course that was the largest in the country. On one par-three, the golfer chipped onto a small island, then rowed over to putt out. It's still possible to see the estate; the place was grand enough to eventually become the Lichterman Nature Preserve, which is not only extant, it's about the only place in Memphis that has preserved Bill Terry's memory. The golf course is gone, but it's the perfect shrine for those whose interests include both baseball history and ecology.

Saunders wasn't going to give up without a fight. On the day of the scheduled foreclosure, he got an injunction that allowed him several more months to raise enough cash to buy back the estate. In addition to postponing the proceedings, Saunders had his lawyers sue Terry for illegally "ordering one of the subtenants on the property to vacate," according to the Memphis *Commercial-Appeal*. As a result of all of these moves, Terry would not be able to take possession of the house until after the 1938 season. When Saunders acted, the paper reported Terry was "in Chicago on business," which, in fact, was where he had gone to attend the winter meeting. When he heard what Saunders had done, in an apparent attempt to catch him with his hands full, it couldn't have improved Terry's mood, which had been lousy all week because he'd had no luck with trades. He'd also been getting heat from the reporters and photographers, with whom he'd been able to spend little time, and he'd had to host the annual dinner the winning National League manager gave for the league's losing teams. Joe McCarthy was also at the dinner, since he could hardly be excluded if he wanted to come, which probably nettled Terry even more; in any case, as he walked by McCarthy's table, the Yankee boss, who thought pipe smokers were complacent loafers, made a crack of some kind about the pipe Terry was smoking. To make matters worse, the reporters around McCarthy—who was very popular with the press—laughed.

Terry blew up. He stopped and yelled at McCarthy, blurting something about the Yankee manager drinking too much beer. One report claimed they had to be separated. The incident certainly wasn't immediately forgotten; Giants' coach Pancho Snyder angrily said he *would* punch McCarthy, should McCarthy get wise with him. The Associated Press' Paul Mickelson took an economic view, predicting that the mercantile battle, at least, would be won by Terry, and some enterprising tobacconist would come out with a "Bill Terry Pipe." "For if there ever was a King Midas in baseball," Mickelson added, "it's Colonel Terry. Like him or not, you've got to hand it to him as one smart guy."

Mickelson's amusement indicates that not all the writers took Terry's occasional explosions all that seriously, and, in fact, Terry treated many writers quite cordially throughout his life. Most of the writers in Terry's time, though, did not expect athletes to be uppity. Reporters were entirely convinced, in this pre-television era, that their columns could make or break an athlete's career. As a result, they were intolerant of players who would not accommodate them automatically, in virtually every area.

Terry was different, a player of a newer stamp, much closer to today's athlete-entrepreneur than most of his contemporaries. First, he was far from being just another dumb jock; second, throughout Terry's career in baseball, he felt certain he could always have found work elsewhere, even when the Depression was at its worst, because he always had a subsidiary career to fall back on. He was never in any way dependent on the writers for either his job or the successful performance thereof, and he knew it. He let the writers know it, too. Many of them didn't want to hear it. Terry was the first important baseball figure to rebel against a star system created by and for reporters, and they responded by trying to make an example of him.

Although Terry's battles with the press didn't climax until 1938, they had begun right after he took over McGraw's job in 1932, when a writer asked him for his home phone number in case questions arose when he was writing a piece. The writer was Joe Williams, and his paper, the *World-Telegram*, came out in the afternoon. Williams, therefore, would be working at night to make a morning deadline, which meant he might call Terry's home late, after the kids were asleep. Terry, always protective of his family, kept his number to himself, and, when Williams objected, Terry became, as he later put it, "more emphatic."

From 1932 on, many of the New York papers treated Terry without the *politesse* that was normally accorded more accomodating stars, like Ruth or Terry's friend and teammate, Mel Ott. In later years, Terry accused the writers of treating him with a bias, and, while he may have been over-sensitive, he had an argument. As early as 1933, some writers had even taken the unusual step of warning him in print. After the Giants clinched the pennant that year, a properly exultant Terry needled the press because they'd picked the Giants to finish in the second division, and Westbrook Pegler, writing in the *Post*, called for more discretion:

> Mr. Terry is a cold man and disinclined to woo the favor of the press. But I do not think a man who finds himself momentarily way up there ought to let the height go to his head. He will be coming down again to the gas station and there will still be reporters rattling around the National League and climbing the ramps to the press-coops who can out-knowledge him in all polite respects and out-manner him, too.
>
> The young man seems to be not quite major-league in some respects. And if it is trouble he wants with the newspaper boys I am sure he need only write his ticket. There have been other champions who uttered the same challenge and thought themselves bright enough to out-repartee the working press but learned to whine persecution before they got through.

Pegler marked the end of an old era and the beginning of a new one, and he did it, as anyone living it would, unconsciously. Terry, when tractable, was beloved; once he started speaking up, something was wrong—he was "sudden," "young," "not quite major-league." When Pegler said Terry would eventually complain about being persecuted, it obviously wasn't a prediction; it was a threat. And as far as not being "major-league," Terry must be given his due—he was creating a new conception of what "major-league," meant, something that had more to do with the players and the game than with the chroniclers.

By 1938, Terry couldn't take the journalistic bullying any more, even though he was coming off two great seasons. He got hold of Arthur Mann and arranged to have him ghostwrite an article for *The Saturday Evening Post*. The piece was called "Terrible Terry," in reference to the nickname that was first given him because he was a terrific hitter, but was now being used regularly by the press as a pejorative. Terry got a lot off his chest in the article, explaining, for example, how his own days of extreme poverty made him fiscally wary, and he offered his side of his feud with the press. He started with his refusal to give his phone number to Joe Williams, insisting that the resulting animosity was more Williams' fault than his own (he was probably right). He said the writers invented a phrase that is still ascribed to him, "What's in it for me?" It was supposedly his response to an invitation to a benefit (he was probably right about that misrepresentation, too). Pretty soon, however, the article began to start sounding defensive, too much like Pegler's whiner imagining persecution, and eventually it got downright snippy, talking about how "personal barbs and aspersions" had replaced real baseball news, while suggesting that the fans would stop reading the columnists long before they stop coming to the ballpark to see him play. So there. Take that. In fairness, though, years before sports columnist Jimmy Cannon called them "chipmunks," Terry apparently recognized that sportswriters who doubled as ethical philosophers were out of their depth.

On Christmas Day in 1914, on the Western Front in Europe, both sides quit firing and met in "No Man's Land" to wish each other well. The Baseball Writer's Dinner was and still remains like that, too—an annual demilitarized zone, almost a "roast." In 1938, as usual, Terry showed up. There's no published indication that he walked out on the annual skit, so he probably didn't. Tom Meany of the New York *World-Telegram* pretended to be ventriloquist Edgar Bergen playing Terry, and Arthur Daley of the *Times* sat on his lap and posed as Charlie McCarthy, Bergen's dummy. (There was undoubtedly also the suggestion that Charlie McCarthy was supposed to represent Joe McCarthy.) In any case, Bergen/Terry was looking for advice from the dummy. James P. Dawson was there on a busman's holiday, and he reported the scene in the *Times*:

> "Suppose," he asked, "the Giants and Yankees were in the seventh game of a world series."
>
> "Now, Bill," McCarthy shot back, "I'll answer questions, but don't ask me how to get your Giants into the seventh game of a world series."
>
> Terry tried again. "Suppose the bases were filled and Joe DiMaggio was at bat, and you were the Giants' manager, what would you do?"
>
> "There's always suicide," the dummy suggested. "Then again, you might get DiMaggio to autograph the ball. That would take time. You might have Mr. Stoneham autograph a new five-year contract. That also would take time. Then you might—oh, hell, Bill, I'd catch the next train to Memphis."

The most upsetting thing about Terry's article in *The Saturday Evening Post* was how it suggested things were getting to him. He'd popped off before, but he'd never gone to such an elaborate length to strike back at anybody. He might start to take a swing at Stengel or McCarthy, but, because he was a reasonable man, he always snapped out of his funk quickly. Did his article indicate that the tension of Terry's job was beginning to tell?

By the time the 1938 spring camp opened in Baton Rouge, Lousianna, Terry seemed fine again, determined to present a more cheerful face to the public. He signed autographs for fans and posed genially for their cameras. He even called frequent press conferences, making sure the news was always equitably distributed among the writers. When one photographer complained that some of the players refused to take time out to pose for head shots, Terry said, "you'll get them," and the photographer did. The *Times* reported Terry even told the newsmen why they sometimes read his efficiency as aloofness: "I may be sharp at times, but I've got work to do. You wouldn't charge into a businessman's office and start firing questions at him before he opened his mail, would you?"

Spring training began typically, with injuries and other assorted hassles. Old Dolf Luque retired, sending Terry a wire that said, in impossibly good English, "I do not intend to report." The *Times'* John Kieran noted that, if Luque had really written the message, it would have said, "Skippy, I no report." Luque always called Terry "Skippy." Castleman, who had been operated on by the omnipresent Dr. Speed, said he was still too frail to pitch, although there was much disagreement both as to when he could return and what kind of exercise program he should undertake. The injury to Whitehead presented a more ticklish problem, since it was not physical alone. He was in fine shape all winter long, but on February 19, Whitehead, feeling poorly, had been taken by his brother Louis to a doctor in Rocky Mount, North Carolina. The doctor found appendicitis so acute that gangrene had already set in, and Whitehead was operated on immediately, barely surviving the illness. Worse, the experience scared the daylights out of him, putting him in very precarious emotional shape for most of the subsequent year. Although, shortly after the surgery, Louis told Terry that Burgess would be fine in time for opening day, and although Louis wrote him a letter to this effect a week later, Terry apparently never heard from Burgess himself. On March 30, he told the *Times* he'd "received word" that Burgess Whitehead would be on hand the next day, and that he'd be "accompanied by his physician." Terry, who now knew how mentally fragile his second baseman had become, said it would be great to see him, that he'd be worked lightly, and that the doctor was welcome, too.

With all this going on, it's little wonder Terry took whatever time he could find to go to New Orleans for Mardi Gras.

Terry was never a blusterer—he'd picked his own team to finish second in 1936, and it had won—so his annual prediction could be taken as the sincere bet of a knowledgeable baseball man. This year, after a spring in which they had gradually improved, he picked the Giants. He was confident his fine pitching would continue, his hitters would only get better, and the McGraw-Terry approach to baseball would pay off as it had so often in the past. After opening day, Terry's view of the matter looked very reasonable. The Giants beat poor Casey Stengel's Boston Bees, 13-1, behind Cliff Melton and three homers, one by Ott. And the good times persisted. By early May, the Giants had won eleven straight games, they were 12-1 overall, and they were in first place, three and a half games ahead of the Cubs. On the day they won their eleventh in a row, however, there was one piece of news that was disappointing, if not ominous; the crucial Whitehead was sent home indefinitely, and the phrase "nervous breakdown" was used candidly for the first time.

The 1938 All-Star Game was played on July 6, and Terry was more determined than ever to win. Joe McCarthy, who was trying to win, too, kept the majority of his starters in for the majority of the game; Terry left them all in for the entire nine innings. Pitchers, of course, were still limited to three innings apiece, and Terry did pinchhit once, sending Hank Leiber up in the third inning for Johnny Vander Meer, who had thrown two consecutive no-hitters just prior to the All Star Game. Even that wasn't a substitution, however, since the pitcher had to come out anyway. In effect, Terry used what he felt was his best team for the entire game. In the top of the fourth inning, when the Cubs' Bill Lee walked the first man he faced, Terry got Hubbell up and throwing in the bullpen; Hubbell never made it into the game, but Terry knew the mere sight of him out there would be discomfiting. The final score was 4-1 in favor of the

National League which, like Terry himself, had finally regained a little pride.

After the break, the Giants were still four and a half games up and they looked formidable. They had been the National League champs for two years, but now they looked even better than they had in mid-July in either 1936 or 1937. Further, when Terry beat McCarthy in the All-Star Game, he seemed to be serving notice that the 1938 Giants would give the Yankees an even tougher test than they had in either of the two previous World Series.

But then the Giants started a slow slide, showing their old dominance only once in a while. They were losing as much as they were winning, while the Cubs, Reds, and Pirates all gained on them. On July 12, they crossed the river to Ebbets Field, where one Brooklyn fan, distraught because his club hadn't beaten the Giants in the last dozen tries, had scrawled a prayer to the Brooklyn starting pitcher in chalk on the sidewalk just in front of the rotunda, the main entrance to the park: "POSEDELL, PLEZZ BEAT THE GIANTS."

And that's exactly what Bill Posedell did, knocking the Giants out of first for the last time. They'd always be close, and they'd never be out of the race entirely, but, from then on, the Giants would always be underwater, looking up at the surface from one depth or another. The next time they would be in first place after the All-Star break would come a full thirteen years later, after Bob Thomson came to bat on a particularly sunny afternoon in October 1951, winning the pennant for the Giants with the most memorable home run in the history of the game.

A month later, the Giants suffered a loss that suggested to everybody that the great years were indeed finished. Hubbell's arm had been sore; now it started hurting so badly he couldn't pitch, and he had to ask Terry to take him out of one game. He said, the *Times* reported, that the arm felt "as though knives were cutting through it" every time he threw.

He was immediately flown to Memphis to be examined by

the Galen of baseball, Dr. J. Spencer Speed, and, on August 20, the doctor said there was a loose piece of bone floating around in Hubbell's left elbow. An operation would be necessary. A little more than a year after Dizzy Dean ruined his arm trying to pitch with a sore toe, Hubbell had to face the possibility that his days of glory were over, too. The reporters, who had been there during the examination and had heard Dr. Speed give Hubbell the bad news, noted that he took it as quietly as he took everything. When somebody asked him what he thought about his future, he smiled and said, "I don't know," but he pointed out that he was thirty-five, that he'd been throwing his screwball for sixteen years, and he said he was well aware he wasn't likely to heal as fast or as well as a nineteen- or twenty-year-old might. Although Hubbell would occasionally return to his old form, he'd never win more than eleven games in a season from the time of the injury until he called it quits in 1943—this was the end of his career as a consistently great pitcher.

The Giants were not officially out of it, however, and, on September 2, Terry made some more additions to his roster, bringing up, among others, Tom Baker from Jersey City and, in what seemed a very desperate gesture, Blondy Ryan again, from Baltimore. As soon as he had made these moves, he received more unpleasant news: his father had died in an Atlanta hospital.

They had been much less than close. While there is no public record of Terry either speaking to or visiting him in the years prior to his death, this could simply be one more indication that Terry was a private family man. Still, if there was any commerce at all between the two men, it was most likely infrequent. The elder Terry died on a Friday. Terry left for Atlanta as soon as he heard; the *Atlanta Constitution* noted that he "attended the services," but the paper reported nothing further. Presumably, neither did Terry. When Terry said he'd given both parents "a good wedding—a good funeral, I mean," a layman might conclude that, in addition to the child's poignant wish for happier parents, there was a determination, however perfunctory, to do right by them in the end. Bill Terry's father is buried on a small rise, not far from the present interstate, in a poor, slightly hilly section of Atlanta. The place has been neglected for years, and is overgrown with weeds; if there were walks, they can't be found now, and the aggressive snarling of dogs penned behind chain-link fences in the neighborhood is hardly suggestive of rest, harmony, and bliss. The family plot includes old Tom Terry, murdered by the Wilsons, and his wife; even little Jasper is there. Jasper's stone reads, "He has gone to be an angel," and then, "our darling baby." Terry's grandparents are there: Ella Heath Terry, Terry's grandmother, who died in 1922 when Terry was playing in Toledo, is given, "Dear wife and mother, we miss you so much." Terry's grandfather, William M., died in 1926; his inscription reads, "Tho lost to sight, to memory dear." The stone over Terry's father is simpler and more functional, and there is no inscription, flowery or otherwise, beyond the name. But a stone does stand, and Terry himself apparently had it placed there.

Meanwhile, the Giants kept trying. Compared by James P. Dawson to "a courageous fighter backed to the ropes, weary and stung," they were actually gaining some ground. On September 10, they played one of their best games of the year, scoring twenty runs for Cliff Melton, who would have needed only three of them to beat Brooklyn. It was the biggest transpontine blowout in history. On the September 15, the fired-up Giants took two games from the Pirates, behind a Schumacher shutout in the first contest and a seven-run inning in the second one. Halt, lame, and aging though the Giants were, they were now only three and a half back.

But Terry and his men had exhausted their stock of miracles, and, on October 1, while the Giants were beating the Bees at the Polo Grounds, the Cubs clinched the pennant. New York finished in third place, five games back. It was by no means a bad performance, all things considered, but the handwriting pertinent to subsequent years had appeared on the clubhouse wall.

As the season wound down, a couple of Giant fans wrote their own warnings in letters to the editor of the *Times*. One complained that, when he wasn't winning, Terry never coached; he stayed out of view in the dugout, hurting team morale. The second fan worried that the Giants had gone "permanently stale" because they hadn't developed any young talent. The Giant machine "creaks with age," he continued, saying that when Hubbell retired they'd have no first-rate pitchers left at all.

These fans made sense. Hubbell wasn't clinically finished, but he wasn't going to be much of a factor in the future, and Terry, who didn't like to lose, would begin to sit glumly in the dugout more than ever before. Terry had done a terrific job of bringing his hobbled team to only five games back in third place, but, in the years after he quit playing himself, he began losing touch with the reality of his situation and, worse, with some of his players. The newer players, especially, felt unwanted. Pitcher Bill Lohrman, who joined the team in 1937 and was 9-6 in 1938, thought Terry was only interested in the older Giants, his personal friends—men like Hubbell and Ott and Moore and Schumacher. Alex Kampouris signed on with the Giants in mid-1938, and he agreed to a point. "Some guys he might have been a pain in the ass to," he said to me. "He was rather difficult to get along with." But then Kampouris added that when he joined the Giants, Terry had given him "a few additional dollars for living expenses, which I thought was pretty damn nice." Even Lohrman, who thought Terry treated unproven players with unwarranted contempt, had to give him this much: Once, when his wife had a thumb so seriously infected that amputation was a possibility, Lohrman said he couldn't go with the team on a road trip. Terry asked if he'd go if his wife could come along, and Lohrman said he would, so Terry bought her a train ticket, arranged for medical care *en route*, and even gave the young couple his own drawing room. Stories like these make it seem that part of Terry's apparent moodiness was a growing inability to communicate with the next generation; the father who misunderstands his sons may himself be misunderstood.

The Giants closed shop on October 2, picked up their last paychecks, and took off for home. Terry headed for Memphis, where he settled with Clarence Saunders out of court. Saunders agreed to vacate his estate by December 15, pointing out that Terry was getting the place for a song, probably only a sixth of what it was actually worth. Castleman was in Memphis when Terry finally closed the deal, and he told me he went with Terry to the Union Planter's Bank, watching as his boss "plunked down thirty-nine thousand dollars for the final payment on the place." Terry told me that, after he had made the million he had promised his wife, he sat her down in their house and showed her the figures to prove he'd done it. Although he didn't say when he did that, or where, it may very well have been this year, right after he moved into the Saunders estate.

In December, Terry started making trades. He acquired a new pitcher, signing a kid from San Diego named Manny Salvo, but he gave up another pitcher to get a big slugger, the Senators' Zeke Bonura. Bonura was an archetypal lummox who drove Terry crazy with his slow play around first, and, one day after returning in 1939, Whitehead protested, too. Harry Danning was catching in the game, and he looked up: "And there was Bonura," Danning told me, "and right behind him was Whitehead, playing in the same position! So I says, 'What in hell are you doing over there?' He says, 'I'm over here all the time anyhow, I might as well *stay* here!'"

But Terry's biggest deal that winter occurred when he gave Bartell, Mancuso, and Leiber to the Cubs for Ken O'Dea, Frank Demaree, and the great shortstop Billy Jurges. The wisdom of this trade was debatable, since he lost three prominent players, only one of whom, Mancuso, could be considered over the hill. He received only one star, Jurges, in return. The writers didn't see the logic, but when one of them grilled Terry about the deal, he did it in such a damnfool manner that he elicited a typical Terry response. The writer asked Terry what he thought of the trade. Terry, undoubtedly looking skyward for sympathy, said, "What do you *think* I think of the trade? I just *made* it!"

If that writer deserved the response, Terry also deserved the question. In fact, Al Lopez said this was the only trade Terry made that he ever admitted was a bad one. In any case, if the deal was a mistake, Terry had, by 1942, corrected it; Mancuso, Leiber, and Bartell were all Giants again, and of the other three, only Jurges had not been dealt away.

Terry was enjoying his new spread during the winter of 1938–39, and, when reporters stopped by, he was downright cheerful, clearing brush, looking and acting very much the country squire. The troubles of the previous season were in the past, and, after a little rest and with a little luck, his skill might bring the Giants another flag. It wasn't an unreasonable hope: Terry's club had been hurt badly by injuries, but it had still finished close in the race. If Hubbell, Schumacher, and Castleman all could come back healthy from their various operations, they could certainly make more than a five-game difference over an entire season. In fact, if any of the three did well, it could make the difference. Terry was possibly thinking in these terms when he traded for a fine infielder and a powerful slugger, rather than to improve his pitching. When he came to the Giants' office in February, Terry picked the Giants to finish no lower than second, and he thought first place was more likely. He found support from a surprising quarter: Leo Durocher, who had just taken over as manager of the Dodgers, said "Bill Terry has the pennant all racked up for the Giants," and Durocher apparently meant it. Durocher's reasoning was interesting; he said Terry would win "because he has more life among his players than any other team in the league." Durocher wasn't clear about what he meant by "life," but whether he was referring to youthful energy or team loyalty, he was a few years late with the compliment.

Burgess Whitehead, not fully recovered, was still an unknown quantity in 1939. When the Giants arrived at spring camp in Baton Rouge, Terry received word that Whitehead would join them there. He'd been examined by a doctor in Tarboro, North Carolina, and had been pronounced fully recovered. Without apparent irony, the paper referred to Whitehead's doctor as the "head physician" at the Tarboro hospital. When Whitehead didn't show up as scheduled, Terry became worried, but he kept his real concerns to himself, although he did make these encoded remarks to the *Times'* John Drebinger:

A funny fellow, this Whitehead. He's pretty high strung and appears to be a little nervous about getting started. But once he gets here, I don't think I'll have any trouble bringing him along. I'll give him all the time he wants to get his hand back in the game.

For a translation, consider the brief answer Terry gave me when I asked just how nervous Whitehead was during this period. Terry stared as though he couldn't believe anybody could miss something so obvious, and simply said, "He was *crazy.*"

The Giants opened at Ebbets Field in 1939, and the early Brooklyn arrivals watched Terry hit practice balls to infielders; every time somebody flubbed a grounder, they'd either boo loudly or honk one of the old-fashioned, Harpo Marx-style automobile horns many were carrying. It was the first day that local regular-season games were ever broadcast over the radio, and Red Barber, whose new show had been badly promoted by the media, needed to get the public's attention, so he invented the pre-game interview on the spot. His first guest—the first guest on any such program—was Terry, who didn't hesitate to oblige the young announcer. Barber, in turn, never forgot the man he found to be "courteous, pleasant, cooperative, intelligent, anything you want," and, in later years, he had some advice for those who would judge the Giant manager:

Terry had a reputation for being a cold, tough man, but it was not true. It is always wise, when you hear something about a man, to remember who told you and why he told you. Newspapermen created Terry's reputation.

By the time the game was half over, the horn-tooting fans subsided, particularly after Giant first baseman Zeke Bonura hit a three-run homer in the third inning. Billy Jurges was perfect in the field, and so was Whitehead; the former got a couple of singles, the latter got a double and then scored. Perhaps this accounts for Durocher's enthusiasm: with Joe Moore added to the equation, the 1939 Giants may have been fielding the best shortstop, second baseman, and left fielder in the league.

Early in the season, Terry went out to the World's Fair in Flushing, where he, Ott, and Hubbell inaugurated a baseball school for kids at the Court of Sports. He probably wished he could enroll some of his players, since, with the exception of the three men mentioned above, his team seemed increasingly lousy in the field. Late in May, he benched Harry Danning, apparently because he was allowing too many stolen bases, and Bonura, ostensibly because he was too elephantine around first. Both men were hitting well, and they were replaced by Ken O'Dea and Johnny McCarthy, who were much weaker offensively. Tom Meany of the *World-Telegram* wondered why Terry made the move, since Danning and Bonura had accounted for "more victories with their power than losses through fielding lapses," and he implied that Terry's insistence on McGraw-style errorless baseball might be blinding him to a larger view. Another possibility, of course, was a general souring. Was Terry also beginning to emulate McGraw's scapegoat-seeking biliousness? By June 1, the writers were characterizing him as impatient, frustrated, even depressed by the club's performance.

The benching of the good-hitting Danning and Bonura might also indicate that Terry wasn't sufficiently aware of the kind of team he possessed. One of the ironies of history's misperception of Terry's Giants in the 1930s was the notion that it was only a pitchers' outfit. People forget about Ott, Leiber, Bonura, even Joe Moore—and Terry himself before 1937; they forget that the Giants led the league in home runs from 1937 through 1939, and that they were second in that category in 1936. From time to time, this power surfaced all at once in a single game. On June 6 at the Polo Grounds, for instance, they beat the Reds, 17-3, on seven homers, with five coming in a fourth inning that Arthur Daley said "will live long in the memories of those who saw it." With those five homers, the Giants broke a record that had existed since 1894, and it's only fair to name the hitters who provided the heroics: Harry Danning, Frank Demaree, Whitehead, Manny Salvo and Moore.

But there were also some beautiful days for the pitchers. On June 21, Bill Lohrman shut out the Reds, 7-0, on two hits and no walks. Terry, however, didn't say a word to Lohrman, either during or after the game. Some of the papers even noted this odd and uncharitable lack of rump-patting. Whatever was bothering Terry that day, his lack of encouragement is something the young pitcher never forgot. Years later, he still brings it up when discussing what he considers to be the negative aspects of Terry's character.

The Giants had fallen all the way to seventh place on the day Terry snubbed Lohrman, and that dismal fact might have been what caused his ill-humor or absent-mindedness, whichever it was. Around this time, Reds manager, Bill McKechnie told John Kieran the Giants were too good to be that far down. McKechnie's Reds were comfortably in first, and he could afford to be kind, but he was also right. With about a week remaining before the All-Star break, Terry moved his club all the way up to second place, only four games back. At this point, they played a doubleheader against the Dodgers that was one of the highlights of this season, as far as comic drama goes.

On July 2 at the Polo Grounds, Durocher's Brooklyns won

the first game, 3-2, despite Hubbell's four scoreless innings in relief of Lohrman. In the second game, Durocher himself came up in the fourth inning with a man on first and one out. Schumacher, who had already given up three runs in the inning, pitched him inside, sufficiently so that Durocher dove for cover. In one sense, the ploy worked, since, on the next pitch, the aroused and offended Durocher hit into a double play; in another sense, it didn't, since the Dodger manager was perturbed enough to go after the Giant first baseman, the very large Zeke Bonura, as Zeke ran out the ground ball. John Drebinger said Durocher "seemed, in his excitement, to mistake Bonura's foot for the bag." Bonura, however, thought this was no mistake. He threw the ball at Durocher's head, then followed him down the foul line into short right. When he caught up with him, he started belting the Dodger manager, or so the papers said. Durocher himself didn't remember any punches being thrown. Years later, he told me:

> When I went to first base I tried to step on Zeke, on Bonura. And I was about twenty-five, thirty feet away, down the line, you know, 'cause I was going just as hard as I could, trying to get there quick and step on him. He was stretching for the ball, you know. And, boy, the next thing I knew, the ball was going by my ear. Well, here comes the Zeke. Well, he wasn't going to—the minute he got to me, I put a big bear hug on him, so there's no way he's going to hit me, you know, 'cause he'd break me in half. No way I'm gonna win *that* argument. And it was all over in two seconds. And no punches thrown, nobody hurt…but the idea was that in those days, that's the way we played.

This seemed harmless enough, particularly since it was the norm, "the way we played," but it took a bit longer than two seconds for the rhubarb to subside. Both teams came onto the field, as was to be expected. Then the fans got into it, providing the obligatory sprinkle of pop bottles, but that was no surprise, either. And it was no surprise that Terry would complain when the umps tossed Bonura, whom he chose to view as merely an innocent bystander. The problem was that after the game was over, Larry MacPhail, who had succeeded Bob Quinn as the Brooklyn general manager, raised a real rumpus. This should probably be viewed as traditional, too, a repetition of Quinn's stagy 1934 outrage, especially since the target was again Bill Terry. In fact, the statement MacPhail sent to the National League's board of directors was remarkably similar in tone to the interview Bob Quinn had given Marshall Hunt of the *Daily News* five years earlier. If anything, this one was harsher; among other things, MacPhail accused Terry of "getting away with murder," and insisted that baseball commissioner Ford Frick "tell Terry he isn't running the umpires and that he isn't running the National League."

Terry said MacPhail's charges were "too ridiculous" for comment, and he disdained reply. Durocher claimed most innocently that Bonura's enormous foot had been in the way. By coincidence, the same *Times* story that reported these comments contained another item about another game, one that sheds light on how baseball was played "in those days." Casey Stengel, who was about to turn fifty, was fined for starting a fist-fight with Pinky May, the Phils' twenty-eight-year-old third baseman. Why, if such behavior was so common then, would so astute a baseball man as MacPhail object so strenuously and publicly? Was his timing in any way related to the upcoming weekend series between the Giants and the Dodgers at Ebbets Field in just four days? On the day before the first game of that series, the *Times* printed this headline:

WILD RECEPTION PLANNED TODAY
FOR SHIFT IN GIANT-DODGER WAR
Police Detail for Ebbets Field
Is Enlarged as Feeling Runs High
in Interborough Rivalry

Beneath that, it was announced that the only seats left were boxes for the Saturday doubleheader; the single game on Friday was now entirely sold out. John Kieran offered his metrical views in the *Times:*

> A Giant's toes and a Dodger's nose
> Were mangled in a clash;
> Ho! Let 'em swing while I laugh and sing
> And the magnates get the cash!

The final attendance tally for the first game was 36,444, not bad for a small park like Ebbets Field. The *Times,* understanding what the important story was, printed that number first in its July 8 headline.

The Giants' first series after the All-Star break was against the league-leading Reds, and, as usual, their play was spotty. They lost the first game big, 7-0, but won the second in proper Giant fashion, 4-1, behind Lohrman and Hubbell. On July 15, though, in the third game, their frustration began to show. They were ahead by a run in the top of the eighth when, with one man on, Harry Craft hit a drive into the not-so-distant left-field stands. The ball started out in fair territory, but it curved sharply to the left. Home-plate umpire Lee Ballanfant called it a fair ball.

It probably wasn't. The Giants were not the kind of team to instigate a riot without sufficient cause. Harry Danning, who the *Times* said was capering around Ballanfant "like an enraged bull" and who'd had a good view of the ball, was the first to be thrown out of the game. Joe Moore, who'd stood under the ball as it landed in the stands in foul territory and who certainly wasn't known as a hothead, was the second to be ejected. The third was Billy Jurges, who received the hook from "Major" George Magerkurth in memorable fashion: Jurges thought Magerkurth was intentionally spitting on him, so he spit back; then they started a fistfight. Actually, Magerkurth wasn't trying to spit on Jurges; when he chewed tobacco, which he always did while on the job, he sprayed everybody as he talked. When Jurges looked back, even he found the humor in the incident: "He was chewing tobacco, and I was chewing gum," Jurges told me. "And he splashed my face with chewing tobacco. So I say, 'Don't spit on me,' and I spit back at him. And I was chewing this gum, it was all white, and it foamed. And Bill Terry was there, he was in back of me, and he started laughing. And I said, 'What the hell are *you* laughing at?'"

Jurges' question to Terry had a point, since this colossal dispute cost the Giants the game, maybe even the championship. So many Giants were eventually thrown out of the game that Terry had to field a makeshift lineup. "I think Hubbell and I wound up in the outfield," Hal Schumacher told me. "Greatest defensive outfit in the business!" Jurges was suspended for ten days, Danning was out for a week with an injury sustained in the melee, and the Giants, who had been a close second to the Reds, proceeded to drop nine straight.

Just how bad was Ballanfant's call? Harry Gumbert who was pitching that day, said "it was foul by three feet." Harry Danning said he followed the ball all the way to the wall, that he could see it as it passed in front of the foul pole and fell into the seats in foul territory. Harry Craft, the man who hit it, was too busy running to look, although when he rounded third, he told me, he "couldn't even see home plate," since there were so many angry Giants in that vicinity. After the game, Craft asked Bill McKechnie where the ball had landed. McKechnie, who had been coaching at third, had been in a perfect position to see it. He looked at Craft over his eyeglasses and said, "My son, the plate umpire called it, and he called it fair." Craft never asked him about it again.

Danning was the first man ejected in the fracas, which is certainly one of the biggest rhubarbs in major league history. He was well aware of the damage it had done to the Giants' chances, both through suspension and injury. "It kicked us out of the pennant," he said to me. "So the next time I had an argument with the same umpire I really told him off. They fined me two hundred and fifty bucks. It was worth it, though. Fuck it, I was so mad—everything just blurted out. He says, 'I'm going to tell Frick.' I said, 'You can tell Frick to stick it up his ass.'" The only Giant who didn't seem concerned was Carl Hubbell, who could be seen throughout the melee calmly leaning against the wall in his corner of the dugout—Hubbell, who once said, "It's a fast game, but you have to slow down to play it."

One of the attendees that day was a youthful Roger Angell, the baseball writer for *The New Yorker* who later wrote the classic book, *The Summer Game*. He saw the fan who caught the ball, a man who was sitting in foul territory, two seats away from the pole. The fan was facing home plate, holding up the ball in his right hand and frantically pointing to his left with the other one. It was an epiphany for Angell. "Life, I had seen for the first time," he said, "is not fair." This monumental donnybrook had one positive result, however: no ballpark before then had foul-pole nets; pretty soon, every park would have them.

Through the rest of July, August, and finally September, the decline of the Giants was smooth and relentless. They looked good in the last game of the season shutting out Boston, 5-0, but by then they were in fifth place, eighteen and a half games behind the Reds. To make matters much worse, the Dodgers had finished third, two floors up.

15

DECLINE AND FALL: 1940–1941

As the collapse became all the more apparent, Horace Stoneham quickly
shelled out $125,000 to equip the Polo Grounds for night baseball.
But the ball that was played there would have been better left in darkness.
Even shrewd Bill Terry couldn't reverse the slide.
— Noel Hynd

Eighteen and a half games—the Giants hadn't been that far
back since the Federal League year of 1915. It was a given that
Terry would try to locate new personnel somewhere. He did gath-
er some new faces, Johnny Rucker, Babe Young, Harold "Hy"
Vanderberg and Mickey Witek, but none of them would make
much of a difference. His most dramatic move was typical of
Giant thinking then—he drafted Paul Dean. Although Dean was
still only twenty-six, he was washed up. His last good year had
been 1935, after which he'd won a total of only eight games.
Terry's rationale for the signing seemed as weak as his enthusiasm. "Frank Snyder and Paul are just like *that*," he told the *Times*.
"Snyder thinks he can come back." Paul Dean was only the seventh man on the 1939 Giant pitching staff, and, although he won
his last four major league games for Terry, he lost the same number, finishing with an earned run average of just under four. He
wasn't the help the Giants needed. The problem was twofold:
first, as John Kieran had recognized back in 1936, while Terry

was a great manager and a knowledgeable trader, he could be faulted for not being a "builder" who recognized and cultivated young talent; second, Terry had a conservative tendency to favor the proven player, even when that player was demonstrably over the hill.

Terry remained out of touch with his men, too; even Joe Moore noticed this, surmising it was due to the new job as general manager. "He went up into the office, and it took a lot of his time," Moore told me. "You get a little bit far away from your players when you're not close to 'em every day." The Giant players who dated back to the McGraw era formed a kind of elite on the club. This division was not discouraged by Terry, so it was natural for the younger men to feel excluded, sometimes angry. If Alex Kampouris had mixed feelings, and if Bill Lohrman didn't much like Terry, Rube Fischer, who arrived in 1941, openly hated his guts. Lohrman thought Terry grew more and more aloof in direct proportion to losing and suggested his growing isolation might be another parallel to the career of his mentor and predecessor, McGraw.

The era was also different. With the beginning of the war in Europe and the concurrent boom in defense spending, the Depression was history at last. By the time the season started, Poland, Denmark, Norway, and the low countries had fallen to Hitler, and much of China belonged to the Japanese. In 1940, the Memorial Day doubleheaders coincided with the evacuation of Dunkirk, and Paris itself fell a month before the All-Star Game. Beyond that, Giant management announced it was going to install lights at the Polo Grounds. That last bit of news upset Terry enough to prompt him to abandon the bat for the pen once again, and he wrote the article for *Collier's* attacking night baseball.

The Giants started Hubbell against the last-place Phils in the opener on April 16, and John Kieran said that was as sporting as "striking an old woman with a basket of flowers on each arm." The game, however, didn't go well, although it was less Hubbell's fault than the hitters' (they got him only one run) and the fielders' (Mickey Witek made two errors, and, after his second one, Philadelphia scored all three of its runs). Hubbell, in fact, was "pitching as well as he might have done in days of yore," John Drebinger said, adding he was "the Meal Ticket of old." The persistent references to the days of past glory whenever Hubbell's name came up shouldn't have been lost on Terry, but it's tempting to think that they were. In an ominous emphasis on the importance of youth, Hubbell's twenty-one-year-old rival, Bob Feller, had a pretty good opening day, too; he no-hit the White Sox.

Hubbell continued to pitch very well on occasion. On Memorial Day at Ebbets Field, he pitched what he later said was his best game, allowing only Johnny Hudson's single in the second inning. What Hudson spoiled that day was not just a no-hitter, but a perfect game. Hubbell threw only eighty-one pitches and faced the minimum of twenty-seven men as Hudson was doubled up after reaching base. Only three balls were hit past the infield, one of them, of course, being Hudson's. "Every ball I threw went just where I intended it to go," Hubbell said. "I never had such control before or since, and I can't explain it." On June 4, he won his fifth game in a row, and Drebinger suggested he'd done it because it was the eighth anniversary of Terry's replacing McGraw as manager.

Hubbell couldn't keep it up, though, and you can identify a turning point in a year that would end badly, it was his start against the league-leading Reds on June 23. Before the game, the first of a doubleheader, the Giants were in second place, one game back. Hubbell was leading by two runs with two out in the Cincinnati ninth; one more out and the Giants would be tied for first. Instead, Hubbell fell apart. The Reds rallied for five runs on six hits, the Giants couldn't score in their half of the inning, and the game was lost, 7-4. With their sails so dramatically deflated, they lost the second game, too, 2-0.

Even worse, they lost Billy Jurges again, and this time it

would be for more than ten days. Arthur Daley of the *Times* saw (and heard) what happened:

> Bucky Walters fired his high, hard one to Jurges to open the seventh. The ball skidded out of his hand and there was a crack that sounded almost as if a base hit had been made.
>
> But instead the ball caromed off the back of Jurges' head with such force that it bounced beyond the pitching mound. While the crowd of 52,657 watched in horror, Billy collapsed. Walters was one of the first to reach him. "I'm sorry, Billy," he muttered over and over.

Even though his response was gentlemanly and sincere—"that's all right, Bucky, I know you didn't mean it"—Jurges and the Giants were the ones who should have felt sorrowful, because their season had just ended.

Now Jurges was gone, and the fact that Hubbell suddenly began feeling his years helped matters not at all. On July 2 at the Polo Grounds, he lost to the Dodgers, 7-3, and the *Times* subhead read, "Hubbell Tires in Eighth." Still, Carl had been pulled before the worst damage was done. The *Times* added that the "young Dodger shortstop," Pee Wee Reese, hit a three-run homer in the ninth off one of Terry's new men, Hy Vandenberg.

Hubbell could still turn in good games—he won his first night game, 6-1, on July 18, at Forbes Field—but the victories came much less frequently. Hal Schumacher was a similar case: he beat the Pirates on the afternoon following Hubbell's night game, allowing only two runs, but that made his overall record even at 7-7, and he'd end the season the same way, 13-13. Further, his earned run average of 3.25 would be more than a run above his career best.

By August 18, the team was twelve and a half games back. Terry even brought Bill, Jr., who had been a college star at the University of Virginia, to the Polo Grounds and had him work out with the club. Bill, Jr., couldn't help, either, although it's doubtful Terry ever seriously thought he might. It's also unclear whether the younger Terry was still devoting some of his time to running his father's Greenwood, Mississippi, club in the Cotton States League. If he was, he had his own problems; Greenwood finished in next-to-last place in 1940, and, in 1941 the franchise was shifted to Pine Bluff, Arkansas. On September 19 in New York, the Giants lost their eleventh straight game; it was the longest losing streak Terry would ever have as a manager. They finished twenty-seven and a half games back, in sixth place.

John McGraw's first full year as manager had been in 1903, and no Giant team since then had ever been twenty-seven and a half games back: Terry's 1940 squad had just set the modern record for Giant ineptitude. In 1941, the team would remain substantially the same, as would its record; there was little question that Terry's unwillingness or inability to bring along younger players was beginning to show. It could also have been that Terry's final effort to win a flag was not whole-hearted, that his desire had left him. The Depression had been defeated, and that had always been the more important fight, anyway, particularly for those teammates who were his close friends, the ones who had shared with him the personal knowledge of hard times. Maybe the younger players couldn't conceive of just how hard those times had been, or how strong the bond was between the men who had known that era. Or maybe "Memphis Bill" just thought he was getting too old to dress up in a costume and play a game: he always knew he could make more money in the private sector than in the public arena, and, in fact he would soon prove it. Or maybe he was painfully aware that a new fight was about to replace the battle against poverty, and that baseball might not be the best line of work to pursue. A moratorium had nearly been declared on the game in 1918, and, if war came again, the same thing could happen.

Although Terry went to spring training without having made any important changes in the team, he hadn't entirely given up on the idea. He needed an outfielder, and he considered taking the Cubs up on their suggestion that he take Hank Leiber back from them. It would have been a complicated, three-cornered deal in which the Giants would also receive the Dodgers' catcher, Babe Phelps, while they sent Harry Danning to the Cubs. The deal was nearly completed when Terry announced he was turning it down, which was a little odd, since he was the one who had proposed it. Brooklyn's volatile Larry MacPhail was upset, dispatching a long wire to the papers accusing Terry of having lost his mind. In reality, Terry probably was forced to retract a proposal the front office had deemed too expensive, and the traditionally close-mouthed executives wouldn't let him say it hadn't been his idea to call off the deal. Harry Gumbert thought this was the case, and he had a pretty good idea who was behind the Giant volte-face. Gumbert told me, "Terry made a deal over there, and Bondy, he called the deal off, he didn't like it. It would've won the pennant for Terry. Everybody, all the news writers knew about it."

Leo Bondy, the team lawyer, must have advised Stoneham to be frugal. Stoneham, in turn, must have told Terry that the deal—and, if Gumbert was correct, the pennant—was off; Stoneham had begun to assert himself, to veto Terry on occasion. After this transaction fell through, Terry announced a move that required neither a trade nor the acquisition of a new player—he said he'd go with the old Gabby Hartnett (Hartnett had been signed in the fall of 1940, after Chicago fired him as manager) and the young Ken O'Dea behind the plate, and, since he couldn't get Leiber, he'd shift Harry Danning to the outfield.

The move puzzled everybody. Terry was certainly acting boldly, undoubtedly thinking of how well Mel Ott had played third base in 1937, when many thought Terry's shift had been responsible for the pennant. Catchers, however, were notoriously poor runners and, therefore, poor outfielders. Additionally,

Danning was one of the best catchers in the league. His powerful bat would remain available, but wouldn't he hurt them defensively? Charitable writers questioned Terry's judgment, while uncharitable ones, remembering that Danning was "currently out of favor with his employers," wondered openly about his motives. Maybe Terry was trying to shame Danning into docility.

Nobody liked it, but were there any reasons for the shift that made sense? Of course. Other players had been successfully shifted to the outfield with beneficial results, even though they usually trotted out there on healthy knees. The most recent example was Detroit first baseman Hank Greenberg. Further, Danning had already played the outfield, albeit briefly, and, in two seasons at Bridgeport in the Eastern League, he'd posted the respectable fielding averages of .967 and .965. He also had the dimensions of an outfielder: he was 6' 1" and one hundred and ninety pounds, and, next to a catcher like the two-hundred-and-thirty-pound Ernie Lombardi, he looked downright svelte. If Jurges couldn't come back, Joe Orengo would have to move from third to short, and Ott would have to come in from right to play third again. In other words, the shift was far from being as crazy as it initially sounded. If these reasons weren't solid enough, Dan Daniel of the *World-Telegram* developed an interesting theory based on Terry's acknowledged mastery as a public-relations man:

> There is still another angle in the Danning story. Terry is not devoid of abilities in the line of psychology. He had to do something to dispel the gloom cast by Jurges' recurrent dizzy spells and create a divertissement for press and fans. At least this he has achieved.

If this theory pushes credulity, it does show that the writers had become convinced Terry was, in the promotional line, anyway, a clever fellow. Whatever the motives behind it, however, the Danning experiment failed, and, by the time the season opened, he was back behind the plate.

Terry did make one important move a third of the way through the season: he got back Dick Bartell. He had been traded from the Cubs to the Tigers, and Bartell, who had helped Detroit capture the pennant the year before, could always win games for a team. On June 8, for example, it was Hal Schumacher day, but Schumacher did not respond to the adulation; after being given a bouquet of roses and a thousand-dollar defense bond, he went out and gave up five runs. He was losing, 5-0, when Bartell came up in the ninth and knocked in a couple of the five runs needed to tie the score. Then, after the Giants did tie it, Bartell batted again in the tenth inning, homering to win the game, 7-5. Ironically, Bartell was in the game as a substitute for Jurges, who had been his entirely devoted enemy when they played on opposing clubs. When he brought Bartell back to the Giants in the middle of the 1941 season, Terry was well aware of this animosity, and he apparently faced the problem squarely by assigning Bartell the locker next to Jurges'. For the record, Jurges didn't remember it that way. He said he was sandwiched between two coaches, Luque and Logan, and he remembered being enthralled with their stories of the old times. He did admit to getting along passably well with Bartell, however. Bartell himself may have encouraged reconcilation, since Jurges was not a man to be messed with at close range; born in the Bronx and raised in Brooklyn, he had once roomed with Bill Lohrman, who told me he caught him shirtless one night and noticed he was badly scarred. "Oh, that," Jurges said. He explained that the scars were bullet wounds, the souvenirs of an encounter with an angry lady.

The season, another mediocre one, wore on and on. Terry's great Yankee counterpart at first base, Lou Gehrig, died on June 2, and Terry was one of the handful of players invited to the private ceremony in the Riverdale section of the Bronx. But there was a laugh once in a while. On June 17, Hubbell beat Frisch's Pirates, but Frisch wasn't there—he was recovering from an operation on his toe to correct the damage done by a spiking some twenty years back, when he was playing for McGraw. While Frisch was confined, one of his visitors was Casey Stengel, who, shortly after the visit, ran into Terry and filled him in on the melodramatic self-pitying of the stricken Frisch. Stengel had the undemonstrative Terry roaring with laughter, and John Drebinger heard Stengel wrap up the story: "On the level, Bill," said Stengel, "it's a sight you've really got to hear to appreciate."

As week steadily succeeded week, the Giants' slow, undramatic, quiet slide in the standings became as predictable as Hubbell's winning ways in 1936. On August 22, the team was in fifth place, eighteen games back; on August 30, they were twenty back. By September 21, after *winning* two from Boston, they were twenty-five and a half behind, which is exactly where they finished the season. The team twenty-five and a half games ahead of them was the Brooklyn Dodgers.

After the Yankees beat the Dodgers in the Series, Terry went home to Memphis, where he stayed through the autumn, working his farm. In early December he went to Jacksonville for the minor-league meeting. The first thing he did was to sit down with Horace Stoneham, Leo Bondy, and Eddie Brannick, who had been considering a proposal he had made to them. Then the four men called in Mel Ott, and, after a three-hour meeting to iron out the details, they called in the press. Henceforth, Terry was only going to head up the farm system. The new Giant manager was Mel Ott.

Some of the writers, inveterate Terry-bashers, insisted Terry was forced out by Stoneham, but Terry always denied this, simply and vehemently. The account of the announcement that day certainly made it seem as if Terry was behind the change. Drebinger, in saying "the move is one Terry has been pressing vigorously on Stoneham for more than a year," indicated that it was not only Terry's idea, but that Terry's wishes were common knowledge in the press box. Terry himself was said to have looked "cheerful," and he even gave everybody a lengthy prepared statement in which he claimed to be "delighted" with the new arrangement.

The switch was by far the biggest Giants news of the year. The *News* even treated the story to a banner headline on page one.

Stoneham, Terry, and Ott all said Ott would be his own man, that he wouldn't take orders from Terry, but the writers weren't so sure. Bob Considine of the New York *Journal-American* had already said he didn't remember Ott ever having taken a stand on anything regarding the running of the team. Dan Daniel of the *World-Telegram* came right out and said the promise that Ott would run things all by himself was "difficult to believe." Ott (or someone) decided he had better assert himself fast, so he started right in with a couple of decisive-looking moves: he took Danning off the trading block on which Terry had displayed him, he sent Bob Bowman and cash to the Cubs for Hank Leiber, and he transferred Frank "Pancho" Snyder to Terry's new bailiwick in the farm system. All of this business was concluded in the Jacksonville hotel room of Jimmy Gallagher, the Cubs' general manager. They broke up after 2 a.m., an hour so late for Ott that, as Kieran said, "he was practically in a coma."

Were these decisions really Ott's? The idea to retain Danning may have come from someone other than Terry. Terry, however, was given Snyder, whom he respected, and the team received Leiber, whom Terry had tried to snag the previous year. These two moves, at least, looked as though they originated from Terry, not Ott; it may well have been that Terry had advised Ott as to which decisions might best allow him to become his own man.

Two days after Ott took over, he was still actively dealing, although he continued to be shadowed by the man he'd replaced; Drebinger said that "Master Melvin, accompanied by Bill Terry, who continues to aid in an advisory capacity, bearded the Brooklyn moguls in their own lair and remained locked with them for more than three hours." Mel Ott had been manager for less than a third of a week. He had never before been heard to express an opinion on the game, he was as mild-mannered as they came and he respected (and had for years depended on) the brilliance of the predecessor who was showing him the ropes. It seems likely that Ott would at least consider Terry's suggestions.

No important deal was struck with the Dodgers, however, by the Terry-Ott team; the final important move came with the acquisition of Johnny Mize. The winter meeting began in Chicago right after the Jacksonville sessions ended, and, since Terry left Florida for Chicago before Ott, the Mize trade was almost certainly Terry's, as both he and Mize claimed. Although Mize wouldn't officially sign until the next Wednesday, which was December 10, Branch Rickey came to a verbal agreement with Terry on the Sunday before that. Terry remembered that they were sealing the bargain with a handshake in the bar of a Chicago hotel when a news bulletin came over the radio announcing the attack on Pearl Harbor.

The first week of December 1941 had been an important time in Giants history. The naming of Ott was incidental; he was made manager because Terry couldn't handle two jobs anymore, and he knew which of the two positions was no longer responding to his touch or maintaining his interest. The significant decisions made before Ott was called into that hotel room were these: Terry could call all the shots regarding trades and hirings, and Stoneham would free up more money to attract class players. The subsequent trades, from the acquisition of Leiber on December 3 to the signing of Mize a week later, looked as though they would vastly improve the team. Drebinger applauded the week's moves, making it clear that he understood Terry, not Ott, was in charge. "The old Colonel really rolled up his sleeves and went to work," Drebinger said, adding that now the Giants had to be favored to win the 1942 pennant. In other words, the last major service Bill Terry performed for his team was to present his old friend, Mel Ott, with a contender.

PART IV

NICE GUYS FINISH LAST

16

RETIREMENT?

Baseball's too cheap, says Memphis Bill,
Who jumps from cows to cotton.
The handsome Giant pay he drew
He seems to have forgotten.
            —The Old Scout

In tones of deep sarcastic hue
On how the game is run
Cool Willy Terry says: "Adieu,
My baseball life is done.

The salaries they pay today
Are picayune and cheap:
In cotton realms I'll soon hold sway
Great fortunes will I reap."

Although we wish Cool Willy speed,
The way his statement shapes,
Instead of cotton minus seed,
He's selling sour grapes.
            —Tim Cohane

Like most Americans, Terry was touched by World War II. Bill, Jr., would serve; fortunately, he would get through the war unscathed. However, there was a stateside family tragedy in 1942. On March 19, Terry's uncle, Milton Lysle, who had been commissioner of the Memphis Freight Bureau, jumped out of the window of his tenth-floor hotel room in Montgomery, Alabama. Lysle, who was sixty, had left a thick sealed envelope for his wife, Terry's aunt, Ella Mae; she never revealed its contents, and, of course, the privacy-minded Terry wouldn't have talked to any writers who might have read the obituary and recognized the connection. Lysle was better known in Memphis than in Montgomery, so the *Commercial-Appeal* ran a fairly long story, but, even there, nobody seemed to know he was Terry's uncle.

Terry, meanwhile, was beginning to fade into the baseball background. He did show up at the All-Star Game in Cleveland, since all proceeds were going to the military's Bat and Ball Fund, a charity he wanted to support. The papers explained that he had come to Cleveland from Memphis, adding that he was en route to Florida to meet with Horace Stoneham. Although there should be no further need to stress this point, it's hard to characterize Terry as merely mercenary when he would stop in Cleveland to attend a benefit game on his way from Memphis to Miami.

Terry was in the papers a little later in the season, simply because he told reporters that he gave a National League club (not the Giants) a very good chance to beat the Yankees, should they win the pennant, which he expected to happen. The reason the press took particular note was because the team he was praising (he said the club was "smart") was Brooklyn. Terry, a man known for his blunt candor, was objective, lauding not only the team, but manager Durocher and general manager MacPhail, two men he personally disliked. He said Durocher had done "a remarkable job," and that "you've got to give Larry MacPhail credit" for the team he'd assembled. He even complimented the borough, saying "that town really makes a player hustle," so there is at least one recorded instance of Bill Terry speaking well of Dodger fans.

The Dodgers never made it to the Series, though, finishing second, two games behind Stan Musial's Cardinals, who went on to dethrone the no-longer invincible Yankees. Because of the war, it would be easy to believe St. Louis beat a Yankee team weakened by conscription or enlistment, but that was hardly the case. DiMaggio, for example, whose Series average was .333, was still very much in evidence, as was Phil Rizzuto, who led everybody on both teams at .381. Rizzuto even hit one into the left-field stands in Yankee Stadium. Still, the Cards won easily. In one game at the Stadium, they even shut out New York (the first time the Yanks had been shut out in post-season since 1926), and St. Louis took the Series, four games to one.

Terry had no comments on the Yankees' loss, but he did make the papers once more in 1942, on the last day of November:

TERRY RESIGNS FROM GIANTS
Ex-Manager Ends Old
Link With Club
Parting Amicable, He
And Stoneham Assert

Only twenty years after Terry had excitedly called Elvena to tell her McGraw had hired him, he was no longer associated with the New York Giants in any way. Despite the declaration that the "parting" had been "amicable," some reporters were suspicious. The National Baseball Library has a clipping of an article by Minneapolis writer George Barton, who never liked Terry, in which Barton said he'd "learned from conversation with several major-league owners" that Terry had not resigned, that he'd been fired, and Barton added, in capital letters, "BILL IS ONE OF THE MOST DISLIKED PERSONS IN THE NATIONAL GAME." Back in Memphis, George Bugbee of the *Press-Scimitar*, who knew Terry better, was as fair as Terry would have wished. Yes, Terry was "brutally frank, often taciturn and downright truculent, sometimes bitter and always scornful of what passes for diplomacy, which he regards as duplicity," he said, but he added that New York would "miss this last of the rugged individualists—this guy with the hyper-sensitive soul under that bluff exterior—more than it knows."

Terry had sometimes said he was in baseball for the money and nothing else, and he did occasionally make people believe that. Now that he had quit the game for good, he might have been expected to turn his attention exclusively to his several other profitable ventures, restricting his interest in baseball to the occasional sunny afternoon in some owner's private box, but he didn't do that. On the day he made his announcement, there was a "leaked" rumor that the Phillies wanted him as their general manager. When Terry was asked by the *Times* about this, he said that he would "be interested" in an offer, if it were a "satisfactory" one. A week later, he announced an offer had been made, but in order to accept, he would need to have full control of the club. "If I take the job, I want to handle everything," he said, "and I'd be quite willing to be an active manager on the field, too." In fact, he added, "I wouldn't take one job without the other."

Unfortunately, Gerry Nugent, who owned the Phils, thought Terry was demanding too much. Terry wasn't hired.

In the spring of 1943, Terry tried to return to the game. He contacted both National League President Frick and Commissioner Landis, volunteering to manage a USO-style barnstorming team that baseball was thinking of sending abroad to play for the troops. The plan was never effected, however, and only a few token big-leaguers (Ott and Frisch among them) were sent. Ott may have gone overseas simply to get away from his team, which would finish last, a dismaying forty-nine and a half games behind the winning Cardinals. It would be the worst season in Giant history.

Whatever Terry thought about the utter collapse of the club he had built and that had been picked to win only two years earlier, it didn't discourage his efforts to get another job in baseball, which were becoming stubbornly persistent. In October, he had a lengthy meeting with the Cubs General Manager Jim Gallagher, and it was reported that Chicago was considering offering him an important job. Then Branch Rickey, who was now the general manager in Brooklyn, began playing a shrewd game. He wanted his manager, Durocher, to stay on, but Durocher was beginning his life-long infatuation with the fast-paced Hollywood crowd. Rickey felt he'd better hint to Durocher that, while his services were desirable, they weren't absolutely necessary. He refused to give Durocher an automatic extension on his contract, spreading rumors reported in the *Times* that, if the manager chose to "sign a movie contract" rather than return to Flatbush, Bill Terry would be the Dodgers' second choice. All three men were at the World Series that year (Terry was covering it for the Memphis *Commercial-Appeal*), and, after one of the games, they met in Rickey's suite. Although none of the three would say what had been discussed, the meeting lasted three hours.

Soon, however, the process started to become tedious and frustrating. Rickey, especially, would not get off the fence, and the papers began to treat his stalling with irony. Terry was, of course, more direct; he simply said "it doesn't seem that they have anything to offer me." Three days after Terry's comments, on October 25, the Dodgers re-hired Durocher, but so much had already been said about the possibility of Terry getting the job that Rickey felt obliged to defend his choice, and the *Times* said he "again insisted that at no time had he considered any other candidate while weighing Leo's retention."

Terry had negotiated for jobs with the Phillies, the Cubs, and the Dodgers, and he had offered to take a team overseas for the troops, but he had failed in each case. Even though it had been his idea to quit, he may have felt a twinge of envy when, late in 1943, Hubbell retired as a player and took over his old job as the head of the farm system, which was going to be expanded to include five teams. He might have even felt snubbed. In any case, he decided he'd had it with baseball, and, in a statement he released in January 1944, he gratified his enemies by sounding huffy. He said baseball was "too cheap a business for me," and that he was quitting the game "for good" to launch a career in the cotton business. He said:

> With the low salaries they're paying players, managers and front-office men, there's nothing in the game

for me. There's no turning back now. I gave the idea of returning to baseball a lot of thought before I finally made up my mind. Now it's definite. I intend to devote myself entirely to the cotton business and watch baseball from the outside.

He also said "no business in the world has ever made more money with poorer management," adding that this proved "it can survive anything."

The writers were delighted. Terry had popped up in range again, like a duck in a shooting gallery, and, if they were the guys who could "God you up," they were also pros at defamation. The first thing they did was to edit out any comments that made Terry sound human, and the following sentences were deleted in many papers: "I love the game, and I always will. I intend to keep up my interest always, but only locally."

To make sure the reporters knew he wasn't simply trying to jar owners into better proposals, Terry told them he'd sold his "304-acre plantation" near Memphis so as to have the cash to buy into "a large cotton-manufacturing firm." What he had sold was the dairy farm he'd made out of Clarence Saunders' golf course, as well as the cedar-wood home he'd lived in since 1938. Although he wasn't eager to leave the house, there were two good reasons to do so: one was the business aspect; the other was that Elvena had felt out of touch in Germantown, which was a long way from downtown in pre-beltway Memphis, and she wanted to be closer to the city. So Terry moved his family to a new place on South Highland Avenue, which was near his country club and the center of the city.

Now he was strictly a cotton trader. He'd met Lytle McKee either at St. Luke's Episcopal Church or at the Memphis Country Club (they were each members of both congregations, and McKee was president of the latter), and it was McKee who talked him into working in the cotton trade. McKee was the second in command at Sternberger & McKee, and cotton was very big business in Memphis. Terry didn't stay with the firm for very many years, but he was successful while he was there; on one occasion, he sealed a million-dollar deal, and he was proud of that transaction. Coaxed at last into the conventional business world, Terry was starting to look like the archetypal self-made success he'd always been ready to become. McKee's son, Lewis, took over the firm after his father's death in 1948, staying in the cotton business for some time; in 1952, he was named "King" of the city's annual Cotton Carnival. He later became an Episcopalian minister in Memphis. He told me admiringly that Terry "had a very special sort of business mind," and he remembered Terry as a man who seemed forbidding, but really wasn't. When asked if he thought Terry was emotionally vacant, McKee said emphatically, "That's absurd, that's absurd." He admitted Terry "could give you a stony-eyed look," but he said this look was designed more to add emphasis than to convey distaste, and he agreed the look was often used ironically.

For the second time Terry had said he was quitting baseball, and, on this occasion, he had added that there was no turning back. Later in the year, however, he was asked about another rumor. Bob Quinn, who was now the general manager of Boston (by the early 1940s, the team was called the Braves again), was said to be interested in hiring him. Significantly, Terry said nothing about being absolutely, positively finished with baseball. "You know as much as I do about it," he told the *Times*.

A year later, it looked as though Bob Quinn's smoke might indeed have concealed some fire. Terry went to Detroit to watch a couple of games of the 1945 World Series between the Tigers and the Cubs, and he huddled with Quinn, who was known to be looking even more seriously for a new manager. A number of papers reported that Terry might be the man.

Once again, nothing came of it. If Terry was ever given an offer, it was probably not good enough; the Braves were not a wealthy club. From then on, although Terry always remained receptive to reasonable overtures, there would be few occasions on which he would actively seek a job in baseball.

Meanwhile, as Terry looked on from the outside, the Giants were relentlessly collapsing. In 1946, Ott became the first manager ever to be thrown out of both games of a doubleheader. In 1946, Ott's Giants finished last again, thirty-six games behind one arch-rival, the Cards, who had won the pennant in a playoff with another arch-rival, the Dodgers. It was the season during which Durocher, pointing across the field to Ott as an example, told writers that nice guys couldn't expect to do any better. Then, halfway through the 1948 season, with the team only one game below .500, Ott was replaced by Durocher himself.

Seldom has the myth of baseball provided a clearer sign of change: the gentlemanly Ott deposed by the brawling Durocher, the "nice guy" who finished last superseded by the very man who had called him just that. John Drebinger, noting the contrast between "Mild Melvin" and "Loud Leo," said this was "the most amazing managerial shake-up that the major leagues have ever experienced." He was right then, and he's still right; he even borrowed some of F.D.R.'s war rhetoric when he said it was "a day that will live long in baseball history." Terry undoubtedly felt that Drebinger needn't have weakened F.D.R.'s phrase, and that he should have stayed with "infamy."

Nonetheless, it would turn out that Terry had done Durocher at least one substantial favor. Before he quit the Giants, Terry had encouraged the development of a big kid on the roster of the Giants' class D team in Bristol, Tennessee. The team wasn't playing him, and Terry, who thought he had great promise, made a call and told the Bristol manager to put him in more regularly. It was an ununusually insightful act on Terry's part, since he had always been so poor a judge of young players. Maybe he was thinking of his own experience back at Dothan. In any event, and partly because of Terry's encouragement, the kid persevered although he went off to war and didn't get a real chance to play until 1945, when he was promoted to Jersey City. He did well enough there to earn a shot with the parent club, debuting with the team in September of the 1946 season, and he stayed a Giant for seven more years. Bob Thomson remembered Terry's help back then, when he, as Terry himself told me, "got him out of the woods in Bristol." Many years later, after Thomson had quit playing, the two men came across each other in Baltimore. Terry was standing in front of his hotel, and Thomson was on the other side of the street; when he saw Terry, he crossed over to say hello. Thomson was by now far better known than Terry, but he was, and is, an unusually modest man, and this is how Terry described the meeting to me: "And he came over to me. He said, 'Do you know who I am?' I said, 'I sure *do* know who you are, Bobby. How could I miss *you*?' And he said, 'Well, I was just wondering.' And we stood there and talked quite a bit." Thomson, who also remembered that meeting, was always grateful to Terry for the help early in his career. There was, then, *some* continuity in even the most dramatic change; the hero of the Giants' first pennant since 1937 was not *entirely* Leo Durocher's boy.

Athough Terry had been mentioned as a possible candidate to succeed Billy Evans as president of the Southern Association after the 1946 season, nothing came of it, and it's not likely an agreement to his financial satisfaction could have been struck, anyway. Now he finally became his own boss; he left the cotton business and bought a small car dealership in West Memphis, across the river in Arkansas. By 1949, he wanted to expand, and he looked to a warmer climate, a place that could eventually serve him well for retirement. He decided on northern Florida, which was an area he knew, since he'd been taking his family on vacation there since 1943. He bought J. C. Carter's Buick dealership in Jacksonville. Bill, Jr., who was now a lawyer, helped close the deal, announcing that their agency in West Memphis already had a buyer. His father started looking for a house right away, although Elvena stayed in Memphis until the summer, so as not to uproot their youngest child, Ray, who was finishing his senior year in high school. Terry told reporters he still enjoyed going to the World Series, adding that he'd turned down three offers to get back into the game in 1949 alone. (One of those offers may have been from Cincinnati, since he served as a hitting coach for the Reds that spring, instructing, among others, the slugging Ted Kluszewski.) But he *had* turned down the offers, saying, "I've forgotten about going back to baseball."

Bravely said, but it calls to mind the Yankee pitcher Jim Bouton's famous comment in his book, *Ball Four*, about how the baseball ends up holding *you*, and not the other way around. As a matter of fact, Terry *was* back in uniform only six months later, although he wasn't getting paid. It was "Ed Barrow Day" at Yankee Stadium, and the eighty-two-year-old baseball pioneer and ex-Yankee general manager was being honored by some old friends. Later on, Barrow remembered how happy this day had made him, and he particularly singled out one of these friends: "Even Bill Terry showed up for my day!" he said. Terry had breakfast with ex-Cardinal Terry Moore the morning before the event's old-timers' game, and Moore told me how he had asked Terry a question: "'There's one thing, Bill, that I never could understand about you, when you wasn't playing but you were pinch-hitting,' and I says, 'every time you had a tough spot, or men on base, that you always put yourself in against Dizzy Dean.' He says, 'Yeah.' And I says, 'Every time I've seen you,' I said, 'he'd usually strike you out, or you'd pop it up.' 'Yeah,' he says. But Terry, he says, 'I always *thought* I could hit him.'" After the breakfast and the game, Terry headed back to Jacksonville, where he was named head of that year's Community Chest drive.

Although Terry had become a well-known figure in Florida, he wasn't in the national news much in 1951, a year when the second of the three great players of his Giants era was inducted into the Hall of Fame. Hubbell had made it there in 1947 (Terry received forty-six votes that year); now Ott was inducted. Terry was gaining—he'd garnered 105 votes in 1950, and in 1951, he received 148 to Ott's 197—but he was still excluded, even though he had preceded the two others as a player and managed them, too. Even the press was beginning to think this was an injustice, and Arthur Daley wrote a column in *The New York Times* saying, despite Terry's reputation as a "cold, calculating, shrewd business man" whose "personality wasn't as heart-warming as it might have been," he was, nonetheless, "a whale of a player" who "belongs in the Hall of Fame." Terry made no comment, but the writers elected players to the Hall, and he was starting to feel, understandably, that he was being kept out for reasons both personal and petty.

In 1953, Terry accepted some part-time baseball work, signing on as a spring-training hitting coach for the Dodgers at Vero Beach. Once, he even posed for photographers in his uniform and cap. If Bill Terry was willing to be seen during daylight hours in Brooklyn attire, there was little doubt that baseball was entering a new era. In fact, it would be only a couple of years before Horace Stoneham would take his club to San Francisco, leaving, some might say, its heart in Harlem. In times like these, who could afford old loyalties? Having been cajoled into wearing Dodger blue, Terry was now approached by the new Brooklyn owner, Walter O'Malley, and, this time, definitely offered a job as manager. Terry turned the position down because, by now, his price was far beyond what any owner was willing to pay. A year later, he told Dan Daniel of the *World-Telegram* that, when O'Malley said he could go as high as sixty thousand dollars, Terry said he'd need at least one-hundred and twenty-five thousand dollars. That, of course, was the end of the discussion. Terry went on, laughing as he remembered O'Malley's startled reaction. "You know, I would have been out money even at one-hundred and twenty-five thousand dollars," he said, "but it would have been a lot of fun. I often wonder how I would have come out if I had taken the Brooklyn job."

Later the same year, Terry finally did get back into baseball, albeit in a relatively small way; he accepted the presidency of the class A South Atlantic "Sally" League. He had already turned the day-to-day operations of his Buick agency over to his three sons, and there wasn't a great deal of work involved in this new job, anyway. He received only five thousand dollars a year, but, as he said, that was an expense account; he figured his expenses would exceed that, anyway, and he would end up having to pay a little for the privilege of doing volunteer work. He noted that his motives in taking the job were obviously not business-oriented, explaining in the *Florida Times-Union* that "once you've been in the game, it's tough to break away for any length of time." Then, in 1954, he was finally elected to the Hall of Fame.

17

BEYOND THE HALL OF FAME

Those fools! How could they keep out Berra when they'd let in Gabby
Hartnett who was never half the catcher Yogi was!...Well, it took Rogers
Hornsby six years to make it, didn't it—with a lifetime of .358! And Bill
Terry and Harry Heilmann eleven years apiece!
—Philip Roth, *The Great American Novel*

Terry's first reaction to being told the writers had finally condescended might have been petty, but it was understandable, delivered in a characteristically terse manner: "I have nothing to say about it," he said. "I have no comment to make." When reporters pressed him, he loosened up and went a little further. "Any time a fellow in my position says something at a time like this, he usually says the wrong thing." But, by the time he arrived at Cooperstown, he was considerably thawed. After Ford Frick, who was now the baseball commissioner, admitted he "had a feeling Bill Terry should have been in the Hall of Fame a long time ago," Terry responded with the following speech, a short one, naturally, which was excerpted in the *Times:*

> "I know it's hard to get into the Hall of Fame. I don't know what kept me out—maybe it was the writers—but I finally made it and I thank God for it. I didn't know I'd ever feel like this. This is a very wonderful occasion to me."

Then Terry directed his remarks to the widows of McGraw, [Bill] Klem and [Rabbit] Maranville, all of whom were present. Bill, flashing a delightful sense of humor, told Mrs. McGraw of an incident during his playing days.

"I used to hold out a lot," Terry said. "One year, following a long siege, your husband sent me up to pinch hit. It was the ninth inning, we were a run behind, the bases were loaded and two were out. I fanned. In the clubhouse later Mr. McGraw told me, "You can ask for more money in the winter and do less in the summer than any ball player I know."

To Mrs. Klem, Terry related how "the only time I ever was thrown out of a ball game it was by the Old Arbitrator." And to Mrs. Maranville, Bill told about a ball game in which he slid into second base, where the Rabbit was waiting with the ball and "bit me on the ear."

The self-absorbed Terry created by the press would certainly never have taken the trouble to prepare those comments, to make such an openly deliberate effort to cheer three widows. The real Terry, however, did precisely that.

A few days later at the Stadium, before a regular game between the Yankees and the Red Sox, the new inductee played in another old-timers' game. The legendary broadcaster Mel Allen was introducing the players, and, when he got to Terry, he broke off and called for Ted Williams to take a bow: the fans were able to see baseball's last .400 hitters on the field at the same time, although virtually none of them were aware that the older man had been the younger one's boyhood idol. When the exhibition got under way, Frisch led off, grounding out. The next man up was Terry, who looked over a couple of pitches, then drilled a line drive into the right-field stands. The crowd reacted in stunned silence momentarily before roaring. Terry trotted around the bases, laughing and flexing his muscles. Not bad for a fifty-five-year-old.

By 1955, Horace Stoneham had made it plain he wanted to move the Giant franchise to San Francisco. Terry didn't approve of the relocation, and he sought to keep the Giants in New York by following the most logical method a wealthy businessman could: he tried to buy them. In late September, just after Durocher had been fired, he heard Stoneham was talking to prospective buyers, and he made some calls. Then Terry ran into Dan Daniel of the *World-Telegram*, telling him he was going to try to buy his old club. He said he could very likely raise sufficient cash, his and that of several men he had already consulted. "I mean every word of it," Terry said. "If Horace Stoneham wants to sell the Giants, let him put a price on them." Terry added that the Polo Grounds, badly in need of repair, would present no problem, since the park would no longer be used. If he used only one park for two teams that never played in town on the same days, he would greatly reduce overhead, anyway. "We would move into Yankee Stadium," said Terry. "And if they ever let me in this Stadium, I am pretty sure I could field a team that would give the Yankees a run for the patronage."

There was precedent for such an idea, of course; the Yankees had shared the Polo Grounds with the Giants until Ruth's stadium was built in the 1920s. Stoneham, however, knew of Terry's low opinion of baseball management, and he also knew it emphatically included him; he was not in a mood to bargain, not with Terry. His response was icy, as a headline and story in the *World-Telegram* suggested:

GIANTS ARE NOT
FOR SALE EVER
TO BILL TERRY

Horace Stoneham is not going to entertain offers for the Giants from Bill Terry. He made it quite emphatic today. Stoneham said: "The New York Giants are not for sale."

"If they are for sale, the negotiating will be done with one of several New York City individuals or groups who

from time to time have expressed an interest in the New
York Giants."

The article had to have made Terry smile, with Stoneham indig-
nantly denying any intention to sell the team, then quickly saying
he might negotiate with those who had "expressed an interest."
Stoneham had apparently never been approached by Terry before
Terry called in the press, so his umbrage might have been partly
justified. Stoneham wasn't right, however, in assuming that Terry's
only motive had been to embarrass him, that Terry had never
intended to make a serious offer in the first place. After
Stoneham's statement, Terry admitted that no formal offer had
been made, but he repeated his initial comment to the press:
"Yeah, I'd like to have the Giants," he said in the *Times*. And, as
Terry said again to Dan Daniel a year later, that's what he had
meant: he told Daniel that "he never was more serious in his life"
than when he tried to buy the team. Terry repeated one other
thing, saying that if he had been able to buy the team, it would
have stayed in New York. If a strong-willed man like Terry had
taken over the Giants, partly with a desire to keep them in New
York City, would he have wavered in his resolve within two years?
If the Giants hadn't joined the Dodgers in asking for permission
to move, would Walter O'Malley have gone it alone? If O'Malley
had been forced to stay in Brooklyn for a year or two more, would
powerful city officials and lawyers who could help with financ-
ing—Robert Moses and William Shea, to name a couple—have
recognized what they were about to lose and accommodated him?
And, even they didn't remain in the Polo Grounds or Ebbets Field,
would not the Giants still be in New York, and the Dodgers still
be the Brooklyn Dodgers?

Now that the writers had finally voted Terry into the Hall of
Fame all was, more or less, forgiven. From then on, he attended
every Hall-of-Fame ceremony that he could. At the 1955 ceremony, Terry took his usual back seat. In fact, the center fielder who

was being inducted that year was a man who always seemed to upstage Terry, Joe DiMaggio. DiMaggio had made the Hall after only four years of retirement, as opposed to Terry's eleven. Terry, however, made no wisecracks; in fact, he was one of only five previous inductees who had shown up to welcome the new boys on board, and two of the others, Ott and Frisch, might have been there at Terry's prodding. Terry had accepted the honor of being in the Hall, and he was going to take it seriously. A week later, on Stengel's sixty-fifth birthday, Terry played in another old-timers' game at Yankee Stadium. He went 0-for-1, but he had five putouts and was in the forefront of the event: he appeared in the middle of a picture in the *Times,* sitting next to Al Simmons and listening while Cobb kidded Stengel about being so old.

In 1956, there was rumor that the Indians were interested in getting Terry to manage, but it remained unsubstantiated. A little later, Terry tried to quit as head of the Sally League, claiming he didn't have time to do what amounted to baseball charity work while running his own affairs, too. At a three-hour meeting two months after he resigned, however, the league directors, happy with the job he'd done, talked him into coming back, and the *Times* said this "spiked rumors he would manage the Cleveland Indians."

Terry still wasn't through with his old game, though, because, in February 1958, he bought his town's Sally League team, the Jacksonville Braves. This was, however, his last real excursion into the baseball world. He and a number of other local businessmen came up with the twenty-five thousand dollars asked by Sam Wolfson, a well-known Jacksonville figure after whom the Braves' new stadium, an exact copy of Chicago's former Comiskey Park, had been named. As soon as the sale was final, the stockholders held a meeting and elected Terry president of the club.

He ran the Braves for the next two years, but, after their 1959 season, Terry found an opportunity to sell them to a young Houston oil millionaire, Craig Cullinan. Cullinan, like Terry, headed a group of which he was the principal investor; Terry agreed to continue to represent Cullinan's group, to act as local caretaker for the absentee landlords. He drew pay for this service, of course. Additionally, the selling price was $40,000, a $15,000 appreciation on his investment, or 37.5 percent; it wasn't a bad arrangement. The deal didn't work out for Cullinan, though, and, in 1963, when the team nearly went out of business, Terry joined forces with a number of other people who didn't want to lose the Braves, devising a profit-sharing plan. Soon, 4,553 Jacksonvilleans owned various proportions of the team, which was by then called the Suns. Some of the new owners had invested no more than ten bucks. The new manager was Harry "the Hat" Walker, a former Cardinal, and *Jacksonville Magazine* interviewed him and Terry regarding their chances not simply of winning, but of survival. Terry said to survive they'd need an average daily gate of three thousand, and, to attract that many people they'd need a winning team.

Unfortunately, they got neither, and a lot of wistful gamblers lost their ten dollars. The last year for the Jacksonville franchise and the old Sally League itself was 1963. It was replaced in 1964 by a new double-A organization, the Southern League. The new league kept some of the old franchises, like Asheville, Charlotte, and Knoxville, but Jacksonville was dropped, and the city wouldn't field another baseball team until 1970.

Although he was certainly financially comfortable enough to do it, Bill Terry never retired from anything but baseball. He remained conscientiously active in his church (he attended every Sunday, and his contributions were generous) and in his community. In 1960, Jacksonville needed a sports personality to dedicate its new coliseum, and Terry obliged. The arena was across the street from the Gator Bowl and seated twelve thousand; like many such venues, it was a smaller version of Madison Square Garden in New York. In his remarks, he said the new stadium would give local kids "a bigger chance to grow up clean and strong and self-reliant," and he added that it wouldn't hurt Jacksonville's continued growth and prosperity, either.

His town's growth and prosperity (and his own) occupied him for the rest of his life. Houston wanted to make him general manager of its new National League expansion team in 1961. Harry Craft, who was Houston's first field manager—the same Harry Craft whose home run precipated the great rhubarb at the Polo Grounds in 1939—said it was a definite offer, one that Terry considered, even flying from Jacksonville to Houston to consult with the team's front office, but that he finally turned the job down. From then on, his connection with baseball was restricted almost exclusively to his dealings with the Hall of Fame. In 1973, when his old pal and teammate Frisch died, he was elected to the Veterans' Committee, and he immediately let his feelings be known. He felt, for example, that members of the Hall, once inducted, had an obligation to show up every year, and that staying away constituted a dereliction of duty to the game and fans alike. He decided to do something about it by exposing the no-shows, singling out one player with a particularly high profile.

"Quite a few come up to be inducted and never come back," Terry said. "Ted Williams is one. He's a fellow who should be a leader in this regard, and isn't. People should be able to see these players without charge. I've always offered to go any place for this sort of thing, and I've gone to a few places." Williams took this reprimand gracefully, and his attendance at the annual ceremony improved after Terry's criticism. There was never known to be any bad blood between the two men—each spoke very highly of the other—and there is no evidence that Terry knew he had been Williams' hero.

Terry also felt good fielding was not duly considered by the Hall's electors, that a good fielding shortstop could win many more ballgames than the writers were willing to admit. One result of his view was the election of Terry's own great fielding shortstop, Travis Jackson, in 1982. Terry, who argued for the principle, not the man, insisted that Jackson was elected entirely on his own merits; Terry said he figured he had helped, but only in getting those merits acknowledged.

Another inductee in Travis Jackson's year was Albert "Happy" Chandler, the ex-commissioner of baseball. Chandler, who was also an ex-senator and an ex-governor of Kentucky, made his acceptance speech sound like a declaration of some new candidacy. He claimed he had created the player's pension fund and said he had integrated baseball:

> For twenty-four years, my predecessor did not let the black man play. If you were black, you didn't qualify. It wasn't entirely his fault. It was what the club owners wanted. But I didn't think it was right for these fellows to fight at Okinawa and Iwo Jima, and then come home and not be allowed to play.

Judge Landis was dead and couldn't defend himself; Jackie Robinson and Branch Rickey were also dead, unable to say, "Hey, what about us?" and Terry thought Chandler was taking credit for the accomplishments of others. He said nothing during the ceremony, but he later cornered Chandler at the Otesaga Hotel. It was Terry at his most typical, curtly dismissing Chandler's claim as bluntly as he could; Al Lopez told me he was a witness, and, although it may have been the wrong time to confront Chandler, Terry just could not tolerate fakery when he thought he'd detected it. Chandler also remembered the incident, and he wrote to me, saying simply, "Bill Terry was not a fan of many folks; he was not a fan of mine as you know. Al Lopez was." Considering that Lopez indicated he thought Terry was not wrong, just unkind, this probably meant Lopez simply kept his mouth shut during the confrontation. Should Terry be faulted for his grim honesty, or Lopez for hanging back? Hall-of-Famer Billy Herman knew Terry, and when I told him this story, he said, "Sounds like him; that's him. I mean, there was no bullshit about him, he just said what he thought. If you liked it, all right, if you didn't, the hell with you. He just spoke his mind."

Terry must be given credit for his remarkable consistency, which probably bordered on honesty more than meanness; he was simply a debunker who saw no reason to tolerate phonies in silence. In 1983, the Giants, now in California, retired his number 3. Terry's comment? "They should have done it years ago," he said.

Although Terry continued his annual trips to Cooperstown (he was last there in 1987, a year and a half before his death), his remaining years were centered more than ever on home. Terry's four children were grown, healthy, and successful. He often had lunch with one or the other of them, and there were grandchildren. Additionally, they all lived nearby; of the four, only Kenn was not in Jacksonville, and he was only a couple of hours away in Vero Beach. Then, not too long before Terry confronted Chandler in Cooperstown, Elvena Terry fell ill.

She was soon confined to a wheelchair, and Terry wanted to make her as comfortable as he could. Although they were living in what he called "a lovely house by the river," which was their second Jacksonville home, he wanted to give her seclusion. He found a house at the very end of a dead-end street, just across from their country club, and he started negotiating to buy it. However, since the house had not been designed to accomodate a handicapped person, he was really only interested in the land, in its quiet location across from a golf course. By the afternoon of the day of the closing, Terry had levelled the house. The new one, built on the old foundation, went up very quickly. It had no doors between the living room and dining room, or the dining room and kitchen; there was a square table in the middle of the kitchen floor, with plenty of room to accomodate the wheelchair, along with a concrete ramp leading from the kitchen down to the floor of the garage. In the garage, Terry had installed an elaborate contraption used to lift a wheelchair into a car. This was the house from which Elvena watched the duffers with delight, the one in which she lived, Terry told me, "a year and a day." She died on December 19, 1983, and was buried in the Garden Cloister in Evergreen Cemetery in Jacksonville.

Terry kept living and working—"battling," as his son Ray said in the *Times-Union* obituary—until he died. He had moved his dealership from its old site, downtown on Fourth and Main streets, to a sprawling modern lot on one of the highways south of the city. By the time he reached the last year of his life, he was worth nearly thirty million dollars. It was in that last year that Joe Moore, a ranch owner and by no means an impoverished man, kidded him by telling Terry he'd be very happy to keep an eye on that thirtieth million for him, once it was made. Still, it would be wrong to say Elvena's death didn't greatly affect him. There were more of her paintings hanging in the house than souvenirs from his career—many more.

Terry still drove to work at least three times a week, he still made it to church every Sunday, and he still tried to show up at Cooperstown every year, but he was starting to decline seriously. After 1987, the year Travis Jackson died of Alzheimer's disease, he needed a cane to get around; friends like Al Lopez remarked on how he seemed to be aging at an alarming rate. At one point, he spent months in a hospital before one of his sons convinced him to get a second opinion from a young doctor he knew. The doctor quickly located the problem and soon had him home. Terry had enough spark left to complain energetically about the hospital's misdiagnosis, not only because it was unprofessional, but because he was on that particular hospital's board. Sometimes he'd hear from old friends. On his last birthday, Hal Schumacher called, and they had a good talk. On another occasion, he received a call from Tom Baker, the pitcher he had acquired from Brooklyn for Freddie Fitzsimmons, and, after Baker hung up, he was delighted. His wife told me he said, "Bill Terry sounded just *exactly* like himself."

He sent Joe Moore "letters" on audio tape, and he still talked to Hubbell frequently on the phone, but, in the fall of 1989, Hub had a bad car accident. According to the *Times*, the police said he'd suffered "an apparent heart attack or stroke"—he'd survived two previous strokes—and then driven into a metal pole. He had critical head and chest injuries, and he died two days later.

If Terry ever did quit battling, and that's certainly debatable, it was not until he heard that news. He lived less than two months after Hubbell's death. When he died, somebody in Jacksonville put up a sign. Significantly, it made reference to the discrepancy between achievement and recognition that had dogged his life; appropriately, it was in front of a gas station. It said:

BILL TERRY WAS BEYOND
THE HALL OF FAME

THE STATISTICAL RECORD

WILLIAM HAROLD (BILL) TERRY
Born October 30, 1898, in Atlanta, Georgia
Died January 9, 1989, in Jacksonville, Florida
Height: 6'1". Weight: 200.
Threw and batted lefthanded

Last National League hitter to bat over .400 (.401), 1930.
Shares National League record for most hits, season (254), 1930.
Hit three home runs in a game, August 13, 1932, first game.
Led National League first basemen in double plays, 1928, 1929, and 1934.
Pitched 2-0 no-hit victory against Anniston, June 30, 1915.
Pitched 0-4 no-hit loss against Ploughs (semipro), July 25, 1920.
Named as first baseman on *The Sporting News* All-Star Major League Team, 1930.
Named to Hall of Fame, 1954.

				Batting Record											
Year	Club	League	Pos.	G.	AB.	R.	H.	2B.	3B.	HR.	RBI.	B.A.	P.O.	A.	E.	F.A.
1915	Newnan	Ga.-Ala.	P	8	...	...	...	...	...	...	...	...	2	11	0	1.000
1916	Shreveport	Texas	P	19	29	3	7	3	1	0	...	.241	2	14	3	.842
1917	Shreveport	Texas	P-OF	95	208	15	48	9	1	4	...	.231	51	61	9	.926
1919-1922		Mercantile	(records unavailable—with semipro Standard Oil Polarines)													
1922	Toledo	A.A.	1B-P	88	235	41	79	11	4	14	61	.336	417	54	10	.979
1923	Toledo	A.A.	1B	109	427	73	161	22	11	15	82	.377	957	57	7	*.993
1923	New York	Nat.	1B	3	7	1	1	0	0	0	0	.143	22	1	0	1.000
1924	New York	Nat.	1B	77	163	26	39	7	2	5	24	.239	325	14	4	.988
1925	New York	Nat.	1B	133	489	75	156	31	6	11	70	.319	1270	77	14	•.990
1926	New York	Nat.	1B-OF	98	225	26	65	12	5	5	43	.289	391	31	9	.979
1927	New York	Nat.	1B	150	580	101	189	32	13	20	121	.326	1621	*105	12	.993
1928	New York	Nat.	1B	149	568	100	185	36	11	17	101	.326	*1584	78	12	•.993
1929	New York	Nat.	1B	150	607	103	226	39	5	14	117	.372	*1575	111	11	.994
1930	New York	Nat.	1B	154	633	139	*254	39	15	23	129	*.401	*1538	*128	17	.990
1931	New York	Nat.	1B	153	611	•121	213	43	*20	9	112	.349	1411	*105	16	.990
1932	New York	Nat.	1B	•154	643	124	225	42	11	28	117	.350	*1493	*137	14	.991
1933	New York	Nat.	1B	123	475	68	153	20	5	6	58	.322	1246	76	11	.992
1934	New York	Nat.	1B	153	602	109	213	30	6	8	83	.354	*1592	105	10	•.994
1935	New York	Nat.	1B	145	596	91	203	32	8	6	64	.341	1379	*99	6	*.996
1936	New York	Nat.	1B	79	229	36	71	10	5	2	39	.310	525	41	2	.996
	Major League Totals			1721	6428	1120	2193	373	112	154	1078	.341	15972	1108	138	.992

(• = tied for league lead; * = league lead)

World Series Batting Record

Year	Club	League	Pos.	G.	AB.	R.	H.	2B.	3B.	HR.	RBI.	B.A.	P.O.	A.	E.	F.A.
1924	New York	Nat.	1B	5	14	3	6	0	1	1	1	.429	43	2	0	1.000
1933	New York	Nat.	1B	5	22	3	6	1	0	1	1	.273	50	1	0	1.000
1936	New York	Nat.	1B	6	25	1	6	0	0	0	5	.240	45	8	0	1.000
	World Series Totals			16	61	7	18	1	1	2	7	.295	138	11	0	1.000

Pitching Record

Year	Club	League	G.	IP.	W.	L.	Pct.	H.	R.	ER.	SO.	BB.	ERA.
1915	Newnan	Ga.-Ala.	8	...	7	1	.875	...	...	...	...	...	...
1916	Shreveport	Texas	19	84	6	2	.750	50	...	10	39	34	1.07
1917	Shreveport	Texas	40	246	14	11	.560	222	108	82	21	116	3.00
1919-1922		Mercantile	(records unavailable—with semipro Standard Oil Polarines)										
1922	Toledo	A.A.	26	127	9	9	.500	147	75	60	35	59	4.26

Managing Record

Year	Club	League	G.	W.	L.	Pct.	Standing
1919-1922 Mercantile (records unavailable—with semipro Standard Oil Polarines)							
1923	Toledo	A.A.	54	16	38	.296	8 of 8
1932	New York	Nat.	114	55	59	.482	6 of 8
1933	New York	Nat.	156	91	61	.599	1 of 8
1934	New York	Nat.	153	93	60	.608	2 of 8
1935	New York	Nat.	156	91	62	.595	3 of 8
1936	New York	Nat.	154	92	62	.597	1 of 8
1937	New York	Nat.	152	95	57	.625	1 of 8
1938	New York	Nat.	152	83	67	.553	3 of 8
1939	New York	Nat.	151	77	74	.510	5 of 8
1940	New York	Nat.	152	72	80	.474	6 of 8
1941	New York	Nat.	156	74	79	.484	5 of 8
	Major League Totals	1496		823	661	.555	...

World Series Managing Record

Year	Club	League	G.	W.	L.	Pct.
1933	New York	Nat.	5	4	1	.800
1936	New York	Nat.	6	2	4	.333
1937	New York	Nat.	5	1	4	.200
	World Series Totals		16	7	9	.438

Terry's Managerial Transactions

Year	Date	Pos.	Acquired	From	Pos.	In Exchange For
1932	Oct 10	C	Gus Mancuso	Cardinals	OF	Ethan Allen
		P	Ray Starr		C	Bob O'Farrell
					P	Bill Walker
					P	Jim Mooney
	Nov		Waiver price	Pirates	P	Waite Hoyt
	Dec 12	P	Glenn Spencer	Pirates	3B	Freddie Lindstrom
		OF	Gus Dugas			
		OF	Kiddo Davis	Phillies	OF	Gus Dugas
					OF	Chick Fullis
			(Part of three-team trade involving Giants, Phillies, Pirates)			
	Dec 29		$25,000	Braves	C	Shanty Hogan
	Dec	C	Paul Richards	Dodgers		Waiver price
1933	April 21	P	George Uhle	Tigers		$20,000
	June 12		(cash price)	Braves	P	Ray Starr
	June 16	OF	Lefty O'Doul	Dodgers	1B	Sam Leslie
		P	Watty Clark			
	Nov 15	2B	George Grantham	Reds	P	Glenn Spencer
1934	Feb	OF	George Watkins	Cardinals	OF	Kiddo Davis
	Nov 1	SS	Dick Bartell	Phillies	P	Pretzels Pezzullo
					SS	Blondy Ryan
					3B	Johnny Vergez
					OF	George Watkins
						(cash)
	Dec 11		Waiver price	Pirates	P	Jack Salveson
	Dec 13	OF	Kiddo Davis	Phillies	P	Joe Bowman
	Dec 14	SS	Mark Koenig	Reds	SS	Billy Myers
		P	Allyn Stout			(cash)
	Dec	P	Leon Chagnon	Pirates		(cash)
1935	May 25		(cash)	Athletics	C	Paul Richards
	Aug 2	P	Euel Moore	Phillies		(cash)
	Sept 24	P	Dick Coffman	Browns		(cash)
	Dec 9	2B	Burgess Whitehead	Cardinals	P	Roy Parmelee
					1B	Phil Weintraub
						(cash)
1936	Jan	1B	Johnny McCarthy	Dodgers		$40,000
	Feb 20	1B	Sam Leslie	Dodgers		(cash)

Year	Date	Pos.	Acquired	From	Pos.	In Exchange For
	Dec 4	IF	Mickey Haslin	Braves	3B	Eddie Mayo
	Dec 8	3B	Lou Chiozza	Phillies	IF	George Scharein (cash)
1937	Jan 27	P	Ben Cantwell	Braves		(cash)
	June 11	P	Tom Baker	Dodgers	P	Freddie Fitzsimmons
	June 15	3B	Wally Berger	Braves	P	Frank Gabler $35,000
	June	P	Jumbo Brown	Reds		(cash)
	Aug 4		(cash)	Reds	OF	Kiddo Davis
	Aug 9		(cash)	Dodgers	P	Ben Cantwell
	Dec 20		(cash)	Cardinals	P	Al Smith
1938	March	2B	Bill Cissell	Athletics		(cash)
	June 6	2B	Alex Kampouris	Reds	OF	Wally Berger
	Dec 6	OF SS C	Frank Demaree Bill Jurges Ken O'Dea	Cubs	SS OF C	Dick Bartell Hank Leiber Gus Mancuso
	Dec 11	1B	Zeke Bonura	Senators	IF P	Jim Carlin Tom Baker $20,000
1939	May 9	P	Red Lynn	Tigers		(cash)
	Aug 23	C	Ray Hayworth	Dodgers	OF	Jimmy Ripple
1940	April 26		$20,000	Senators	1B	Zeke Bonura
	May 14	P	Bill McGee	Cardinals	P P	Harry Gumbert Paul Dean (cash)
	June 15	3B	Tony Cuccinello	Braves	P 2B	Manny Salvo Al Glossop
	Nov 25	IF	Joe Orengo	Cardinals		(cash)
	Dec 5	P	Bob Bowman	Cardinals		(cash)
	Dec 10	OF	Morrie Arnovich	Reds		(cash)
1941	Jan 2	P	Bump Hadley	Yankees		(cash)
	April 30		(cash)	Athletics	P	Bump Hadley
	June 19	2B	Odell Hale	Red Sox		Waiver price

CHRONOLOGY

1823   Great-grandfather, Tom, born in Atlanta

1832   Great-grandmother, Mary Jane Thurman, born in Atlanta

1854   Grandfather, William M., born in Atlanta

1858   Grandmother, Ella Heath, born

1861   Great-grandfather murdered in Atlanta

1875   Grandparents married in Atlanta

1878   Father, William T., born in Atlanta

1897   Terry's parents marry in Atlanta

1898   October 30: Bill Terry born in Atlanta

1903   Great-grandmother dies in Atlanta

1904   Uncle, "Big Jim" Ison, has record-breaking year playing first base at Georgia Tech

1912   June 6: Terry's first amateur league game for Grace Methodist in Baraca Sunday School League in Atlanta

1915   May 4: Terry's first professional league game, with Dothan in Georgia State League

        June 17: Terry's first game with Newnan in the Georgia-Alabama League

        June 30: Terry pitches no-hitter against Anniston for Newnan

1916   June 29: Terry pitches both ends of doubleheader for Newnan

        Terry moves to Memphis

        August 1: Terry's first game for Shreveport in Texas League

        November 21: Terry's marriage to Elvena Sneed is announced in Memphis paper

1917   February 25: Terry pitches in all-star game in New Orleans winter league

1918   Terry quits baseball, starts working for Storage Battery Service and Sales Company in Memphis

Terry quits battery assembly job and joins Standard Oil of Louisiana as salesman

1919 June 15: Terry establishes Standard's semipro team, the Polarines, and umpires first game

1920 July 25: Terry pitches no-hitter against Ploughs for Polarines

1922 April 1: Terry meets John McGraw in Peabody Hotel in Memphis, turns down offer to play for New York Giants

May 10: McGraw meets Terry's price and Terry joins the Giants

May 11: Terry sent by Giants to play for Toledo Mud Hens, American Association

May 21: Terry pitches first game for Toledo

May 27: Terry wins first game for Toledo

September 4: Terry hits inside-the-park homer at Columbus

1923 May 5: Terry breaks ankle sliding into second base

June 29: Terry hits record home run at Indianapolis

August 1: Terry succeeds George "Possum" Whitted as Mud Hens' Manager

September 16: Terry's grandmother dies in Atlanta

September 24: Terry plays first game as New York Giant at Polo Grounds

1924 October 4: Terry homers in his first World Series game

October 10: Giants lose to Washington in seventh game, after McGraw takes Terry out

1926 Terry's grandfather dies in Atlanta

1927 Terry hits the first home run ever over centerfield fence at Memphis Chicks' Russwood Park

1930 Terry leads majors with .401 batting average

1931 September 27: Terry loses credit for a hit and batting title when game with Brooklyn called for darkness

1932 April 19-22: Terry hits six home runs in four games to tie record held by Babe Ruth and Chuck Klein

June 6: Terry succeeds John McGraw as manager of New York Giants

1933 April 24: Terry breaks wrist batting against Brooklyn

July 6: Terry becomes one of four players (with Ruth, Frisch, and Jimmy Dykes) to get two hits in first All-Star Game

July 11: Dizzy Dean strikes out Terry on behalf of sick child

July 12: Terry shows Blondy Ryan's wire to reporters

September 19: Giants clinch National League pennant

October 7: Giants defeat Senators to win World Series in five games

October 9: Terry signs forty thousand dollar contract

1934 January 24: At press conference, Terry says of Brooklyn, "I was just wondering whether they were still in the league."

July 10: National League, with Terry as manager, loses second All-Star Game 9-7, despite Carl Hubbell's pitching.

September 29-30: Brooklyn beats Giants twice, allowing St. Louis to win pennant

1935 March 17: In exhibition game, Dizzy Dean throws four straight fast-balls at Terry's head

July 8: Terry bats in only run for National League in third All-Star Game

1936 April 16: Terry requests police protection at Ebbets Field for Dick Bartell

July 9: Terry announces retirement as player

July 15: Terry comes out of retirement

September 24: Giants win National League pennant

October 6: Yankees beat Giants, 4-2, to win World Series

1937 July 7: National League All-Stars, managed by Terry, lose 8-3

July 12: Terry ejected from game for only time in his career by Bill Klem

September 9: Terry signs new contract that makes him manager and general manager

September 30: Giants win National League pennant

October 10: Yankees beat Giants, 4-1, to win World Series

1938 January 29: "The Terrible Terry" appears in *The Saturday Evening Post*

July 6: National League All-Stars, managed by Terry, win 4-1

September 2: Terry's father dies in Atlanta

1941   December 2: Terry resigns as Giants' manager, is replaced by Mel Ott, but stays on as general manager

1942   November 30: Terry quits Giants organization

1944   January 8: Terry announces that he's given up trying to get a good job in baseball and has taken position as a cotton trader in Memphis

1949   Terry buys Buick dealership in Jacksonville and moves to Florida

1953   Dodgers offer Terry manager's job; he refuses

1954   January 20: Hall of Fame elects Terry

August 14: Terry homers in old-timers game at Yankee Stadium

Terry becomes president of South Atlantic ("Sally") League

1955   Terry tries to buy New York Giants

1958   Terry buys Jacksonville Braves in Sally League

1959   Terry sells Jacksonville team

1963   Group of investors, headed by Terry, buys back Jacksonville team

1964   Jacksonville team and Sally League fold

1983   April 6: Giants retire Terry's number 3

December 19: Elvena Terry dies in Jacksonville

1989   January 9: Bill Terry dies in Jacksonville

NOTES ON SOURCES

During the course of my research for this book I interviewed Bill Terry on several occasions before he died in 1989 and have quoted verbatim from the tape recordings I made at the time. I conducted similar interviews with numerous former players and Terry's contemporaries, whom I've noted in the Acknowledgments. Besides these interviews, I have quoted frequently from the sportswriters and columnists who covered the Giants in the New York and national press during the 1920s, 1930s, and 1940s, relying in many cases on unattributed stories in *The New York Times*. In most cases, the stories were either on microfilm or on file at the National Baseball Library at Cooperstown. As this biography is intended for the general reader, rather than the baseball scholar, and an elaborate documentation of all these quotatations would have weighed it down, I've chosen not to cite date and page placement. Where I've cited magazines, the full citation is included in the notes that follow. Where I've cited books, an abbreviated citation is included indicating the author's name and the page, with the full citation included in the Select Bibliography.

10. *"He could take kids out of the coal mines"*: Quoted in Chieger: 111.

16. *"To illustrate Georgia"*: The information on Tom Terry is from files in the Atlanta Historical Society.

24. *Terry's baseball debut was unimpressive*: In August, 1923, when he was managing Toledo, Terry was sent a form requesting information by the Boston journalist, C. Ford Sawyer. Terry filled it out, and it eventually found its way into the National Baseball Library. In it, Terry claims to have played for Marist College when he was living in Atlanta. Marist is one of several teams on which Terry may have played, although no record remains; two others are Boys' High and Sawnee University, both in Atlanta. On the same form, he lists a stint with Atlanta's Crackers as his first "professional engagement" and, as one of the "clubs since then," the St. Louis Browns. Since he later claimed never to have played for the Crackers and specifically said he had been turned down by the Browns, these two claims probably should be discounted as resumé-padding.

36. *An infant son to feed*: This son was Bill, Jr. Since I was unable to obtain the cooperation of the Terry family in researching this book, and since Shelby County, Tennessee, will release family records only to family members, and finally, since the records in the Terrys' church were lost in a fire, I can't be precise about the birth dates for Terry's four children. I have been able to fix these dates within twelve-month periods based on dated articles that give the children's ages at the time the articles were written. The only exception to this problem involves one of his sons, the youngest, Ray, whose birthday on October 28, 1932, is recorded in an unattributed clipping at the National Baseball Library.

47. *A loss to St. Paul on July 23*: In Terry's defense, St. Paul was a very good team that went on to win the American Association pennant that year. Its record was 107-60, a winning percentage of .641, and it finished fifteen games ahead of second-place Minneapolis—and forty-one and a half ahead of the seventh-place Mud Hens.

52. *He hit .377 that year and nearly won the American Association batting title*: Terry's Toledo teammate Bill Lamar came in first with a .391 average. As far as Terry's Mud Hens themselves, they finished last, fifty-nine and a half games behind Kansas City.

54. *"There's only one way to time Johnson's fastball"*: Quoted in Chieger: 168. Birdie McCree worked in the front office of the New York club in the American League, which was called the Highlanders in 1908, when he said that.

64. *"Terry, you can ask for more money in the winter"*: Quoted in Chieger: 95.

65. *"In this game there is no 'luck'"*: Leverett Smith, "Ty Cobb, Babe Ruth and the Changing Image of the Athletic Hero," in Browne: 78.

65. *"The Age of Play"*: Robert J. Duffus, "The Age of Play," *The Independent*, December 20, 1924: 539.

67. *"Used to hold out all the time"*: Quoted in Connor: 81-82.

73. *"Sit still, kid," Lindstrom said*: Fred Fitzsimmons, "Did the Best Teams

Get Into the Series?" *The Saturday Evening Post.* Undated clipping in National Baseball Library.

75. *"The inhabitants of our country"*: Quoted in Carter: 177.

82. *"I didn't make the mistake that Wally Pipp did"*: Quoted by Tom Clarke in *The San Francisco Examiner and Chronicle*, July 28, 1978.

83. *"McGraw: The Mussolini of Managers"*: Billy Southworth, "McGraw, the Mussolini of Managers," *Baseball Magazine* 39 (November 1927): 533-5.

86. *"McGraw might have been the manager"*: Quoted in Bob Broeg, *St. Louis Post-Dispatch*, April 3, 1976.

89. *"Subtle as a belch"*: Quoted in Chieger: 88.

97. *"I grew up in San Diego"*: Quoted in Connor: 20-21.

98. *"Carries no trace of criticism"*: F.C. Lane, "The Terrible Terry," *The Saturday Evening Post* 44 (April 1930): 495-97.

102. *"Never since then have there been so many so good"*: William B. Mead, "The Year of the Hitter," in Thorn: 254.

102. *The great Hall-of-Fame hitter Johnny Mize*: Mize said that "Bill Terry hit straightaway and he batted four hundred in the Polo Grounds before I got here, and to me that's five hundred, easy, in any other park." Quoted in Curran: 276.

103. *"According to survivors, the fuel behind the hitting binge"*: William B. Mead, "The Year of the Hitter," in Thorn: 254.

103. *Defensive strategies of the game simply grew more sophisticated*: Stephen Jay Gould, "Entropic Homogeneity Isn't Why No One Hits .400 Anymore," *Discover* 7 (August 1986): 60-66.

104. *"I asked Terry what had become of the .400 hitter"*: Walter ("Red") Barber, "Bill Terry Recalls Days with John McGraw," *Baseball Digest* 30 (November 1971): 78-81.

104. *"A fairly light bat, with a long, thin handle"*: Quoted in Frank Graham, "Baseball's Greatest First Baseman," *Baseball Magazine* 45 (November 30, 1930): 548.

105. *"An actress is lucky if she gets two"*: "Why I love the Giants," *The New York Times Magazine*, June 29, 1947: 23.

107. *"In that uncomfortable time"*: *The Sporting News*, February 14, 1976: 37.

108. *"Don't let me ever see you do a damn fool thing"*: Quoted in Lee Greene, "The Little Giant," *Sport* 32 (May 1961): 94.

110. *"Harry," Hubbell said, "I'm just thankful"*: Hubbell's thinking was a little wishful here. He did pitch in some night games. His first was a fine 6-1 win over the Pirates at Forbes Field on July 18, 1940.

111. *McGraw, red with fury*: Graham, *McGraw of the Giants*: 242-243.

120. *McGraw would "tear him apart right in front of the team"*: Quoted in Connor: 94-95.

120. *"The type of fellow who would call all the shots"*: Quoted in Chieger: 111.

134. *"By gum, they missed him"*: Quoted in Klingaman: 340.

135. *"A real good baseball manager"*: Quoted in Wayne Lockwood, "Carl Hubbell Looks Back and Remembers," *Baseball Digest* 31 (December 1972): 72.

135. *"Terry and McGraw are in striking contrast"*: "John McGraw's Capable Successor," *Baseball Magazine* 51 (October 1933): 487-89.

142. *While it was certainly a coincidence*: The great earthquake on the West Coast came on the heels of Roosevelt's inauguration and the subsequent bank holiday. In any event, most historians and economists see the early spring of 1933 as the time the economic rebound began. See Schlesinger, *The Coming of the New Deal*, and Ellis.

150. *After he left the kids' ward*: Quoted in Gregory: 108.

166. *"May God have mercy on the man or group"*: Quoted in Schlesinger, *The Crisis of the Old Order*: 114.

174. *"He hit as good a ball as I ever pitched"*: Quoted in Wayne Lockwood, "Carl Hubbell Looks Back and Remembers," *Baseball Digest* 31 (December 1972): 74.

180. *"If your ballclub had played all season"*: For the dialogue in this exchange between Stengel and Terry and the descripton of what happened, I have quoted liberally from Creamer: 184.

182. *His son was in prep school*: Bill, Jr., had been named captain of the Memphis University School baseball team on March 9, 1934. He was an outfielder.

182. *"Walter Winchell didn't think my real name was an appropriate stage name"*: Quoted from an unpublished letter dated March 22, 1989, from Ruth Terry to Suzanne Gerber of *The Cable Guide*.

190. *"The idol of my early days was definitely my dad"*: Quoted in Chieger: 226.

190. *"Into what other profession could he have jumped"*: Clifford Bloodgood, "The Giants Get a Second Baseman," *Baseball Magazine* 56 (February 1936): 407.

191. *Edmund Wilson wrote about the "barbarism" of the era*: Quoted in Ellis: 142.

191. *Kenneth Burke came up with an idea for a WPA-style boondoggle*: Kenneth Burke, "Bankers Arise," in Giboire: 84-85.

191. *Michigan Senator Arthur Vandenberg*: Ellis: 207.

195. *"Terry passed us in the hotel lobby"*: From an unpublished letter dated March 4, 1969, in the National Baseball Library.

198. *"If I close my eyes I can still see 'Memphis Bill'"*: Curran, Mitts: 123.

201. *"Was motivated by publicity considerations"*: Allen: 155.

220. *"I stopped," DiMaggio remembered*: Quoted in Silverman: 75.

221. *"I've always heard that one player could make the difference"*: Quoted in Moore: 25.

223. *When Cincinnati General Manager Larry MacPhail introduced night baseball*: For a summary of MacPhail's role in the development of night baseball, see Don Warfield, *The Roaring Redhead* (South Bend, Ind.: Diamond, 1987): 56-68.

225. *In a recent baseball newsletter*: Almon S. Ritter, "Life as a Cuban Ballplayer: The Rodolfo Fernandez Story," *Oldtyme Baseball News* 4 (1992): 25.

254. *His father had died in an Atlanta hospital*: Without the cooperation of the Terry family it will likely be impossible to resolve the question of Terry's relationship with W. T. Terry in his last few years. Three months before his death in Atlanta, the elder Terry may have been a guest at his son's home in Memphis, but the evidence supporting this is downright mysterious. It hinges solely on one clipping in the National Baseball Library, with a photo of a man clearly identified as Terry's father. The man is handling a cow. The caption refers to Bill Terry having "stocked his estate" with cattle. Terry didn't replace Clarence Saunders' golf course with his dairy farm until nearly a year after W. T. Terry died, however. Further, the clipping has been dated (in longhand) June 6, 1940, nearly two years after the death of Terry's father. The newspaper is unidentified. Obviously, if the date is accurate, the man is not Terry's father. What makes it worth mentioning, however, is that if the actual date is 1938, not 1940, it would show that father and son met at least once before the former's death.

266. *"As the collapse became all the more apparent"*: Hynd: 314.

269. *"Every ball went just where I intended it to go"*: Quoted in Joe King, *The Sporting News* (September 29, 1954).

277. *In other words, the last major service Bill Terry performed*: This may have been wishful thinking, but it was the assessment of numerous New York sportswriters commenting at the time of the trades. Drebinger went on in the same column to say that "they already appear to stand as the No. 1 outfit to watch when the Spring parade begins."

283. *The National Baseball Library has a clipping*: George Barton was executive sports editor and columnist for the *Minneapolis Tribune* in the 1930s and 1940s. The clippings dateline reads "Chicago."

290. *"Even Bill Terry showed up for my day!"*: Barrow and Kahn: 5.

292. *"Those fools!"*: Roth: 23.

SELECT BIBLIOGRAPHY

Allen, Lee. *The Giants and the Dodgers.* New York: Putnam, 1964.

Barber, Walter "Red", and Robert W. Creamer. *Rhubarb in the Catbird Seat.* Garden City, N. Y.: Doubleday, 1968.

Barrow, Ed and James M. Kahn. *My Fifty Years in Baseball.* New York: Coward McCann, 1951.

Broeg, Bob. *The Pilot Light and the Gas House Gang.* St. Louis: Bethany, 1980.

Browne, Ray, et. al, ed. *Heroes of Popular Culture.* Bowling Green: Popular Press, 1972.

Carter, Paul A. *Another Part of the Twenties.* New York: Columbia, 1977.

Chieger, Bob, ed. *Voices of Baseball.* New York: Signet, 1984.

Connor, Anthony J., ed. *Voices of Cooperstown.* New York: Collier, 1984.

Creamer, Robert W. *Stengel.* New York: Fireside, 1990.

Curran, William. *Big Sticks.* New York: Harper, 1991.

——. *Mitts: A Celebration of the Art of Fielding.* New York: William Morrow, 1985.

Ellis, Edward Robb. *A Nation in Torment: 1929-1939.* New York: Coward McCann, 1970.

Giboire, Clive, ed. *Lightest Blues.* New York: Imago, 1984.

Graham, Frank. *McGraw of the Giants.* New York: Putnam's, 1944.

——. *The New York Giants.* New York: Putnam's, 1952.

Gregory, Robert. *Diz.* New York: Viking, 1992.

——. *The Baseball Player: An Economic Study.* Washington, D. C.: Public Affairs Press, 1956.

Hynd, Noel. *The Giants of the Polo Grounds.* New York: Doubleday, 1988.

Klingaman, William K. *1929: The Year of the Great Crash.* New York: Harper and Row, 1989.

Langford, Walter M. *Legends of Baseball.* South Bend, Ind.: Diamond Communications, 1987.

Mead, William B. *Two Spectacular Seasons.* New York: Macmillan, 1990.

Moore, Jack B. *Joe DiMaggio: A Bio-Bibliography.* Westport, Conn.: Greenwood, 1986.

Reichler, Joseph L., ed. *The Baseball Encyclopedia.* 1st Ed. New York: Macmillan, 1969.

Roth, Philip. *The Great American Novel.* New York: Holt, Rinehart and Winston, 1973.

Runyon, Damon. "Baseball Hattie." In *Romance in the Roaring Forties and Other Stories.* New York: Beech Tree, 1986.

Schlesinger, Arthur M., Jr. *The Coming of the New Deal*. Boston: Houghton Mifflin, 1958.

——. *The Crisis of the Old Order*. Boston: Houghton Mifflin, 1957.

Silverman, Al. *Joe DiMaggio: The Golden Year 1941*. Englewood Cliffs, N.J.: Prentice-Hall, 1969.

Thorn, John, ed. *The National Pastime*. New York: Warner, 1981.

INDEX